STRIKING DISTANCE

STRIKING DISTANCE

BRUCE LEE & THE DAWN OF MARTIAL ARTS IN AMERICA

Charles Russo

UNIVERSITY OF NEBRASKA PRESS | LINCOLN & LONDON

Library of Congress Cataloging-in-Publication Data
Names: Russo, Charles, 1975–
Title: Striking distance: Bruce Lee and the dawn
of martial arts in America / Charles Russo.
Description: Lincoln: University of Nebraska Press, [2016]
Includes bibliographical references and index.
Identifiers: LCCN 2015035013
ISBN 9780803269606 (cloth: alk. paper)
ISBN 9780803290495 (epub)
ISBN 9780803290501 (mobi)
ISBN 9780803290518 (pdf)
Subjects: LCSH: Lee, Bruce, 1940–1973. | Martial artists—United
States—Biography. | Martial arts—United States—History.
Classification: LCC GV1113.L44 R87 2016 | DDC 796.8092—dc23
LC record available at http://lccn.loc.gov/2015035013

Set in Lyon by Rachel Gould.
Designed by N. Putens.

For Angelo and Cel . . .
As Grandpa Charlie told me—
"Keep punching!"

Do not repeat the tactics which have gained you one victory, but let your methods be regulated by the infinite variety of circumstances.

—**SUN TZU**, *The Art of War*

CONTENTS

PART 3. 1964

PROLOGUE
The Dissident

Wally Jay spent the past two days cooking four whole pigs in the narrow confines of his backyard.

A native-born Hawaiian with a bright disposition and vertical build, Wally knew how to construct a proper "Imu," even if the islander earth-oven was poorly suited for mainland suburbia. Following his usual routine, he dug the pit, stacked the firewood, arranged the rocks, and spread the banana leaves. The barbecue's pyre ascended high over his backyard fence, quickly igniting a flurry of 9-1-1 calls on rotary dials. And like clockwork the Alameda Fire Department sent an engine over just as the rich aroma began to pervade Eagle Avenue.

Their inspection, however, was little more than a formality. Wally had been hosting his giant luau parties twice a year for almost a decade now, and the firemen from nearby Station 3 had long since become accustomed to the massive Hawaiian barbecue that preceded the event.

Fire Chief William Hilbish had even become chummy with Wally over the years, noticing that the jujitsu master seemed to exude nothing but humility and good manners. For someone with a reputation for tossing grown men about like rag dolls on the mat, Wally appeared to be a gentle soul. Besides, Hilbish's guys were always fascinated to see the island-style earth-oven blazing away in a neighborhood yard.

"All right, Wally, we'll see you in six months," Hilbish said, as he departed alongside the training studio at the rear of the house. "Enjoy your luau."

In the frenzy of last-minute preparations at the Jay residence, the fire-fighters were hardly noticed. Wally's wife, Bernice, was several days into self-catering a small mountain of food out of her tiny kitchen: huge trays of chicken long rice, ten-gallon pots of poi, platters of lomi lomi salmon, and a tropical orchard's worth of sliced pineapple. She handed these dishes off for delivery as soon as they were ready, grabbing whichever of their children or students were passing through the kitchen at the time and ordering them to load everything into the family station wagon for delivery to the luau's venue, at nearby Colombo Hall.

Even in the bustle, Wally remained excited. His summer luau was looking to draw upward of a thousand partygoers, and the big turnout boded well for his judo students and their next excursion to compete abroad. Wally always used the party's ticket-sale revenue to take his students around the hemisphere for tournaments, tightly packing them all into his station wagon (at present, loaded heavy with platters of teriyaki lingcod) and driving them around North America to compete against whoever invited them out for a match. His team cleaned up straight through to Vancouver on their trip the previous spring, and Wally was itching to get them out again.

Not that he was surprised by the high ticket sales. Wally knew the second he booked "Hawaii's Songbird" Lena Machado to sing at his luau that she would draw a considerable crowd. After her celebrated performances at the San Francisco World's Fair in '39, her soaring falsetto drew Bay Area Hawaiians like an islander incarnation of the Pied Piper.

Better yet for Wally, his buddy James Lee had arranged for a special martial arts guest to come down from Seattle to perform. And that prospect was shaping up to be every bit as exciting as hearing Machado sing. Over the last few years, the martial arts demonstrations had become a big part of the luau entertainment, and this friend of theirs from Seattle . . . well . . . Wally knew the kid to be a showstopper.

Leo Fong drove south from Vallejo along I-80 in his metallic green Ford Fairlane, as the late day summer sun glimmered in gold rush hues on the water of San Francisco Bay. Further out toward the horizon, a vast fog was gathering on the Pacific, threatening to move inland and impose its grayness on the glow of the Golden Gate. The Bay Area was nothing if not atmospheric, and after growing up in Arkansas, Fong still regularly marveled at the California scenery.

Merging onto 24 toward Oakland, Fong thought of how his parish reassignment from Sacramento to Vallejo had cut down so heavily on his commute times, just as how his departure from Chinatown to study with James Lee in the East Bay kept him from suffering Bay Bridge traffic. Fong had been traveling to San Francisco for kung fu lessons for the past few years, first at Hung Sing off of Portsmouth Square, and then at Kin Mon, up on Waverly. These days he was making the weekly trip to practice in James's garage, out toward the Oakland foothills.

Unlike most practitioners of the time, Fong did not derive his martial arts identity from any one particular school or method. Even as his foundation was in American boxing, Fong had studied jujitsu, taekwondo, and a variety of kung fu styles since moving to California. Still, he felt inclined to keep looking and experimenting, to continue chasing down some sort of "ultimate" fighting style.

It was in this regard that he had found a like-minded mentor in James Lee, who was almost ten years his senior, but one of the more forward-thinking martial artists he had met. Not only did James share Fong's interest in various styles, but he was always proactively on the lookout for technique that could prove effective in a street fight. Whereas Fong grew up beating back the racism of corn-fed Ozark boys, James had made a name for himself fighting on the blue-collar streets of Oakland. Different worlds, sure, but they both understood the stark and spontaneous nature of real fighting.

Fong's schedule limited him to only a weekly practice session in Oakland, but the second he arrived James would excitedly convey something new that he had come across that week. Like Fong, James didn't have firm allegiance to a particular style or system but rather always put the emphasis on effectiveness—"Does it work?" The new techniques he related were always something viable, something that could prove worthwhile in a street fight: a streamlined type of kick or a viciously effective choke hold.

It was one of those zealous reports from James that now had Fong on the road to Oakland for Wally Jay's luau, though to check out not a fighting technique but an individual fighter. Fong was somewhat indifferent to the invitation at first, but he was won over by James's enthusiastic descriptions of the guy slated to perform at the luau: some twenty-year-old martial arts dynamo from Seattle.

Some kid named Bruce.

James Lee held a beer and explained why he wasn't breaking bricks.

In the festive, teetering-toward-rowdy atmosphere of Wally's luau, James fielded a stream of lighthearted inquiries about why he hadn't taken the stage yet to crush things with his bare hands. A favorite among the luau crowd for his past Iron Palm demonstrations, James politely shrugged off their questions and explained that he was sitting this one out to make room for a younger martial artist.

The gathering in Colombo Hall was in full swing, with the venue decorated top to bottom with island decor and exotic flowers amid the morphine waltz of island music blaring from the speakers. The luau was a huge draw for the Bay Area's Hawaiian community, as well as the smaller though equally proud contingent of martial artists within Wally Jay's orbit.

James held the heavy hitters in this latter group in high regard. Not only were they formidable fighters in their own right, but they understood where martial arts were heading in America.

He spoke for some time with Ralph Castro and Ed Parker, the kenpo masters with their own Hawaiian roots. Castro talked about his plans for expanding his small but dedicated school on Valencia Street in San Francisco's Mission District. He joked that if he took over the lease for the vacant business next door, it might be cheaper to just let his students kick down the wall that separated the two locations (which they eventually did). Parker operated an ever-expanding network of schools, with his main location down in Pasadena. He often traveled up to the Bay Area to confer with his colleagues and document martial art performances in Chinatown with his Super 8 camera. At the luau he answered the customary questions about how Elvis Presley's training was going—"The kid is tough"—but was far more excited to talk about his upcoming international martial arts conference later that summer. Parker explained that he had secured a venue in

Long Beach. Part showcase, part competition, he said that he was hoping to draw heavy attendance from martial artists around the world.

Leo Fong arrived shortly after in the green Fairlane, and James Lee invited him to sit with everyone at his table. As a once-a-week student, Fong didn't know many of James's other guys too well. He did recognized Al Novak though. A 260-pound World War II veteran who had raided Normandy on D-Day, Novak was a muscled beast of a fighter. Even the old Chinatown guys—highly dismissive of the idea of Caucasian martial artists—had to concede Novak's prowess. James had first met Al at a previous luau a few years back. The two quickly struck up a friendship and had been training together ever since. Fully aware that martial arts could have vast appeal for a wide audience in America, James eventually ran an action photo of Novak, a non-Asian, on the cover of a later edition of his first book.

As the island revelry continued in Colombo Hall, James lit a cigarette and was approached by another guest inquiring why he wasn't up on stage. James laughed the question off. Just wait and watch the kid about to perform, he explained with a boozy smile. It would certainly be something to see.

Bruce Lee ignored the stairs and just leapt onto center stage. Without pause he began to perform a martial arts form, a rehearsed movement representing specific techniques of a particular fighting style. At five feet seven and barely 140 pounds, the young out-of-towner was hardly an imposing figure up on stage. Yet the fluidity of his form, along with the zip and pop of his movements, implied something worthwhile, even potentially formidable. The crowd watched politely, thinking that the young martial artist showed promise in his earnestness.

Leo Fong, on the other hand, watched in complete bewilderment. James was suspect of any martial artist that put too much emphasis on forms, and Fong couldn't believe he'd hype up a guy that was only adept in rehearsed movements. Fighting, as they both agreed, was wildly unpredictable, with little room for dance-like choreography. The constant practice of forms was a key part of where modern martial arts was going astray, they reasoned, producing "locker room" black belts with no sense for (or experience in) a real street fight.

But then, as if he could hear Fong's thoughts, Bruce stopped his movements, turned to the crowd, and in a tone that was at once cocksure and condescending, challenged the audience with a simple and defiant question: "How could you expect to fight like that?"

By the time he had agreed to perform at Wally Jay's luau, Bruce Lee had been giving martial arts demonstrations in America for close to five years. But by 1964 they had taken a far more pointed tone. Whereas he had once demonstrated to merely bring awareness to the obscure Chinese art of kung fu, Bruce now had the specific agenda of advocating for a modern and more effective approach to the martial arts, and he pushed toward this with little regard for the damaged egos that would be left in his wake.

As a result Bruce's reputation was highly polarized. His friends and colleagues found him to be inspiring and infectious, an endlessly energetic individual who kept them thinking and laughing. They marveled at his dynamic martial arts ability and gravitated to the logic and practicality of his viewpoint. For many others, though, he came across as brash and egotistical, an overbearing show-off and a tiresome self-promoter. Across the Bay in San Francisco's Chinatown, the martial arts community regarded him as a trash-talking troublemaker, with one neighborhood kung fu master dismissing him as little more than "a dissident with bad manners."

When it came to the martial arts in America during the early 1960s, the San Francisco Bay Area was the place to be, having benefited from the talent and influence of a diverse array of practitioners who had migrated from southern China, Hong Kong, Japan, and Hawaii. As Al Tracy, a local kenpo teacher and colleague of Ed Parker at the time, would characterize it: "The real significant early development of the martial arts in the United States was heavily based in the Bay Area. Many of the most important people came out of the Bay Area, not just for the Chinese but for so much of the martial arts."

By the spring of 1964, Bruce had been making regular trips from Seattle to Oakland for the better part of two years, to collaborate with James Lee and his colleagues. There in the east bay, Bruce had found them to be a talented group of older and well-seasoned practitioners who were inclined toward innovation. They embraced him as an equal and indulged his around-the-clock fanaticism for the fighting arts. In just a couple months' time, Bruce would fully relocate to Oakland, to further immerse himself in this unique martial arts laboratory.

On the Chinese calendar 1964 was the Year of the Green Dragon. It would be a hard and eventful year for the twenty-three-year-old Bruce Lee. He would drop out of college and stare at his career with uncertainty. He would marry against the protests of his bride's family and quickly learn that his first child was on the way. He would travel to Ed Parker's showcase in Long Beach and defiantly broadcast his dissenting viewpoint to an international audience of martial arts practitioners. And before the year's conclusion, he would face Chinatown's kung fu ace in a behind-closed-doors high-noon showdown.

Standing on that stage in Oakland, Bruce Lee could have likely never imagined that he was also less than a year away from his first foray into American show business, in which he would travel to Hollywood and audition with Twentieth Century Fox for a role in Charlie Chan's *Number One Son* (and be cast, instead, as Kato on *The Green Hornet*). Furthermore, his big challenge match in the months ahead would provide the spark for his greatest evolution as a fighter and cause him to begin tangibly constructing the new martial arts paradigm that he was already beginning to envision. In this regard 1964 was a pivotal moment for him. The Year of the Green Dragon would shape his life in profound and long-lasting ways.

Bruce Lee's demonstration at Wally Jay's luau quickly revealed itself to be actually more of a stern lecture. And Leo Fong was now puzzled for a whole new set of reasons.

"There is no way a person is going to fight you in the street with a set pattern," Bruce declared from the stage, referring to the choreography of his initial form. Stepping back toward center stage, he then worked his way through a Northern Shaolin fighting form. Bruce was impressive in this rendering as well, launching wide kicks that arced up over his head. Again though, he was quick with his critique. "Classical methods like these are a form of paralysis," he declared. "Too many practitioners are just blindly rehearsing these systematic routines and stunts."

A disjointed atmosphere spread through the crowd. Much like Fong, the spectators were caught off guard. Martial arts demonstrations were typically lively affairs with a lot of dynamic ability and maybe a bit of light humor. Instead, the martial artists within the luau crowd were being subjected to a young practitioner dressing them down. He was challenging the worth of what many of the established masters were teaching, and doing so by emulating their styles and then refuting them. Fong wasn't surprised when his quick scan of the crowd around him revealed a fair share of red faces and tense expressions. Martial artists, like so many of the Asian cultures they sprang from, were not receptive to boasts or put-downs, particularly from younger quarters, and Bruce was dealing heavily in each regard.

After concluding his performance—and dismissal—of other fighting styles, Bruce began to explain the dynamics of the style he taught at his school in Seattle. Here, he explained, the emphasis was on streamlining everything to a tangible effectiveness: economy of movement and direct attacks. The focus was on speed and power. No acrobatics, no fancy forms, no excess: the most results for the least effort.

With his peculiar English accent, he began to increasingly punctuate his descriptions with quick bursts of punches and advances. "The techniques are smooth, short, and extremely fast," he said before letting loose a flurry of fast blasts. "They are direct, to the point and are stripped down to their essential purpose without any wasted motions."

Bruce explained that he liked to think of his approach as "scientific street fighting." His acquaintances in the crowd—Castro, Parker, Novak—knew that he was selling his own brand of the Wing Chun style of kung fu.

Finally, he gave a demonstration.

Calling up a sizable male volunteer from the front of the stage—"a big football linebacker-type," by Fong's perspective—Bruce challenged him to block his punch. He explained to the crowd how he would close the gap between them from a wide distance and successfully strike his opponent with a tag to the forehead. The entire move was explained; the volunteer and the crowd knew Bruce's objective. He asked if the volunteer was ready, and then in a tidy blur he was across the stage to tap his opponent an instant ahead of his block.

The crowd murmured. Bruce's speed was stunning.

"Now, let's do it again."

They reset.

"Ready?"

Again Bruce moved with blinding speed, like a fencer going for the final point. His opponent tried to compensate with an early move, and Bruce reassessed in microseconds, waiting for his block to pass before he tagged him again. Same spot.

Bruce left the stage to mixed applause.

Fong took stock. Despite Lee's blazing displays of speed, much of the crowd was unimpressed. Bruce's attitude was contrary to the etiquette of both martial artists and Chinese custom, an immediate deal-breaker for many in attendance. James Lee, on the other hand, didn't appear fazed in the least and spent his time after the demonstration gleefully inviting his inner circle over to his house on Monday, for a meeting with Bruce.

Fong wasn't sure what to think. He got in the ring enough to know when someone had fighting ability, and this kid had speed and coordination like few guys he had ever seen. Fong also knew where he was coming from philosophically. Bruce was tackling the elephant in the room, putting it front and center for everyone to consider: Do these skills and techniques really work? Or are they just a bunch of fancy routines artfully packaged in Eastern exoticism? For Fong it was blunt articulation of the same issues and criticisms that he had discussed with James on numerous occasions.

Still, Fong felt uneasy. The kid's attitude. His attitude was gonna lead to trouble.

PART 1

San Francisco

1 THE PATRIARCH

Lau Bun quietly lit a cigarette along the top end of Portsmouth Square, while his senior students conducted class in his nearby basement studio. He nodded a silent hello to his neighbors as they passed by him along Brenham Place, and although his emphysema was growing worse, he took his time finishing his smoke.

At sixty-eight Lau Bun exuded a formidable presence that belied his years. Slim, with a strong, wiry physique, he possessed piercing eyes under thick-rimmed glasses and hardened features below short gray hair. He carried himself with reticence, his only volume amplified through the intensity of his expression.

Below him the spacious city park along the lower slope of San Francisco's Chinatown sustained its daily bustle well into the late spring afternoon of 1959. Children darted about in dervish-like blurs, as seniors lingered on weathered benches bantering in boisterous Cantonese tones. An anxious deliveryman took a swift shortcut through the park, sidestepping clusters of casual gamblers who populated the plaza hunched over Old World games embossed with Chinese characters. Tourists gawked at the neighborhood racket, fascinated that the scene was at once so alien and so familiar.

The park's moniker—"the Heart of Chinatown"—was apt, yet for reasons far less quaint than the nickname might imply. For all the neighborhood's success as an exotic tourist destination of unique sights and vibrant flavors, Chinatown was, in many ways, a densely packed ghetto. Most of its people resided in impossibly cramped quarters, almost barrack-style, with extended families often existing in what were little more than studio apartments, from floor to floor, building to building. In this sense Portsmouth was really the front porch and sprawling yard of an entire community, providing fresh air and a much-needed reprieve from claustrophobic living spaces teeming with hyper siblings, down-on-their-luck uncles, and screaming babies.

Through the many roles he played in the community, Lau Bun was well acquainted with these closely contained quarters. A skilled herbalist and bonesetter, he made house calls to treat injuries and wounds throughout Chinatown, arriving with his well-worn volume of remedies under one arm and a satchel full of herbs under the other. On occasion he made similar trips, but in a much different capacity, as a "mediator" of disputes for the community orbiting the Hop Sing Tong. The wisdom of his years and the physical feats of his youth proved to be a fitting combination for such a role, and with only a single Chinese officer within the ranks of the SFPD, a well-respected figure like Lau Bun was (after all was said and done) a welcomed alternative to city law enforcement.

In a wider sense Chinatown had long been its own tightly bound universe within the greater city, hemmed in between the financial district to the south, the dockworkers along the bay to the east, the Italian neighborhood to the north, and the financial elite westward up towering Nob Hill. For the Chinese the compass had long pointed toward hostility and racism in most directions, making the boundaries of their neighborhood sanctuary well defined and abrupt, specific even to certain sides of the street. In years past Chinese children who strayed beyond the top end of Broadway Avenue were often met by flying rocks from the kids of North Beach. But those tensions had softened over the past two decades, ever since Pearl Harbor instantly shifted the racial scarlet letter on the West Coast from the Chinese to the Japanese.

If a curious social observation was to be made there at Brenham Place, it was the fact that Lau Bun and his Chinatown neighbors could claim Portsmouth Square for themselves. Not only was the plaza a prime location in downtown San Francisco, but as its ever-oxidizing memorial plaque testified, the park was flush with U.S. history. Portsmouth was where California was first declared American, courtesy of Captain John Montgomery, who raised stars and stripes over the Mexican customs house that sat on the plaza in 1846. As the city's first civic center, it was also where Samuel Brannen, a local businessman with a newfound monopoly on mining equipment, first announced the California gold rush to everyone within earshot just two years later.

The fact then that this park, practically the Plymouth Rock of the west, belonged to a minority of people that the nation scarcely begrudged citizenship was certainly no small irony. Though that's not to say it wasn't fitting. Chinese immigrants were arriving in San Francisco in the earliest days of the gold rush and had continued to weave integral contributions into the fabric of the city (and the American West) through the formative periods to come. These were contributions that, in the face of a century of exclusion and racism, often manifested in ways both silent and unsung.

Finishing his smoke, Lau Bun walked the few steps across the narrow street to his apartment building and quietly descended the steps to assess the end of the evening's class.

Postures became precise, expressions more businesslike, as Lau Bun's students adjusted to his presence before he reached the bottom of the staircase.

With more than twenty-five years of teaching Choy Li Fut kung fu and lion dancing within Chinatown, it was as a teacher—and really, as the neighborhood patriarch—of martial arts that Lau Bun was best known. And if his reputation in the community was notable, it was legendary among his students. They murmured stories of his abilities on their short walks home from class: of his enforcer days in the Tong or his flawless handling of the straight sword. Perhaps it was the tale of the rat that he killed with a dart ... at a sizable distance ... in the dark. Or the most frequently told of them all: the "incident" in Los Angeles.

Not that Lau Bun's school was swarming with students. The size of his classes tended to fluctuate from year to year but always maintained about a core dozen dedicated students, even as others fell by the wayside as a result of either too many movies or Lau Bun's hard-line insistence on foundational abilities. Younger students especially interested in his weapon proficiency—of the straight sword, throwing dart, chain whip, and butterfly knife—quickly learned that months of horse-stance training came first.

Lau Bun's studio, like much of Chinatown's spaces, was Spartan. He had a small burner for cooking beneath the stairs and a tiny adjacent room that was just large enough to accommodate a dresser and a bed with little else, opposite a closet-like bathroom. His main room, the studio space for his classes, was not large either, barely twelve square feet, but he fit them in well enough. In all the location cost him forty-five dollars monthly, with a couple of extra dollars thrown in for utilities. He didn't have a phone. Prospective students caught word of him on the streets and descended the steps to inquire. He charged them fifteen dollars a month, and many of them arrived with bags of change, lunch money saved over time and more sorely needed for means of defense. Young arrivals to Chinatown quickly learned that hostility could come as much from within the neighborhood as without. Native-born Chinatown kids would discriminate heavily against the newcomers, and in a decade's time this would manifest into serious gang violence. For 1959 it was still a matter of fifteen dollars in quarters and dimes, paid to an old master in exchange for lessons on how to beat someone back on the walk home from school. For Lau Bun it was a respectable living and a satisfying way to settle into old age.

In that underground space, Lau Bun was a hardheaded drill sergeant, running endless horse-stance exercises, and visibly impatient if he had to explain anything more than twice. But he wasn't without empathy for his students. He had his own trials on arriving in the United States, and difficult ones at that. This softer side was more apparent to his older students, not just for their tenure in Lau Bun's presence, but for the acquired wisdom that within kung fu exists a duality of hard *and* soft, a yin yang that applies not just to fighting technique but to the individual martial artists themselves. Lau Bun's softer side was apparent in his bedside manner surrounding his medicine and the serene tones he persuaded out of his well-worn butterfly banjo during the school's quieter moments.

Standing beside them now, he sized up his class. They held their horse stances firm, legs strong but split. It was their base, their foundation for fighting. Everything stemmed from your *jot ma*—your horse stance—every advance, every punch. He insisted that they hold that pose for great lengths of time, until it was solid, until it was formidable. It was a practice that wore down many newcomers, imposed on them for months and inspiring internal questions of whether they should have used their lunch money at the school cafeteria instead. Others just couldn't endure the monotony of the training, having joined expecting a fast track toward the mastery of the straight sword, or (in high-hope whispers at least) the Ten Thousand Elephants form.

Lau Bun continued to inspect his students as they held strong in their school clothes. Not bad. Then he settled on a newer student spread too wide. Lau Bun stood closer, looked him over again, and pushed through him till he tumbled to the tiled floor.

A weak foundation wasn't much of anything at all.

The history of Chinatown is uniquely intertwined with the origins of San Francisco itself, and to understand one is to grasp much of the other as well. In fact, just one block to the west of Portsmouth Square, along the busiest thoroughfare in the neighborhood, is where San Francisco took its first formal steps to becoming a city, and in turn, where the history of Chinatown begins.

At the time of its settlement by eighteenth century European explorers, the San Francisco Peninsula was an idyllic seven-square-mile protrusion of coastal landscape dominated by sprawling sand dunes, massive hills, and epic bouts of sweeping fog. It is positioned between a sizable bay to the east and the cold waters of the Pacific Ocean to the west. The area's native people, the Ohlone, spanned the Northern California coast for hundreds of miles, with settlements from Big Sur to Mendocino, and thrived for millennia in the region's mild climate and abundant natural resources.

The Spanish arrived first, seeking to both convert the natives to Christianity and guard against Russian and British territorial interests in the area. They developed outposts on the peninsula in 1776 as part of their system of missions that stretched north from Mexico through California, constructing the Presidio as a military installation on the north end of the peninsula, and then the Mission Dolores along a creek about two miles to the southeast. The settlements were as scenic and pristine as they were isolated and remote, existing with little variation for half a century.

Shortly after Mexico declared its independence from Spain in 1821, William Richardson, the chief mate of a British whaling vessel, stayed behind to marry into a local family. With an eye on the region's real estate, he applied for Mexican citizenship and built the first home outside the Presidio and mission in 1832, in the northeast section of the peninsula along what would soon be called Calle de la Fondacion (later known as Dupont Street, and eventually Grant Avenue, Chinatown's main thoroughfare). One year later Jacob Leese, a merchant from Ohio, built a house just south of Richardson, who saw the advent of a neighbor as reason enough to begin designing a formal street plan for what would be a new, though still sparsely populated, community. Even as Montgomery claimed California for the United States within sight of Richardson's home some twelve years later, San Francisco was a sleepy backwater port in the Pacific wilderness barely numbering three hundred inhabitants.

Events in the spring of 1848 changed the far-flung frontier town forever. The United States finalized its annexation of California from Mexico just days after gold was discovered in the distant hinterlands to the northeast of San Francisco. Within just a few years of Brannen marching into Portsmouth with profits in his eyes and announcements of gold on his lips, the local population would expand to some thirty-six thousand inhabitants, fortune hunters from seemingly every corner of the globe who transformed San Francisco into a booming rough-and-tumble Pacific port. For the Chinese the promise of San Francisco was more than just opportunity—it was fable, spoken of in hopeful tones as Gam Saan, the "Gold Mountain."

By the mid-nineteenth century many Chinese were already inclined to test their fortunes abroad. Oppressive taxes imposed in the turbulent fallout of the Qing Empire's loss in the first Opium War resulted in a systematic bankrupting of China's peasant farmers.

From Havana to Johannesburg Chinese communities began to spring up in cities around the world during the mid-nineteenth century, as the country's impoverished citizenry looked abroad for opportunity to escape the dire social conditions at home under the Manchu government.

Of the many Chinese who emigrated during this period (some two and a half million from 1840 to 1900), the lion's share of those traveling eastward across the Pacific to Hawaii and the United States hailed from Guangdong Province, in southern China. The region, through its city of Canton, already had a long tradition of commercial trade and worker exchange with foreign nations, and by 1850 was suffering a trifecta of catastrophe in the form of widespread rebellion, institutional corruption, and disastrous flooding, pushing many to the brink of starvation. With stories trickling back across the Pacific telling of a pristine foreign land abundant with riches, several hundred Chinese gambled on the "golden romance" in 1849 and 1850 during the prime early years of the rush. When some of these initial adventurers soon returned home bearing startling newfound wealth—evidence that the fable was fact—the migrations began in earnest. By 1852 over twenty thousand Chinese had traveled to the United States through San Francisco, composing almost 10 percent of California's population at the time and nearly a quarter of its labor force.

The Chinese who arrived in San Francisco were quick to set out for gold country, stopping only briefly in their own ethnic enclave along Sacramento Street, a few blocks south of Portsmouth Square. As fortunes were made and new districts developed, William Richardson's old neighborhood along Dupont was increasingly abandoned for better quarters (particularly after massive fires leveled the fledgling city six times in just eighteen months between 1850 and 1851), allowing the nearby Chinese settlement to expand northward block by block, into the area that it occupies still today.

In light of the widespread racism that followed, it's easily lost in the long-term historical narrative that Chinese immigrants were at first well received in America during the nineteenth century. At the federal level, U.S. policy maker Aaron H. Palmer submitted a plan to Congress during this period advocating for increased Chinese immigration to America, deeming them a boon to the domestic labor force. In 1852 Governor John McDougal echoed this line of thought by urging that the Chinese immigrants to California be given land grants. In San Francisco the Chinese were regarded with tolerance and a quaint affection, perceived as an exotic and hardworking portion of the growing local community that was destined for assimilation by Christian missionaries. Chinese migrants dressed in their traditional silk robes to participate in civic events and holiday celebrations in Portsmouth Square, such as in 1850 when U.S. justice Nathaniel Bennett asserted to them: "Born and reared under different governments and speaking different tongues, we nevertheless meet here today as brothers. . . . You stand among us in all respects as equals. . . . Henceforth we have one country, one hope, one destiny." The *Alta California* newspaper echoed his sentiments when it editorialized that the Chinese immigrants would "yet vote at the same polls . . . as our own countrymen." Mark Twain later wrote, "A disorderly Chinaman is rare, and a lazy one does not exist. They are quiet, peaceable, tractable, free from drunkenness."

This honeymoon proved short-lived, particularly as there was less gold to be found yet more and more Chinese arriving to pursue it. The tone soon grew hostile first in the mining camps of gold country and then amid the labor struggles of San Francisco, where the Chinese showed little interest in assimilation and "Little China" grew into a much-larger "Chinatown." Calls for the restriction of Chinese rights and citizenship in America flourished in the coming years, effectively scapegoating the Chinese as the source of myriad labor woes in the West, particularly as a severe depression set in during the 1870s. In San Francisco racist newspaper editorials and cartoons, along with demagogue labor organizers and vigilante mobs, echoed city hall's anti-Chinese attitude in the decades following the gold rush. One San Franciscan characterized the situation by saying, "In 1852 the Chinamen were allowed to turn out and celebrate the Fourth of July and it was considered a happy time. In 1862 they would have been mobbed. In 1872 they would have been burned at the stake."

By 1882 Congress had passed the Chinese Exclusion Act, effectively putting a decade-long moratorium on the immigration of Chinese laborers and prohibiting citizenship for foreign-born Chinese in America. It was a complete turnaround from the positive view taken by Palmer at the federal level a few decades earlier and proved a perfect diversion from the much more complex issues of labor and unemployment in a burgeoning nation awash in resources. The key labor role the Chinese had played in building the West—in the cities, in the farm fields, and on the railroad lines—were brushed aside as support for the act proved high. It was extended in 1892 for ten more years, before being extended again and then made "permanent" in 1904.

Just a few years later, the leaders of San Francisco saw the catastrophic 1906 earthquake, which culminated in the eastern portion of the city burning to the ground, as an opportune moment to relocate the Chinese and Chinatown to a remote corner of the city.

By the beginning of the twentieth century, it was officially government policy—nationally and locally—that the Chinese presence would be curbed in America.

Among the ranks of Chinese adventurers who found financial prosperity in their sojourn in America was Lau Bun's father, who at the turn of the century began sending the results of his labor back across the Pacific to his family in Toi San, a city along the southern coast of Guangdong Province in the Pearl River Valley. The wealth offered the young Lau Bun opportunities in education, as well as the chance to study martial arts with local masters. He dabbled for a time in a variety of styles, until he witnessed a friend's dominant display of Choy Li Fut kung fu—a whirling cyclone of whipping fists and furious punches—which made the young Lau Bun intent on mastering it.

Developed in the early nineteenth century by Master Chan Heung, Choy Li Fut combines elements and techniques of three different southern styles of kung fu to form a unique combat approach: angular stances and extended postures unleashing a barrage of roundhouse punches and elongated uppercuts in a variety of directions, earning the style a reputation for keen effectiveness in fighting against multiple opponents. By 1850 Choy Li Fut had drawn a big following among the peasant class, with students of Heung branching out around southern China and forming a network of schools that garnered heavy enrollment. In time these branches began taking on their own distinctive personalities and unique interpretations of the style.

Lau Bun sought out Yeun Hai, the master of the Toi San school of Choy Li Fut. Retired and settling into his twilight years, Yeun Hai had hailed from the Hung Sing branch of Choy Li Fut in Fut San, a school known for its combat orientation and aggressive fighting technique. In the tradition of the school branching outward, Yuen Hai traveled from the Fut San school to open a new location in Toi San, where he taught for many years and took a young female martial arts practitioner to be his wife.

Persistent and bearing enough resources to be convincing, Lau Bun brokered a deal to take in the aging couple and provide for their room and board in the years to come in exchange for their tutelage. The proximity allowed Lau Bun private and intensive study of the couple's martial arts knowledge and endeared him to them as a son. Under Yeun Hai he learned not only Choy Li Fut but also Chinese herbalism and bonesetting. Before he passed Yeun Hai conveyed to Lau Bun the formidable Ten Thousand Elephants technique, a highly guarded close combat maneuver meant to be employed to devastating effect (and named as such to convey that each finger will strike with the weight of a thousand elephants).

As a young adult Lau Bun eventually departed to seek economic fortune in the United States, just as his father had done before him. With immigration suspended for Chinese nationals, Lau Bun took an alternative route through Mexico (a popular option in light of the now rigid exclusion law) and entered America through San Diego, before traveling to find kin in Los Angeles. He set up a legal identity as a "paper son" under the name Wong On, exploiting—like many other Chinese migrants of the era—an immigration loophole that arose after the destruction of so many legal records in the 1906 San Francisco earthquake and fire. He resided in the Chinese community of Los Angeles for a few years in the late 1920s, when trouble came knocking.

In an incident that would forever be attached to his reputation and would shroud his martial arts prowess in legend for years to come, Lau Bun fought his way out of a raid by federal immigration agents, with nothing more than his kung fu. While versions of the story vary among the tellers (some go as far as saying that Lau Bun took the lives of two agents in the skirmish), it is typically told that he was cornered in an apartment building by a group of four immigration agents. Trapped and outnumbered, Lau Bun—now adept at becoming his own whirling cyclone of whipping fists and furious assaults—fought his way through them before leaping from a second-story window and disappearing into the streets of Los Angeles.

The event made a minor folk hero of Lau Bun in a Chinese community that was constantly under threats and harassment from immigration officials. It also caught the attention of the Hop Sing Tong, which, in a recruiting effort, proposed to him a mutually beneficial arrangement: Lau Bun would be safely relocated out of Los Angeles to the Tong's San Francisco branch, and in return he would teach kung fu to its members and their children. Furthermore, with a resurgence of tong rivalries in Chinatown, his talents would be put to good use as a bodyguard and an enforcer.

As Chinatown grew in San Francisco, the neighborhood structured itself around various types of community groups and neighborhood organizations. Among their many roles these groups provided assistance in the acclimation of new arrivals from China, protection against anti-Chinese hostility, and aid in their brethren's eventual return to their homeland (even if it was in a casket). Others groups were purely social. The organizations often took shape according to regional origins and familial affiliations from China and, in many ways, were the governing bodies of Chinatown itself.

The tongs were modeled after the secret societies and underground rebellious groups that quietly formed in Guangdong during the nineteenth century to foment the overthrow of Manchu rule and advocate for the return of a Chinese-led dynasty. By the 1880s the tongs in San Francisco had veered sharply toward organized crime (causing the up-and-up community associations to add the prefix "Benevolent" to their own title as a distinction), and it was as part of this dynamic that Chinese martial artists were first woven into the social fabric of life in the New World during the nineteenth century. In what was hardly an athletic or social endeavor, early Chinese martial artists in America trained tong soldiers for combat surrounding the governance of vice. It is partly within this context that the martial arts garnered a peculiar status in the community. Unlike the respect and prestige that the martial arts held in Japanese culture as national sport and tradition, in the Chinese community these fighting skills were suspiciously regarded as the covenant of eccentrics, troublemakers, and gangsters.

In its early years San Francisco's Chinatown was a highly law-abiding neighborhood (particularly in contrast to the utter depravity of the red light district to its immediate east, the Barbary Coast). Yet as anti-Chinese hostility peaked in the 1870s and calls for exclusion manifested into federal policy, the lawful leaders of Chinatown lost traction to a rising tide of crime-oriented tong organizations thriving off gambling, opium, and prostitution. The law-abiding residents of Chinatown were soon caught in the crossfire as the tongs competed against one another for these markets, sowing rampant violence throughout Chinatown at the end of the century. The proliferation of murder and vice within the tong wars only inflamed calls for a permanent exclusion act, even as the current policy only further disenfranchised the established leadership in Chinatown. It was a vicious cycle that spilled into the early years of the twentieth century, until the situation was abruptly curbed through extraordinary circumstances.

On the morning of April 18, 1906, the city of San Francisco experienced a massive 8.3 magnitude earthquake that purportedly lasted forty-eight seconds. The earthquake damaged the city's underground water mains and left firemen ill-prepared to battle the raging blaze that developed from its destruction. In the following days an epic inferno consumed the entire eastern side of the city. Chinatown was reduced to ashes. The brothels and opium dens went with it.

City leaders perceived a unique opportunity to relocate the Chinese to a more remote southeast corner of the city (and even organized an official subcommittee for doing so). The leaders of Chinatown, on the other hand, wasted little time in quickly rebuilding in the same location and effectively outmaneuvering efforts of removal. The plan was simple and had already been in the works in the years prior: Chinatown needed to have a contributing effect to the city, and this would be best accomplished by way of transforming it into a tourist mecca and an economic boon to city coffers. The new Chinatown was then strategically rebuilt in a style that would evoke the Orient, with a pioneering style of architecture that was unprecedented anywhere else in the world, combining Western structures with Asian accents: sturdy brick apartment buildings with pagoda roofs, curved balconies, and gilded exteriors. The San Francisco Real Estate Board applauded the early results and began encouraging that all new structures in the neighborhood follow a similar approach. Plans for relocation fell by the wayside.

The level of blatant vice that existed in San Francisco was no longer openly tolerated by the city, neither in Chinatown nor in the Barbary Coast. In the years immediately following the earthquake, the city effectively stamped out the last vestiges of the Barbary for good, while the tongs in Chinatown turned toward political organizing and less visible forms of criminal activity. Opium never flourished again, but gambling and extortion remained just under the surface. Tong muscle never needed to take the shape of such formal soldiering again, but neither was it obsolete. Lau Bun taught Choy Li Fut for many years to members of the Hop Sing Tong, while also working as an enforcer for the organization.

In the Depression-era economic climate leading up to World War II, employment options for Chinese Americans were particularly narrow, and, as one sociologist pointed out, could essentially be grouped into just four categories: chop suey restaurants, gift shops, native grocery stores, and Chinese laundries. Lau Bun unknowingly entered into a new category when he found a small space on Clay Street to operate as a more formal practice studio. He called it the Wah-Keung (meaning the "strong Chinese") Kung Fu Club of Choy Li Fut and opened to interested neighborhood residents. It was a quiet transition of martial arts from the tongs to the public, though it really represented a sea change in how the Chinese martial arts would be both practiced and perceived in twentieth-century America. And unlike the gift shops and chop suey restaurants—which played to Western notions of Chinese culture—Lau Bun was dealing in the real thing.

However, in a mind-set that descended from the tongs' secretive inclinations toward authority as well as their protective nature of the community in a foreign land, martial arts instruction was not only strictly limited to Chinese people; it was also not meant to be flaunted about in public but rather displayed quietly and with reservation, as if one were handling a concealed weapon. This was a deeply entrenched tong code developed over many generations, from the secret societies of Guangdong to the advent of anti-Chinese mobs in San Francisco during the 1870s, and Lau Bun was a staunch proponent of this insular philosophy.

Even still, he was also known to allow occasional exception.

The din of the nearby street noise softened with the evening hour as Lau Bun poured himself some tea and sat quietly in his basement studio. He left the door at the top of the stairs open a while longer, listening for signs of his students' return.

Lau Bun had settled nicely into his humble lifestyle there on Brennan Alley. He made an adequate income and had a spacious outdoor park at his doorstep. Better yet, his school had now lasted a full two decades, with new students regularly wandering down his stairs. With his change of location from Clay Street years earlier, he'd replaced the name Wah-Keung with Hung Sing, to align his school with its origins of his teacher Yuen Hai and their particular branch of Choy Li Fut. He had experienced some hard times and tense moments since his youth in Toi San, memories that were a stark contrast to the tranquility of his subterranean quarters at that moment, there in the oldest part of his strange New World city.

Footsteps echoed down from the stairwell, breaking his introspection, as a group of his senior students descended into the studio at an anxious pace. They quickly removed their shoes at the base of the stairs and bowed to acknowledge their teacher, their *sifu*. Lau Bun put down his teacup and rose to stand before them. Their adrenaline was still palpable, and their expressions (as well as their lack of bruises) suggested that they had been successful in their endeavors this evening.

He had sent them southeast, to test their kung fu skills in a Latino section of the city's Mission District. It wasn't a difficult place for them to pick a fight, and the prospect of police involvement was minimal. He had dispatched them with few instructions, and they had left with zeal.

For all of his relentless insistence on horse-stance drills and rugged practice time, Lau Bun knew that there was a level of training that couldn't be acquired in the studio. He had observed (through close proximity) enough tong incidents to know that the real testing grounds for a fighter were on the streets, and he intended to keep his students—his dedicated, long-term senior students—in tune. They learned a lot from these skirmishes, and for all of Lau Bun's stoicism, he took pride in their victories.

"Boys," he said to them in Cantonese, "how did we do tonight?"

2 NATIVE SON

Bruce Lee stood near the deck railing with a group of fellow passengers as the ocean liner finally entered San Francisco Bay. It had been almost three weeks since the President Lines ship had departed Hong Kong, since Bruce nervously said good-bye to his family and awkwardly boasted to his friends that he would "become famous in America."

The voyage across the Pacific had been long but hardly arduous. Although he was quartered in third class, Bruce passed the time socializing with first-class passengers and giving them dance lessons each evening in the ship's ample ballroom. Bruce was the life of the party, and many of his nights aboard the USS *President Wilson* turned into a blissful sort of limbo as he sailed toward an uncertain future.

With their seafaring revelry now concluded, his fellow travelers took turns posing for photographs with Bruce along the railing, producing a quick memento to remember their dynamic teenage dance instructor. They were all dressed sharp for their arrival, and Bruce was no exception, wearing a dark suit, light tie, and sunglasses that complemented his boyish good looks.

As the passengers prepared to disembark, Bruce felt that same mixture of anxiety and optimism that had nagged him since his departure. While the dance floor had provided a frequent reprieve, he had been deeply introspective throughout the trip, mindful that he was teetering between chapters of his life.

With his childhood abruptly concluded behind the Pacific horizon, he settled his attention on the American landscape that stretched out before him. San Francisco was the city of his birth, and now eighteen years later, it would also serve as midwife to his adulthood. The years that transpired in the interim had, in many ways, proven auspicious. Bruce was a successful child actor of the Hong Kong cinema, appearing in numerous films and gaining increasing fame through the recent success of his first starring role, in *The Orphan*. Tenacious and ferociously motivated, Bruce was a high school boxing champion and promising student of venerated Wing Chun kung fu master Ip Man. Charismatic, social, and seemingly hyperactive, he was also Hong Kong's reigning national cha-cha dance champion.

His present trip to America, however, was not based on these youthful achievements but rather as a solution to his ever-increasing appetite for teenage mischief. Bruce had been immersed in the contentious street-fighting culture of Hong Kong, and his most recent scrape caught the attention of the local authorities, who admonished his mother and warned that he was a step away from being arrested. In turn, she suggested to her husband that it was an opportune moment for their son to take advantage of his American citizenship, an idea that Bruce's father all-too-readily embraced.

And now weeks later, exiled to the opposite side of the Pacific, Bruce was holding a suitcase in the shadow of the Golden Gate Bridge, while his classmates in Hong Kong prepared for their graduation.

San Francisco's Chinatown was a colorful cacophony of bright neon signs and richly painted buildings. An intermingling frenzy of tourists and residents played out in a riotous street-level scurry amid local grocery stores, chop suey restaurants, gaudy gift shops, and ornate theaters. The neighborhood was simultaneously a genuine Chinese community and a consciously orchestrated tourist destination, a unique piece of a vibrant city that had manifested in ways that even the earthquake-era leaders could have scarcely imagined.

Bruce soaked it all in, basking in its newness yet taking comfort in its familiarity. He had been met at the immigration office by his godfather, Quan Ging Ho, a close friend and colleague of his father, who greeted him with great affection before shuttling him off to Chinatown. Mr. Quan, a playwright, poet, and integral member of Chinatown's opera scene, had agreed to put up his godson for the next few months before Bruce moved to Seattle to resume his education in the fall.

His apartment, on the lower slope of Chinatown at 654 Jackson Street, was as simple as it was cramped, offering Bruce a single bed tightly packed between other pieces of furniture in the corner of the main room. The bathroom and kitchen were located down a narrow hallway and shared with the residents of the other units. For Bruce, who had grown up fairly affluent in Hong Kong, attended to by his family's servants, the space was as depressing as it was claustrophobic, a clear reminder that his current circumstances were predicated more on necessity than opportunity.

Before his young guest could dwell on the space, Mr. Quan hustled Bruce back out onto the street for a whirlwind tour of the neighborhood. There was much for Bruce to see in Chinatown, especially since much of his own personal history was intertwined with the community. Mr. Quan hurried him up to Grant Avenue, where a long banner stretched high over elaborate lamp posts, proclaiming, "The Largest Chinatown in the World." After just a moment's walk from Mr. Quan's apartment, the two were now standing before the ornate entryway to the Sun Sing Theater. Bruce knew before Mr. Quan had even said it that this was the theater where his father had performed.

In the autumn of 1939, Bruce's parents, Lee Hoi Chuen and Grace Hoi An, had traveled to the United States on tour with Hong Kong's Cantonese Opera. Hoi Chuen was a well-known and very successful Chinese comedic actor of both stage and screen. His wife, Grace, a beautiful woman with a quarter European ancestry, accompanied him on the trip as a wardrobe manager. For a Chinese couple in the era of exclusion laws, it was a rare opportunity to travel to America, and not long after their visas were extended, they learned of Grace's pregnancy.

Mr. Quan explained how the Sun Sing was originally known as the Mandarin Theater and that his father's time performing there was a great success. Having spent many youthful hours on film sets and in theaters, Bruce was well aware of both his father's stage talents and the adoration he received from audience members. Yet his own relationship with his father seemed perpetually strained by a terse and distant dynamic that played out throughout his childhood right up until the moment he had boarded that steamship for America. In truth Hoi Chuen's rigidness with his son was hardly exceptional but rather typical of Chinese tradition, where a father's authority must eclipse his affections. And Bruce's teenage years had certainly caused ample opportunity for Hoi Cheun's affection to get wholly lost in the shuffle.

Mr. Quan continued speaking, explaining how the rich tradition of the Cantonese opera not only went back centuries in southern China but was a fixture of San Francisco's Chinatown since the days of the gold rush. Bruce examined the entrance to the theater with his father on his mind, knowing full well that his recent troubles had done little to alleviate the tension between them.

As they walked back along Grant, Mr. Quan maintained his role as gleeful tour guide, pointing out random bits of neighborhood color in the late-afternoon sidewalk bustle. He gestured to a newspaper clipping taped up in a window of a street-level storefront and explained how a girl with the name of Lee had won this year's beauty pageant. The article displayed the face of Leona Lee, a twenty-year-old beauty from Hawaii who was recently crowned Miss Chinatown USA. The decades-old neighborhood pageant had recently gone national, requiring organizers to relocate the event from the Great China Theater to the much larger Masonic Auditorium up on Nob Hill. When the judges asked Leona, "Who is the greatest woman in the world?" she replied with charismatic nonchalance—"My mother, of course"—and locked up the top prize.

Before Bruce could dwell on Leona's charms, Mr. Quan gestured north toward Broadway and explained how there was an important bookstore at the end of the block that had just won a major court case about poetry. A published poet himself (his most recent volume, titled *Two Continents*, dealt with themes of identity among Chinese immigrants), Mr. Quan was referring to Lawrence Ferlinghetti's bookstore, City Lights, which had made national news in garnering an obscenity charge for publishing Allen Ginsberg's *Howl*. City Lights was ground zero for the Beat counterculture in San Francisco, and Ginsberg had written his iconic poem just one block to the east, in a tiny apartment on Washington Avenue.

Bruce had barely begun to make sense of the bookstore topic, when Mr. Quan again shifted gears, pointing to a building across Grant Avenue and explaining how it housed The Lion's Den, one of the neighborhood's many great nightclubs. Since the late thirties San Francisco's Chinatown had boasted an array of popular venues that showcased Chinese singers and dancers in elaborate floorshows and costumes. Mr. Quan rattled off many of these places for Bruce as they crossed the street. Among the best was the Chinese Skyroom, located on the top corner floor of a building at the far end of Grant, where shows would often end with the house dance troupe—The Wongettes—leading a conga line around the club, while high-stakes poker games would go late into the night beyond the back bar. Yet the most notable of all, was Forbidden City, over on Sutter, where the gregarious owner, Charlie Low, put on some of the most ambitious floor shows outside of Vegas. The entryway of Forbidden City was still lined with dozens of photos showing off the celebrities who had come through—the likes of Gene Kelly, Duke Ellington, Bob Hope—but as spectators, not performers. They came to see the Chinatown talent, like crooner Larry Ching (billed as "the Chinese Frank Sinatra") and Gee Ming, the house magician. There had been many other locations too—Club Mandalay by Portsmouth Square, the Kubla Khan on Grant, and Club Shangri-La on Bush Street—that had since fallen by the wayside.

Ascending Jackson Street's vertical landscape, the pair passed by a curbside newsstand, sporting the *Chinese Times*, the *Chinese Pacific Weekly*, and the *Chinese World*. The neighborhood may have been only six blocks wide, but it had a long tradition of publishing its own Chinese-language newspapers. One of the city's two big English-language dailies, the *San Francisco Chronicle*, blared a headline about the Giants moving into second place in the baseball standings, giving them equal billing with the main headline of President Eisenhower's latest nuclear missile talks with Russia. The Giants had arrived from New York just the year before after being wooed by San Francisco's ambitious Republican mayor George Christopher. The city embraced the team—and its dynamic centerfielder Willie Mays—from the get-go, filling the old stadium at Sixteenth and Bryant while a new one was being constructed at Candlestick Point. (Ironically, Mays had gone 3 for 5 in yesterday's game yet continued to get booed by hometown fans, on account of popping up a ball-four pitch in a key spot earlier that week.) Although the team hadn't even settled into a stadium, Bay Area fans already sensed a championship in their newly acquired ball club (and while the Giants would indeed face the Yankees in the 1962 World Series, it would be almost four more decades before they actually wore the crown).

Jackson Street seemed to ascend infinitely upward. Crossing Stockton Street, Mr. Quan pointed to a large white stone building with curved pagoda-styled roofing at the top, "And this," he explained, as he finally came to a stop on the sidewalk, "is where you were born."

It was a handsome building, particularly for a hospital. Bruce's parents had told him the story, but it was fascinating to finally see it in person. Mr. Quan explained how the hospital—built three decades earlier on community fund-raising—was a cornerstone of the neighborhood and for a long time was the only medical facility in the city that would attend to Chinese patients.

Inching up the block, Mr. Quan shifted his attention past the hospital. "Your parents lived here, on the alley," he said, pointing toward Trenton Street, which ran through the middle of the block. "When your mother was ready, we just walked her across the street."

Hoi Cheun was performing a series of engagements in New York City's Chinatown when Grace went into labor during the last week of November 1940. Her son was born early on the morning of the twenty-seventh, in the Year of the Dragon at the Hour of the Dragon. The name she chose—Lee Jun Fan—carried specific meaning. As his family would later explain, "The true meaning of Bruce's name—JUN FAN—was 'to arouse and make FAN (the United States) prosperous.' The gut feeling of many Chinese at that time, who felt suppressed by and inferior to foreign powers, was that they wished to outshine the more superior countries and regain the Golden Age of China. Bruce's parents wanted Bruce to have his name shine and shake the foreign countries." At the Chinese Hospital the attending physician, Dr. Mary Glover, had suggested that the boy also needed an American name, to which one of the nurses proposed "Bruce." The American name would later confound Hoi Cheun, who admitted he just couldn't pronounce it (more interesting still, Bruce would be entirely unaware of his English name until his early teens). The family remained in San Francisco for four more months with their newborn son, as Hoi Cheun finished his remaining shows on the West Coast and Grace made certain her son's citizenship was in order.

As they turned back down Jackson Street, Mr. Quan pointed across to the Grandview Theater, which housed another of Bruce's early beginnings. Before departing the United States, Hoi Cheun had arranged his son's first foray into show business, with a small role—a prop really—as a newborn baby in the film *Golden Gate Girl*. It was made by pioneering Chinese female director Esther Heng and had proved to be one of her most successful films. In this regard Bruce's show-business career had really begun before he could crawl, and it was just one more facet of his history along these streets—from the Mandarin Theater to Trenton Alley—which did little to lessen the introspective mood that had enveloped him during his trip from Hong Kong.

Ducking into a nearby restaurant for dinner, it occurred to Mr. Quan that Bruce hardly seemed like an unruly adolescent. Rather, he was quiet, polite, and surprisingly shy. He appeared outwardly proud of being Chinese and seemed to express genuine interest in the points of history around the neighborhood. Most surprising to Mr. Quan, however, was that Bruce seemed far less interested in talking about his film career than about his passion for martial arts. More than just some teenage hobby, Bruce characterized it as the main interest in life, and he was entirely serious when he told Mr. Quan that he would like to express to the entire world the greatness of the Chinese martial arts.

After dinner the two stopped to inspect the fourteen-foot statue of Sun Yat-sen that stood tall over the small neighborhood park opposite St. Mary's Cathedral. The "Father of Modern China" (or, as some historians characterize him—"China's George Washington") Sun Yat-sen was instrumental in orchestrating the 1912 overthrow of the Qing Dynasty and the toppling of China's last emperor. While in exile during the years leading up to the revolution, Sun Yat-sen had spent time in San Francisco's Chinatown raising money via the Ghee Kung Tong on Spofford Alley to fund the rebellion at home. Bruce was familiar with the historical figure, knowing that his mother's side of the family—a greatly influential Hong Kong clan—also worked to support Sun Yat-sen's revolution.

For many other residents of San Francisco's Chinatown, the statue had a more recent significance. Mr. Quan explained how this was where Madame Chiang Kai-shek came when she visited Chinatown, and that the city received her like royalty.

After many decades of experiencing hostility and exclusion, the Chinese in America were quickly embraced—literally overnight—as comrades-in-arms in the face of the Japanese attacks on Pearl Harbor. Madame Chiang had traveled to the United States on a goodwill tour in March 1943, at the height of the war, to drum up support for China's struggle against Japan. To say that she was received like royalty was an understatement. Rather, she was treated like a beloved female heroine who had magically stepped from one of history's epic sagas, like some Asian amalgamation of Scarlett O'Hara and Joan of Arc. Educated in America and evoking the Western ideal of exotic Eastern beauty, Madame Chiang captivated audiences around the United States during the length of her tour. In Washington her address to Congress was met with a booming ovation and beaming press, while in Los Angeles, she drew a capacity crowd to the Hollywood Bowl for a glitzy affair beset by A-list movie stars. In San Francisco her tour stopped traffic across multiple neighborhoods as thousands of spectators packed entire city blocks to get a glimpse of her at the Civic Center and in Chinatown.

Although she never spoke about the Chinese Exclusion Laws while in America, President Roosevelt rescinded them months later (while, for all practical purposes, restriction on Chinese immigration stayed in effect until 1965 and didn't fully resume until a few years later).

From a more behind-the-scenes historical viewpoint, her visit was hardly pristine. By the end of her tour she was drawing increased criticism for lavish shopping trips at a time when her countrymen were literally starving. FBI director J. Edgar Hoover suspected that she was embezzling large amounts of the money she was raising, and Americans who hosted her were typically appalled by the overly entitled behavior of her entourage. Yet this undercurrent was mostly lost in the applause. Madame Chiang's visit heavily altered American attitudes toward Chinese people, as the sum total of her intellect and beauty proved the perfect equation for reshaping viewpoints within the current historical circumstances.

However, this change in perceptions that Madame Chiang had affected was hardly all-encompassing, as derogatory caricatures of Asians would still dominate the American media for years to come: stereotypes of laundry men and rickshaw drivers or conniving villains in the mold of dragon ladies and Fu Manchu. Socially, Asians Americans (like other racial minorities in the United States) were still widely treated as second-class citizens, lacking voter protections and housing rights. Bans on interracial marriage and immigration remained in place. In San Francisco the Chinese were still relegated to living in Chinatown and lacked any representation in political office.

But Bruce was returning to America as the nation's social landscape was poised to shift. Recently, the city of San Francisco had sworn in Herbert Lee as the first Asian officer within the ranks of the police department. Nationally, Hiram Fong would soon be the first American of Chinese descent elected to the U.S. Senate, just as Daniel Inouye would be the first Japanese member of the House. Yet even as these figures made essential contributions, Asian Americans would never have a civil rights leader in the vein of Martin Luther King Jr. or Cesar Chavez. This would be a curious vacuum that caused heroes and inspiration to emerge from some unexpected places.

As they walked back toward Jackson Street, Bruce looked again toward the Sun Sing Theater. He could scarcely imagine it at the time, but the venue would mark his time in Chinatown just as it had his father's. Yet he would not take the stage at the Sun Sing Theater for a few years, and much would happen in the interim.

3 THE GOOD LONG FIST

Two blocks west of Portsmouth Square, down the steps to the other subterranean kung fu school in Chinatown, the altar within the Kin Mon Chinese Physical Culture Studio bore the inscription:

To vanquish humiliation and get revenge
One should study the martial arts industriously

The proper use of the good long fist
Is to punish lawbreakers and to eliminate violence

Wong Tim Yuen sat in his basement studio at 142 Waverly Place as he often did on most afternoons before class, smoking cigarettes and reading the newspaper. Known to some as just "T.Y.," he looked as meticulous as ever: neatly pressed shirt and pants, dark tie, suspenders, jet-black hair oiled back. He had well-defined features anchored around wide, inquisitive eyes, and a tall, solid frame that by itself implied proper use of "the good long fist." The name of his school, Kin Mon, translated to mean "the sturdy citizen," and T.Y. conducted himself as the embodiment of the concept.

Kin Mon was located just across from the Hop Sing Tong, where, like Lau Bun, T.Y. was a long-standing member. Although he was almost fifteen years Lau Bun's junior, the two of them represented core forces of martial arts in San Francisco's Chinatown, dating back to the early 1940s. And just as Lau Bun rendered his abilities in numerous capacities for Hop Sing beyond just teaching, T.Y. made his own contributions as well. During the war years, when U.S. servicemen on shore leave would frequently take their Forbidden City revelry too far on the streets of Chinatown, urgent distress calls requesting Hop Sing muscle most often fell to T.Y. In an era when few Americans had ever heard of—much less personally encountered—kung fu, the drunken GIs could hardly have suspected what the alleys of Chinatown were poised to unleash on them.

But those incidents were insignificant, nonsense really, compared to the encounters of T.Y.'s youth. On the wall behind him, through a mild haze of tobacco smoke, was an aged black-and-white photograph of T.Y. as a teenager at the 1928 national martial arts exhibition in Nanjing, China. At the center of the stage stood his teacher, Leong Tin Chee, with T.Y. and senior student Chew Lung flanking him on either side. The three of them all hold martial poses: the master poised tall at the center of the trio, the acolytes baby-faced, lean, and muscular.

Leong Tin Chee spent many years at the turn of the century as a nomadic master who traveled the Chinese countryside conducting demonstrations, meeting challenges, and generally seeking out martial arts around the nation. It was in this context that a teenage T.Y. watched him as a spectator in the crowd, a witness to the makeshift wooden stage trembling beneath the deep power of Leong's horse stance. Dazzled by the display, T.Y. sought out his tutelage and was taken on as his second student. He studied under Leong for a decade, traveling China and often fighting in his share of brutal *le tai* competitions, the full-contact platform matches that ended for many participants in serious injury or maiming. From location to location T.Y. evolved into a formidable fighter, shaped by the stark violence of one *le tai* after the next.

Later, during the Japanese invasion of China, T.Y.'s father eventually found him passage to America, likely saving him from the fate that befell his classmate Chew Lung, who perished from a sniper's bullet. Upon arriving in San Francisco's Chinatown, the Hop Sing Tong quickly recruited T.Y. for his martial arts prowess, just as it had with Lau Bun years earlier.

Yet despite his old-world origin, T.Y. would eventually play a quiet role in ushering in a modern and very American era for martial arts. In a grand juxtaposition to the first photo, an adjacent image on the wall captured students of Kin Mon smiling with giddy excitement on the set of the *Home* show, the popular daytime NBC program with Arlene Francis and Hugh Downs, where the school performed kung fu on television in 1955 (presumably for the first time in American broadcast history). It was a curious showing in light of the old Tong code—of not exposing martial arts to the non-Chinese—especially from Hop Sing, of all places. But time and time again the sturdy citizen in T.Y. saw it differently. His viewpoint may have been deeply buried beneath hard rules and a stern disposition, but in the long view of martial arts history T.Y. would be a pioneering force in unraveling the racial exclusion that surrounded the Chinese martial arts.

More recently, he began collaborating on an instructional kung fu book with his senior student James Lee, who had pioneered his own martial arts publishing company. An English language book by a Chinese master was unprecedented and followed on the heels of T.Y.'s decision to allow James Lee's close friend and protégé Al Novak to train at Kin Mon on a regular basis. The hulking Novak was the first white student to train within San Francisco's Chinatown (in 1960), and T.Y. would maintain the trend with a slow trickle of other non-Chinese students throughout the decade.

Sitting there smoking between those two photographs, between NBC and Nanjing, T.Y. was a conduit linking the still-emerging modern era of martial arts to the deep origins of old world China. After all, T.Y.'s system was Sil Lum, which in Cantonese translates as Shaolin. And, as the saying goes, "All martial arts under heaven arose out of Shaolin."

Or so it would seem.

Located along the Songshan mountain range in China's Henan Province, the Shaolin Temple is one of the most famous Buddhist monasteries on the planet. Originally constructed at the turn of the fifth century, the temple carries great religious significance, marking the arrival of Chan Buddhism (more often known by its Japanese name, Zen Buddhism) from India to China. However, Shaolin's global fame is more readily derived from its association with the Chinese martial arts, through its reputation as a kind of kung fu Mecca. Majestically situated and mystically oriented, Shaolin is regarded in global popular culture as the storied wellspring from which the Chinese martial arts have flowed to the entire world.

Yet to really understand Shaolin's martial arts legacy, it is necessary to understand its most notable detractor. Tang Hao was a Chinese historian who today is scarcely known beyond a small circle of academia. Beginning with his work in the 1920s, Tang Hao was really the first modern historian to examine the origins of martial arts in China. Through the numerous books and articles that he wrote, Tang Hao dismissed much of the prevailing history surrounding the Chinese martial arts as fanciful folklore, particularly with regard to Shaolin. In drawing sharp lines between mythology and fact, Tang Hao's work was met by the Chinese martial arts community not with interest and gratitude but rather with hostility and outrage.

It is in this precarious balance, between the much-celebrated folkloric legacy of Shaolin and the once-unwelcomed scholarship of the ostracized Tang Hao, that the history of the Chinese martial arts still teeters. It is a peculiar dynamic with few parallels in the modern world, especially as Shaolin's martial arts mythology continues to thrive well into the twenty-first century.

The early folklore attributed to Shaolin's connection to the martial arts is tied to the origins of Chan Buddhism in China. The popular rendering asserts that in the fifth century, the monk Bodhidharma traveled from India to spread Buddhist teachings, and that his place of conveyance in China was Shaolin. This made the monastery, in the words of Shaolin historian Meir Shahar, "the symbolic crossing point between the realm of the Buddha and China."

The martial arts, as the story goes, were a byproduct of this interaction. Noticing the adverse physical effects that long periods of meditation were having on the monks, the Bodhidharma is said to have passed along a series of exercises that the monks could perform to cultivate their physical health, stimulate their mental state of being, and (if ever necessary) employ for the defense of the monastery. Having an abundance of time, the monks honed these exercises into highly refined fighting techniques.

Centuries later, when the monastery was supposedly burned to the ground by the invading Manchus, it is believed that the handful of monks who escaped later disseminated their fighting techniques throughout China. This is said to have led to the formation of a southern Shaolin Temple, which gave rise to the regional styles of the south. Over time the fighting techniques that emerged from Shaolin's legacy would spread even further, eventually extending well beyond the borders of China to the entire world.

Tang Hao dismissed much of these Shaolin story lines as legend, particularly the notion of the Bodhidharma as the initial source of kung fu. Through intensive research and reporting, he began the process of building an evidenced-based timeline regarding the origin and evolution of the Chinese martial arts that was predicated on historical developments across China's social, military, and intellectual landscapes. Ironically, the factual history that emerges from Tang Hao's scholarship is every bit as compelling as the folklore.

While the monastery's connection to Chan Buddhism is sound (despite debate over the actual existence of a Bodhidharma figure), Shaolin military activity does not surface in the historical record until the early part of the seventh century, when the monks successfully defended their temple and then their adjacent cropland from bandits. Shaolin fighting technique at the time was a far call from the elaborate unarmed hand-combat systems that they are now known for, but rather involved a sort of ritualistic black magic in which younger monks would fight in the field while the elders would stay behind and invoke vengeful Buddhist demons to annihilate their foes.

Later, when Shaolin did earn a reputation for martial methods, it was for its practitioners' superior aptitude in staff fighting. Under the Ming Dynasty, the Shaolin Monastery became a kind of war college, training future officers in a variety of combat skills. The emphasis on pole fighting (more than half the classes at Shaolin specialized in this area) conveyed a core capability for future officers who would have to train their soldiers in armed battlefield techniques, such as long-spear combat. Shaolin thrived in this role and gained a reputation throughout China for aspects of its military training program. However, the emphasis on staff fighting as core training eventually shifted around the time of the pioneering military theories put forth by a renowned commander.

Qi Jiguang was a celebrated Ming general, national hero, and arguably one of the great military minds in human history. Known for instilling iron discipline throughout his ranks of soldiers by way of rigorous training methods, Qi Jiguang (pronounced gigi-kwan) had considerable impact on military thought at the end of the Ming Dynasty (and on many subsequent generations, as well).

Beginning in 1560, Qi successfully led forces in fighting off marauding pirates all along China's east coast, enlisting peasant farmers and miners into effective battalions with great success. Where other military leaders proved impotent in dealing with the pirate threat, Qi began to score a series of victories that, by 1564, would result in the pirates withdrawing from China. Later he would have a successful tenure overseeing the bolstering of Great Wall defenses in the far north, preventing any Manchu incursions during his watch.

Over the course of his career, Qi published a pair of books on military strategy that would have considerable impact on training institutions such as Shaolin. In his *New Treatise on Military Efficiency*, Qi devotes an entire chapter (with the wonderful title "Fist Canon and the Essentials of Nimbleness") to the topic of unarmed fighting techniques and the benefits of teaching them among the combat ranks. These skills would be not for application on the battlefield, he argued, but for the physical conditioning of troops, and most notably, for their acclimation to the nature of actual combat.

Savvy to the prevailing military currents of the times, Shaolin adapted to this new viewpoint and maintained its relevance as a training institute by featuring unarmed fighting techniques as a primary part of its curriculum.

As martial arts historian Ben Judkins explains: "The popularity of the unarmed martial arts exploded [in China] between 1580 and 1640. . . . Already by the 1580s some Shaolin monks were practicing boxing with the aim of 'perfecting' the unarmed arts, much as they had done with the pole." Most notably perhaps is the unique nature of the period in which these unarmed fighting styles began to emerge during the Ming Dynasty. Historians refer to it as Ming syncretism, an era of a special intellectual atmosphere in China, which saw a harmonious cross-pollination of the three great Eastern philosophies and their practices among the educated classes: Buddhist religious thought was combined with Confucian doctrine and integrated with Daoist philosophy.

This fostered a unique atmosphere for the Shaolin monks and other upper-echelon segments of Ming society to contribute to the development of open-hand fighting styles. (Despite all prevailing story lines, Shaolin wasn't actually inventing fighting methods at all but rather absorbing them from the peasant class and honing them in its own fashion). Within this context of Ming syncretism, traits of Buddhist meditation, Confucian medical practices, and Daoist calisthenics all appear to have had some role in shaping and integrating the Chinese martial arts.

Yet away from the elite circles and the much better documented segments of dynastic life, the peasant class in China was embroiled in day-to-day currents of violence that, in reality, contrasted profoundly with the image of orderly dynastic society that the Ming architects were inclined to portray. Widespread banditry and other forms of petty crime, combined with flourishes of rebellion, infused common life with a degree of steady violence that would have given the martial arts a simple and widespread relevance at the time. The need for militias and crop-watching units, as well general protection for homes, businesses, and individuals was considerable.

So it was on the heels of the military theories of Qi Jiguang, during the Renaissance-like atmosphere of Ming syncretism among the elite, and in the steady and stark violence of peasant life that the unarmed fighting techniques of the Chinese martial arts began to flourish. Despite all lingering tales of the Bodhidharma, this is the historical point at which Shaolin first specialized in the open-hand combat techniques for which it would be famous centuries later. And in a wider sense, it is when kung fu—as we know it in a modern sense—first began to surface in the historical record in China.

Throughout history the Chinese martial arts have been known by many names: *wushu* (which translates to "martial methods"), *kuoshu* ("national art"), *chuan fa* ("boxing method"), *Chinese boxing* (a reference to open-hand fighting styles, not Western boxing), and in more recent times, as *kung fu* (meaning "effort" or "hard work").

The list of different styles and schools within the Chinese martial arts is long, varied, and extremely colorful: Tiger Claw, Buddhist Palm, Northern Praying Mantis, Southern Praying Mantis, Monkey Style, Bear Style, White Eyebrow, Drunken Fist, Five Animals, Five Ancestors, Six Harmonies Boxing, Cotton Boxing, Ax-Hitch Boxing, and hundreds more. With different features, approaches, and emphasis, these styles have varying regional and familial backgrounds and ultimately compose a diverse and expansive field of techniques. Eagle Claw, for instance, is a northern style that is grappling oriented, showcasing joint locks and pressure-point attacks. By contrast, White Crane is a southern style known for sophisticated hand techniques applied at close range with swift striking motions that are derivative of its namesake animal. Conversely, the globally popular and well-known practice of tai chi chu'an is often described as an internal or soft style of kung fu; the slow movements and meditative nature of the art typically speaks to a greater emphasis on spiritual, mental, and energy-related concepts, as opposed to a more martial orientation.

By the late nineteenth century, the otherwise obscure regional and familial fighting systems around China begin to rebrand themselves in the face of growing peasant class interest in the martial arts. As historian Ben Judkins explains:

> During the early 19th century, China had a huge number of local fighting styles. Most of them were very small village or family affairs. Many of these styles did not actually have names, though there were some notable exceptions.
>
> They were not studied so much as a particular "style" of fighting. They simply were fighting. Later in the 19th century as the demand for martial instruction increased, and the number of reasons it was pursued diversified, it became necessary to market these skills on a broader scale than had been undertaken in the past. Names and shiny new creation myths began to appear as the fighting techniques of the previous generation were increasingly repackaged as a "martial commodity."

The martial brands of the late nineteenth and early twentieth centuries were developed in a similar style to Shaolin's creation myth of the

Bodidharma as the early source of the temple's fighting-art tradition. Just as the Bodidharma martial arts legend emerged long after the supposed interaction would have taken place, many of the modern creation myths were developed long after the actual genesis of most styles.

As martial arts historian Brian Kennedy writes: "The goal of most martial arts systems' histories is to give that system prestige—what the Chinese refer to as 'face.' Some hope to impress the general public or prove that the system is combat-effective, while others simply aim to inspire students of the system. Still others are concerned only with relating some interesting folk tales. 'Truth' rarely factors into the equation." Scholars refer to this as "invented tradition." By developing a compelling (and often semimystical) origin story, the school or style could draw new students by hooking onto their martial arts imagination. Essentially, it was highly savvy advertising.

For Wing Chun it was a priestess designing a streamlined defense technique to aid a younger woman fending off a belligerent warlord. For White Crane it was when the patriarch of a southern family tried to scare off a crane and observed the bird's sublime movements. For Monkey style it was when an imprisoned man observed the agile movements of primates in the nearby trees from his cell window. While some martial artists acknowledge the folkloric nature of these stories, many others, to this day, regard them as fact.

It was in an era of ever-increasing hyperbole that Tang Hao applied a skeptical eye to the Chinese martial arts. By the late 1920s the fledgling republican government in China had created the Central Guoshou Institute as a formal body to promote and organize the Chinese martial arts as a pillar of national physical culture. (Indeed, it was the Central Guoshou Institute that organized the 1928 national competition in which T. Y. Wong fought and performed during his early twenties.) Following an era of widespread martial branding, as well as an explosion of fanciful literature, the Chinese martial arts were ripe for a sober historical assessment. A lawyer by trade and an experienced practitioner of martial arts, Tang Hao was assigned as a lead editor for the publication division of the Central Guoshu Institute.

Like the governmental organization that he worked for, Tang Hao was a reformist who believed that the martial arts could play a key role in the physical culture of a modern twentieth-century China. In 1920 Tang Hao published *Study of Shaolin and Wudang*, in which he tackled the disparity between fact and folklore in Chinese martial arts history, taking aim, as Judkins put it, "at as many sacred cows as possible." He dismissed the folklore surrounding Shaolin and criticized much of the quasi mysticism that had been attached to the martial arts in his time.

Immediately, Tang's work was received with hostility, and as a friend of his would later write in a memorial essay, "some ruthless and self-proclaimed practitioners of Wudang and Shaolin made a plan to attack Tang Hao and beat him up." This was only prevented when a reputable third party intervened on his behalf (and the fact that people within the Central Guoshu Institute didn't defend him, suggests he may have been insulting people in-house, as well).

Later in his career he would continue to write about and promote an evidence-based history of the Chinese martial arts, debunking the highly popular book *Secrets of Shaolin Boxing* and disputing the trend of invented traditions. Later, as he endured periods of bankruptcy and near homelessness during a career that was hardly lucrative, he continued his studies and published books along the same lines for close to two decades.

Yet even as Tang Hao was striving to accurately portray the factual historical origins of the martial arts in China, these fighting systems (and their folklore) were already taking root in foreign nations around the globe.

4 THE LITTLE DRAGON

A few audience members let loose a yelp when Bruce shot out a blast of punches. He did it again—the blur, the pop—and garnered a few more exclamations.

Having caught the crowd's attention with his dancing, Bruce was now taking the opportunity to show off his kung fu skills. He had gotten in the habit of seizing intermission for his demonstrations (a strategy that he would employ for years to come), and as he had been learning over the past two months, few people in America—even within the Chinese community—had ever heard of Wing Chun. His current audience, at the Chinese American Citizen's Alliance in downtown Oakland, was no exception. As a result he gave them a flashy combination of different styles: "The showmanship, not the killer," as his classmates in Hong Kong would have called it.

In the summer of 1959, Bruce was slowly learning to navigate his way in America. Although Mr. Quan had found him a job at the Kum Hon Restaurant just across from their apartment, Bruce had quickly proved that he was poorly suited for work in the service industry, and he lasted little more than a week. Mr. Quan, however, responded with a savvy alternative strategy: if Chinatown was the land of Forbidden City nightclubs, then surely a national dance champion could earn some money giving dance lessons.

Bruce's freelance employment as a dance instructor quickly gained momentum as the local Chinese community offered him many opportunities for work, not just in Chinatown but on the other side of the Bay in Oakland as well. He charged one dollar per couple and taught at local dances in the KMT Building, the Claremont and Leamington hotels, and in numerous association halls. He often made as much as thirty dollars per outing, which, he reasoned, was pretty good money for attending a social affair.

Not far from the stage, George Lee, a forty-year-old machinist from Alameda with a big Buddha-like smile, stood in awe of Bruce's demonstration at the Citizen's Alliance lodge. George had learned kung fu years earlier in China, but none of what he had been taught seemed as fluid or as practical as what this kid on stage was doing. And the speed . . . it was jaw-dropping.

Although Bruce appeared half his age, George quickly approached him after the demonstrations to inquire about lessons, only to learn that Bruce was leaving the Bay Area soon to attend school in Seattle.

"Any chance you'll come back here?" George asked. "Because I can get some people together and you could open a school."

Bruce had already considered the idea while traveling to the United States. With only five years' experience in Wing Chun, he couldn't have dreamed of teaching in Hong Kong, but in the sparse martial arts landscape of America, it was appearing increasingly possible. Before Bruce could reiterate the priority of his studies in Seattle, George inquired further.

"What style were you doing on stage, with the punches?"

"It is Wing Chun," Bruce explained with pride, "from Hong Kong."

Located along China's southern coast, Hong Kong Island sits at the base of the Pearl River Delta eighty miles from Canton in the South China Sea. Once a sparsely populated fishing village that England's foreign secretary dismissed in the early nineteenth century as a "barren island," Hong Kong was eventually taken as a British colony in the wake of the First Opium War. Like San Francisco what had started as a remote port (of only about seven thousand inhabitants at the time of British possession in 1841) would experience a huge influx of settlers around 1850, when Hong Kong received vast numbers of refugees fleeing the civil war struggle of the Taiping Rebellion. In 1860, with Hong Kong's population surpassing one hundred thousand, China also ceded control of Kowloon, the adjacent mainland peninsula, which was subsequently integrated by the British into the colony.

The place that developed over the next century was overpopulated, racially diverse, and heavily influenced by geopolitical currents. In time the colony would become a dense metropolis marked by tightly packed skyscrapers (the most vertical city in the world) as well as an intricate finance and banking system that would become a key component of the global economy.

In the spring of 1941, Hoi Cheun and Grace had returned home to Hong Kong from San Francisco and introduced their other children, Phoebe, Agnes, and Peter, to their pudgy five-month-old baby brother, Bruce (their youngest child, Robert, would be born years later). They had arrived home during World War II in the tumultuous atmosphere of the Pacific theater, where the Japanese invasion of mainland China in the summer of 1937 instituted a brutal campaign against the civilian population and quickly sent waves of refugees into the British colony. In 1938 alone half a million people flooded into Hong Kong as Japanese forces swept through Canton and the rest of nearby Guandong Province. The inevitable finally came on December 7, 1941, when Japanese forces toppled the British colony with little resistance during the same offensive that simultaneously launched an attack on the American fleet in Hawaii's Pearl Harbor. The occupation that followed lasted until the summer of 1945 and involved widespread food shortages, loss of public utilities, and the general disruption of day-to-day society.

The Le family weathered this period at their home on Nathan Road in the Kowloon section of Hong Kong, with a Japanese military encampment directly across from them. Nonetheless, Hoi Cheun's wealth from his acting career got them through the war without incident, and his return to show business in its aftermath afforded his children an affluent upbringing in a place where rampant poverty was readily on display. With the passing of his brother, Hoi Cheun held firm to tradition by taking in his sister-in-law and her five kids, effectively creating a rambunctious and noisy home environment swarming with children and pets. For as rigid as he could be with Bruce over the years, Hoi Cheun was a generous man who often intervened financially to help friends and family.

After becoming smitten with him from her orchestra seat at the opera, Grace had eloped with Hoi Cheun at a young age. Although raised in Shanghai, she belonged to the very prominent and multiethnic Hong Kong family of the Ho Tung-Bosman clan. Her grandfather, Charles Maurice Bosman, was a prosperous Dutch merchant and consul with a wide range of business ventures throughout Hong Kong. He married a Chinese woman, Lady Tze, and had several children, including Robert Ho Tong, who would become a well-known philanthropist and businessman and is historically regarded as a Hong Kong incarnation of Andrew Carnegie. Grace's father was Ho Kom Tong, who in photographs looks noticeably full-blooded Chinese compared to his very Eurasian-looking siblings, and was likely the offspring of an affair that Lady Tze had with a Chinese servant.

Ho Kom Tong made an already labyrinth-like family tree exceedingly horizontal by having seventeen kids with numerous wives and concubines. A recent book written by Ho Kom Tong's great nephew, Eric Peter Ho, on the subject of their family tree, refers to Grace as "the final piece in the jigsaw of Ho Kom-tong's family," citing her as the daughter of his mixed-race Shanghai mistress. Yet even as it is typically cited that one of her parents was German, Grace's exact racial makeup remains ambiguous. In fact, during interviews with U.S. immigration officials prior to leaving San Francisco in 1941, Grace formally stated that her father was Chinese and her mother was English. Whatever the particulars, Bruce descended from a Hong Kong family in which racial integration had long been regarded as a nonissue.

Grace and Hoi Chuen's first son had died shortly after childbirth, a bad omen in Chinese tradition that stoked great fears in them about displeased ancestral spirits. More than just some casual superstition, this would play out in tangible ways over the years. Since these beliefs implied that the second child should be a girl, they adopted Phoebe in an effort to put the procession into proper order. With Bruce there existed a general concern that the spirits sought to take away Grace's sons, so in an effort to confuse them, he was often referred to at home by the female name *Sai Fan* (meaning "Little Peacock"). This gender misdirection played out in colorful ways during his early years with girl's clothing and an earring right up until his ninth birthday, when it was deemed that the spirits had been adequately outmaneuvered.

With the 1949 victory of the Communist Party in China, Hong Kong experienced a renewed influx of refugees, this time fleeing their own countrymen rather than an invading force. (Oddly enough, Chairman Mao echoed the early British foreign secretaries when he dismissed Hong Kong as "a wasteland of an island.") With Communist control of China, nearly a million Chinese people fled to Hong Kong in this period, overwhelming an already overpopulated area and severely impacting life in the colony. As Bruce's childhood friend Hawkins Cheung would later reflect: "Hong Kong in the 1950s was a depressed place. Post–World War II Hong Kong had suffered from unemployment, a poor economy, over-crowding, homelessness, and people taking advantage of each other. Gangs roamed the street, and juvenile delinquents ran rampant." This environment contrasted starkly with the wealth and privilege that Hoi Cheun provided his family at home. It was a dichotomy that was literally evident at their front door, where they would often find homeless people sleeping in their entryway. In this regard Bruce came of age in a curious dynamic of comfort by way of a movie star father set against the looming poverty and strife of his urban environment. It would shape him in his early years and steer him to martial arts.

As a child Bruce was as bright as he was rambunctious. His family nicknamed him *mo si tung*, meaning "never sits still," as his early years kept his mother constantly occupied. Later, the sum total of his mischievous personality, stubborn disposition, and hyperactive body would eventually get him expelled before he was a teen from the English-language La Salle Intermediate College. His parents then rerouted him to the equally prestigious St. Francis Xavier College, where Bruce continued to dig out his share of mischief and trouble.

In the Kowloon section of Hong Kong in the early 1950s, mischief and trouble ran rampant on many fronts. In addition to the large homeless population fending for itself, many teenagers who failed to pass an entry exam into the colony's secondary school system were left with merely an elementary-level education in the face of a consistently languid economy.

Adrift with little prospects of employment, they formed juvenile gangs and perpetrated a wide range of petty crimes on the streets. Further exacerbating this environment, Hong Kong had also inherited vast numbers of professional gangsters who had fled Communist persecution on the mainland, and who now perpetrated a far more serious and organized form of local vice within the colony.

Bruce exhibited a tough disposition in his early years, often rallying his preteen friends to scrap with the British boys from the nearby King George V School. Even still, he had traits that could prove magnetic to bullies: he was physically small and possessed pretty-boy good looks to match his movie-star privilege. Although his family didn't blink at racial integration, his mixed heritage was yet another point of contention when navigating the gauntlet of Kowloon's streets. It was this constant day-to-day street strife that would spark his initial interest in martial arts.

Many of Bruce's classmates at St. Francis Xavier were already studying with a master whose studio was close to the school. The teacher was known for a style that was modern, easy to learn, and—best of all—had a reputation for being effective on the streets. Although few of them could conceive of it at the time, this master would become a martial arts legend in his own right.

The combined impact of Japan's 1937 invasion of China and the subsequent Communist victory in 1949 caused a widespread dislodging of the mainland population. Families who had lived in one place for generations suddenly had to relocate to other parts of the country or even the world. In the process China's martial arts masters were also reshuffled from their places of origin, taking their regionally based styles to areas where they had never previously been encountered. Furthermore, in a Marxist effort toward modernization, Mao banned China's martial arts practices as an antiquated and superstitious tradition. It was in this context that the colony of Hong Kong saw an array of kung fu masters from all over China brought into unprecedented proximity for the first time.

Ip Man arrived in Hong Kong in 1950, penniless, widowed, and close to sixty years old. The son of a wealthy merchant, he was raised in prosperity and privilege on a manor farm in the southern town of Foshan, where as a teen he studied an obscure southern style of kung fu known as Wing Chun. After continuing his training during secondary school in Hong Kong, he returned to an idyllic lifestyle on his family's estate at the age of twenty. Like many of his countrymen, he found life as he knew it upended in the war years, as the Japanese invasion of World War II steadily eroded his wealth and security. Having worked as a policeman for the Nationalist Forces, Ip Man eventually fled southern China in the face of the Communist victory and, in time, made a living in Hong Kong teaching his one great skill.

Economical, swift, and direct, Wing Chun has little of the flare seen in some other kung fu styles. There are no acrobatic forms or grand, sweeping movements, just stripped down techniques seeking an almost mathematical effectiveness in their application. The emphasis on "in-fighting" positions the practitioner to attack along the opponent's centerline, often using short kicks and flurries of quick punches in close proximity. In Hong Kong the simplicity and streamlined nature of the style often proved itself most effective during the rapid chaos of a street fight.

The folk history attached to Wing Chun asserts that a priestess of the southern Shaolin temple had designed the style to be employed by a female peasant who needed to fend off an aggressive suitor. This notion, that the style was developed for females by females, would only add to Wing Chun's reputation as a singularly unique incarnation of kung fu.

Ip Man's approach, like the style he taught, was all based on minimalism. Unlike many other masters (such as Lau Bun, for instance), he had no interest in the more peripheral traditions of Chinese martial arts, such as medicine or Lion Dancing. His art's purpose was for the boiled-down intention of combat effectiveness, and in postwar Hong Kong, that would work just fine.

At the time Ip Man was slowly getting his business running in the early 1950s, Wing Chun was an obscurity, and he was one of the last known accomplished practitioners of it in China.

Bruce had taken up Wing Chun with Ip Man in the Kowloon section of Hong Kong in 1954 at the age of thirteen and set himself to it with a fanatical ambition. His peers marveled at not only how hard Bruce trained but also how single-minded he became in his devotion to learning. Bruce committed only sporadic diligence to his studies at St. Francis Xavier each day, but he never skipped a Wing Chun class and put in dedicated hours while he was there. Outside class he got into the habit of practicing his punches while holding dumbbells and filling his walks to school with sharp kicks to undeserving trees along the way. Even while sitting at the dinner table, he would occasionally throw out a punch to some phantom opponent. His classmates saddled him with the nickname "Upstart," while Ip Man's son referred to him as "fighting crazy."

However, the atmosphere between students in Ip Man's studio could be casually contentious, as ego and competitiveness drove them to outdo one another. Younger students sought to glean techniques that were above their skill set, so that they would have an advantage against their rivals. As Hawkins Cheung put it, "Everyone wanted to be top dog."

A core practice of Wing Chun training is the sensitivity drill of *chi sao* ("sticking hands"), in which two practitioners move interlocked hands and forearms to develop contact reflex. This exercise seeks to imbue Wing Chun practitioners with keen awareness of the movement and balance of an opponent, allowing for disruption and the ability to counter any attack. In class students engaging in *chi sao* had the opportunity to best a rival by landing a solid blow in the process. Like every other aspect of his training, Bruce took to *chi sao* practice with considerable zeal.

But his industriousness was a trait that soon backfired on him, when older students took offense at being bested by a fledgling practitioner during *chi sao*. They responded by pointing out Bruce's mixed-race heritage to Ip Man, citing it as a violation of Chinese martial arts etiquette, and urging his dismissal. Ip Man was reluctantly obligated to do so but found a loophole by allowing two of his most senior students, William Cheung and Wong Sheun Leoung, to continue Bruce's training on the side. For Bruce the issue of his mixed-race ancestry, as well as this Chinese-only code, would surface again and again for many years to come.

In training now with the senior students, Bruce was given a more hands-on view of fighting, in which the streets of Hong Kong were often employed as the perfect environment for an extended bit of martial arts practice. With the colony housing a variety of instructors, students would test the legitimacy of what their masters were teaching against practitioners from other schools. This grew into a culture in itself, since many of the gangs on the streets of Hong Kong were affiliated with a particular style of kung fu. As a result a street fight was never hard to find, and as the challenge culture grew between rival styles, the colony's police force began to regard these young martial artists as deviant youth gangs engaging in illegal violence. In response the teens began taking the fights off the streets and up to the rooftops, where they could find a decent amount of space and conduct their showdowns uninterrupted.

The "rooftop fights" of Hong Kong in this period became a unique fighting culture all its own, and Ip Man's Wing Chun students made a name for themselves within it. "As he taught us," Hawkins explains, "Yip Man said, 'Don't believe me . . . Go out and have a fight. Test it out.'"

This facet of Bruce's Hong Kong training would forever shape his martial arts philosophy as William Cheung and Wong Sheun Leoung kept him in firsthand proximity to the hard realities of actual street fighting. He saw what worked versus what was mere extravagance, and he got a sense for the peripheral factors—stamina, instinct, and grit—that transcended both fighting technique and theory. In the short term, however, it meant scrapes, black eyes, and calls from the police. As a result Bruce's teen years were marked by navigating the wrath of his father as much as the wrath of rival gangs. His sister Agnes notes that Bruce didn't cope well with coming out on the losing end of a street clash, and the unbearable anguish of such losses manifested in his drive to train harder and harder. If it was a matter of being unbeatable, Bruce reckoned, he would work to become unbeatable.

This deep-seated drive and ambition began to pay off during some of Bruce's more innocuous pursuits as well, such as his late-teen championships in boxing and dancing. While his victories in the ring could be seen as a convenient extracurricular (and less troublesome) context to apply Wing Chun–style punches, his interest in cha-cha dancing was quite genuine and fit nicely with his social scene at St. Francis Xavier.

Bruce also thrived in the acting roles that his father got him, and beginning from the age of about six, Bruce had over twenty roles in Hong Kong films, billed under the name Lee Siu Loong—Lee Little Dragon.

In the face of his street mischief, these more positive accomplishments rounded out the polar extremes of Bruce's adolescent behavior. He could be gregarious, charming, and highly motivated. Although never a star in the classroom, he was an avid reader of books and a devoted student of the philosophical side of Ip Man's teaching. Conversely, he could seem arrogant and egotistical, with an antagonistic streak that quickly created enemies. These traits had gotten him expelled from a prestigious school and increasingly placed him on the radar of local law enforcement. This duality would mark Bruce's social relations for years to come and create both lifelong friends and bitter enemies.

"He was a little hyper, but a lot of fun," explains his childhood friend Ben Der. "I liked him a lot; he was very honest and very humorous. But if you didn't know him, you could get the idea that he was too cocky and too much of a showoff."

Whatever the exact balance, the sum total of these features would eventually bring his childhood to an abrupt end. Fellow students assert that it was Bruce who picked the particular fight that would prompt his return to San Francisco. It was a rooftop bout set up against a member of a rival Choy Li Fut school and had been arranged by senior students to last two rounds. Bruce took multiple punches to the face during the first round, and during the break in between, he urged his classmates to stop the fight, since he wouldn't be able to hide his wounds from his dad. Convinced to keep going, Bruce rallied back and beat his opponent to the ground in victory. Shortly afterward the parents of his vanquished foe wasted little time in contacting the police.

Popular urban mythology asserts that the true issue with Bruce's victory was that his opponent was actually the son of a well-known gangster and therefore Bruce's departure to the United States was predicated on dire circumstances. Whatever the specifics, these run-ins had been serious enough that before Bruce or Hawkins could obtain overseas visas, their parents were forced to first wrangle with the authorities (purportedly in the form of a bribe) to get their children removed from a list of known local troublemakers.

With high school graduation approaching, jail was appearing as likely as college. For Grace and Hoi Chuen, the decision to send Bruce to the United States was not a difficult one.

Bruce walked along Portsmouth Square in the early summer evening, as the sun slumped west behind Nob Hill. Like anyone else in Chinatown interested in martial arts, he had been eventually pointed in the direction of Lau Bun.

If Bruce's time in San Francisco had started with uncertainty and insecurity, he was now approaching the entrance to Hung Sing with his Hong Kong swagger back in order. Perhaps it was all the praise he was receiving after his demonstrations at the local dances. Or maybe the fact that during his last big fight in Hong Kong, he had been victorious against a practitioner of Choy Li Fut, the style that was being taught by Lau Bun at the bottom of the stairs. Whatever the case, he descended those steps far too quickly and with more zeal than humility, clueless not only to the fact that Lau Bun had been teaching longer than even Ip Man but that Bruce was hardly the first hotshot to come down with something to prove.

"When Bruce came to Hung Sing, he didn't know anything about San Francisco," recounts Sam Louie, one of Lau Bun's senior students at the time. "There were 7 or 8 of us in class. He came down to show off some hands, and tried to say to us that Wing Chun was the best. So our *sifu* threw him out."

Lau Bun could surmise by the heated language coming over the partition that he had an interloper in Hung Sing. The school had had its share of them over the years, and in his younger days he may have been more inclined to engage them. (Once, during a particularly contentious incident, he whispered to a senior student, "Don't worry; if you lose, I'll take him out.")

The reputation of the Hong Kong Wing Chun students had preceded Bruce to San Francisco's Chinatown. Long before Bruce had returned to America, Ip Man's teenage students were already regarded in San Francisco

Chinatown as disrespectful, belligerent, and (in the eyes of Hung Sing, at least) horribly overrated. Lau Bun had governed the Chinatown martial arts culture for years, preventing it from devolving into the sort of unruly fight culture that had emerged in Hong Kong. He had no intention of that changing any time soon.

The room went quiet as Lau Bun stepped into the practice studio, and the look of alarm and consequence on the faces of the younger students quickly conveyed to Bruce the gravity of the situation. The older students looked to their teacher for permission.

"Don't bother," he barked, in abrupt Cantonese.

Lau Bun peered down at Bruce with condescension and hostility from behind thick glasses. He spoke slowly and deliberately.

"Did your teacher allow you talk like that at his school in Hong Kong?"

Bruce stammered, realizing now he was in over his head. Lau Bun pressed him.

"There is no street talk in here," he said. "Take your mouth back up to the street."

Bruce hesitated. Lau Bun pressed again.

"Now!"

Bruce stormed back up the stairs. Smirks surfaced on the faces of the older students, as relief emerged on those of the younger ones. In both short- and very long-term contexts, Chinatown's martial arts scene would remember this incident with Bruce . . . among others . . . for years to come.

Just as when he was a newborn, Bruce spent only a few months in San Francisco before moving on. But he had begun to make a name for himself, for better or worse, in Chinatown . . . and slowly, in Oakland as well. For now he was on his way to Seattle.

5   THE SOFT ARTS

At the start of the 1960s, the Asian martial arts were still largely an obscurity in America, though to varying degrees. The Japanese art of judo had enjoyed some international popularity throughout the century, and in many ways was the best known and established of the arts in America. The Okinawan striking art of karate had made inroads among U.S. servicemen stationed overseas during the past two decades and was quickly gaining popularity in recent years. The Chinese martial arts, on the other hand, were almost entirely unknown at the time Bruce Lee returned to America from Hong Kong in 1959.

In San Francisco, Chinatown began the decade with little variation to its own well-established structure of the neighborhood's insular kung fu culture. Lau Bun's Hung Sing and T. Y. Wong's Kin Mon were familiar institutions in the community and were moving into their third decade of local operation. Their presence within Chinatown was most noticeable during Chinese holidays, neighborhood festivals, and business openings, when their schools would perform lion dance ceremonies as a ritualistic blessing (in which "the spirit of the lion chases away evil spirits"). This made them not only visible but also essential to the spiritual customs and traditions of the community.

However, there was a third and final foundation to the neighborhood's martial arts culture, which was less visible yet every bit as relevant. The Gee Yau Seah—"The Soft Arts Academy"—was located down Old Chinatown

Lane, a narrow and inconspicuous alleyway along the ascending slope of Washington Street. Known to many longtime residents as "Horse Stable Alley," Old Chinatown Lane extends northward between closely situated apartment buildings deep into unseen Chinatown. It was there, in the furthest recesses of Chinatown, that the Gee Yau Seah was located. Far less a formal school environment than Hung Sing or Kin Mon, the Gee Yau Seah was more a gathering place, a martial arts social club with an emphasis on the soft arts of kung fu. Appropriately enough, it was formed around the same time as the neighborhood's other two martial arts institutions.

In 1939 the Chinese Consolidated Benevolent Association funded Choy Hak Pang, an accomplished practitioner of Yang style tai chi chuan, to relocate from Hong Kong to San Francisco to provide a source of exercise and recreation for its local members. Choy was a student of celebrated master Yang Chengu Fu, and his arrival in San Francisco is often heralded as the start of formal tai chi instruction in the United States.

While in Chinatown he established the Gee Yau Seah, modeling it on a similar tai chi social club founded years earlier in Shanghai. Choy traveled often to teach in other Chinese communities around the United States and founded similar clubs in New York and Los Angeles. After close to a decade of instruction within San Francisco (and around America), Choy returned with his family to Hong Kong in 1947, where he continued to teach, and where his career took another fascinating turn in the form of a very unexpected student.

Gerda Geddes was born in 1917 to upper-class society in Norway, the daughter of a prominent national politician. As a young woman she gravitated toward prewar bohemian life in Oslo, training as a dancer and mingling with the local art world. She studied the teachings of controversial psychoanalyst Wilhelm Reich during her time at the University of Oslo and joined the resistance against the Nazis in her midtwenties. With the advent of World War II, she narrowly evaded the Third Reich after a series of dramatic encounters. Escaping to Sweden hidden beneath a cart of lumber, she would have seemed an unlikely (or perhaps perfectly sensible) candidate to one day play a notable role in spreading Chinese martial arts around the world.

Her marriage in the postwar years brought her to Shanghai, where her husband held a new business position. Early one morning Geddes became transfixed watching an old man perform slow dance-like movements in the misty predawn hours alongside a canal. Like most other Europeans, she had no concept of or exposure to tai chi. At the time Geddes had been exploring ways to merge dancing with her university studies in psychoanalysis to develop a sort of physically oriented mental therapy. Now, watching tai chi in Shanghai, she felt as if she no longer had to invent it, since the Chinese had already cultivated it for centuries. She recalled, "As I watched I had a sensation of hot and cold streaming up and down my spine . . . and I remember thinking, 'This is what I have been looking for all my life.'"

Held under virtual house arrest in Shanghai for two years following the Communist victory in China, Geddes and her family were eventually allowed entry to Hong Kong. There in the mid-1950s she approached Choy Hak Pang with an interest in studying tai chi. When she performed an interpretive dance for Choy and his colleague, her efforts were met with much confusion: "They did not seem very impressed," she said. "In fact, they indicated that most of what I did was bad for the body in one way or another." Despite any misgivings, Geddes seems to have won Choy over and soon began training with him five days a week.

In the same culture and in the same time period that a young teenage Bruce Lee was demoted from Ip Man's school for his mixed racial heritage, the elder Choy's decision to take a European woman as a student was nothing short of revolutionary. Classes were in private, and there was an unspoken rule of no physical contact. Geddes learned under Choy until his death the following year, when she then began studying under his son, Choy Kam Man, who at first proved very nervous interacting with an older European woman.

The younger Choy's martial arts evolution was in itself a fascinating trajectory. Engaged in the Hong Kong street-fighting culture of the 1950s as a teen, Choy lifted weights and excelled at Southern Mantis style (learning under local master Yip Shui), but only practiced tai chi reluctantly at the insistence of his father. However, he soon began to notice that the softer arts were benefiting his martial abilities in tangible ways. This awareness culminated in an experience that would shape the younger Choy's career, when he had a sort of transcendental experience while practicing tai chi alone one afternoon, feeling as if his body had "disappeared" in the process. As he committed more time to practice, the experiences continued. He confided not in his father but in other practitioners and meditation instructors, who collectively congratulated him for finding true balance in the yin/yang. Subsequently, the younger Choy felt that his skills were evolving well beyond petty street fights and weight lifting. Soon he anchored all his martial focus around the perfection of the soft arts.

Geddes trained with the younger Choy for a year before returning to England, intent on introducing tai chi to Europe (in 1960 she even had a brief segment performing on the BBC). However, Geddes was routinely met with widespread disinterest and bewilderment. She finally found her niche a few years later when she integrated tai chi into her teaching curriculum at the London Contemporary Dance School, where she would teach for the next thirty years.

(Interestingly enough, this nearly exact scenario had played out with American-born Sophia Delza just a few years earlier. Born to a liberal and artistically minded family in New York City, Delza studied dance as a young adult and eventually accompanied her husband, a UN diplomat, on his new assignment in Shanghai. Like Geddes she successfully sought out a Chinese tai chi instructor. Whereas Geddes learned Yang-style tai chi and returned to teach in London, Delza learned Wu style and returned to teach for years in New York City, at the United Nations and Carnegie Hall. It is one of those peculiar historical synchronicities without any direct connection.)

Meanwhile, the younger Choy returned to San Francisco, where he took up his father's legacy in Chinatown within the Gee Yau Seah, continuing to teach Yang-style tai chi in America. Handsome and studious in appearance, Choy Kam Man—or, as he became known around the neighborhood: Master Choy—rounded out the small group of teachers in Chinatown at the start of the 1960s. Younger, low-key, and unaffiliated with the Hop Sing Tong, Choy was a quiet contrast to the status quo of Lau Bun and T. Y. Wong. Although Choy was a teacher of tai chi, his martial abilities would leave the rare witness in awe. "Master Choy could fold space and time," explains former student Jack Wada. "His movements defied a certain logic. It was as if he could worm-hole his way with a punch or kick. You might see it start, then it would be in and you would pick it up on the way out."

Choy lived in a tiny apartment on Stockton Street with a large family that had a penchant for taking in stray canines. At any given point in the day, their home was a cramped riot of screaming children and barking dogs. Yet Choy never had a proper tai chi studio of his own to retreat to. In addition to the Gee Yau Seah, he taught for years at the YMCA on Sacramento Street, where like the other neighborhood masters, his enrollment was steady, though hardly booming. This changed as the decade picked up momentum, and both martial arts and San Francisco's youth culture gained prominence. In the late sixties, Master Choy would draw a large and loyal following of non-Chinese students, young San Franciscans, and recent transplants who didn't buy into the era's well-known subculture gurus but still sought new avenues toward spirituality, or at least peace of mind.

Within the neighborhood, however, this following would eventually earn Master Choy threatening calls in the dead of night, warning him to stop teaching Chinese secrets to other races, almost twenty years after his father first taught Geddes in Hong Kong. Although known as a teacher of soft style, Master Choy would eventually fend off his critics by taking a hard-line stance.

A genuine glimpse of Old World kung fu could be found with another well-known figure of the Gee Yau Seah, who in his old age had become a legendary figure in early American martial arts circles. Almost twenty years a senior of his close friend Lau Bun, Mah Sek was a well-respected master with a benevolent glow who possessed strange and amazing abilities to match his long and colorful history. Born in a rural Chinese enclave of the Sacramento Delta region in 1876, Mah Sek was sent back to China at the age of seven to live with an uncle in Canton. Once a Shaolin monk, his uncle had assumed a new identity after killing an opponent in a martial arts challenge and becoming a fugitive of the law. Mah Sek was trained by his uncle from a young age in old-style Shaolin kung fu, before returning to San Francisco as a young man. He watched Chinatown burn in the 1906 earthquake and later worked as an instructor and enforcer for a tong in nearby Stockton. Like his uncle before him, he killed a man in hand-to-hand combat and spent years lying low of the law. His opponent's death weighed heavily on him and spurred him to refute using martial arts for the purpose of fighting.

In the years that followed, Mah Sek turned his martial arts abilities inward and used them to showcase feats of the body, becoming a sort of martial arts acrobat and contortionist who would enthrall spectators at demonstrations for years to come. He was a master of Qi Gong, the internal art of cultivating the human body's intrinsic energy. Long an esoteric concept that dates back to Chinese antiquity, notions of Qi (natural energy or life force) would be integrated into medicine, religion, and martial arts throughout Chinese history.

Mah Sek combined his Qi Gong abilities to his iron body training, the kung fu practice of hardening parts of the body through constant and extremely arduous physical conditioning. Over time Mah Sek had rendered his body malleable and impervious, becoming "like a hard rubber ball" capable of withstanding any blow. His Iron Shirt Qi Gong demonstrations were legendary in early American martial arts circles, as he withstood body blows from crushing weights and sharp weapons with no injury.

Historically, martial arts street performers were regarded as the bottom rung of the culture's hierarchy in China, stigmatized as a mixture of charlatans and kung fu circus freaks. Yet they played a key role as provocateurs of the martial arts imagination. In this sense Mah Sek represented tangible evidence, well into the twentieth century, that perhaps the Old World stories were in fact true, that the limits to a true master's abilities were seemingly boundless.

Yet even as these old masters held sway over Chinatown's martial arts landscape at the start of the decade, a more modern era was inevitably set to dawn. And the incident—the fight—that would significantly shape martial art's biggest name of this coming era would be born of the alleyways of San Francisco's Chinatown. Yet for all the grit and badass reputation of Lau Bun's Hung Sing and T.Y.'s Kin Mon, the showdown would emerge instead from Old Chinatown Lane, from within the Gee Yau Seah.

6 THREE MOVES OR LESS

SEATTLE, WASHINGTON | 1960

Bruce let Jesse Glover know. Enough was enough. He would fight his critic.

Deferring to his Hong Kong instincts, Bruce sought to fight on the roof of the school. Glover talked him away from campus and instead set the fight for the courtyard of the nearby YMCA.

Glover was Bruce's first student in Seattle. Just as George Lee had approached Bruce after his demonstration at the Chinese American Citizen's Alliance, so too had interested observers begun to shake out of the crowd during Bruce's showcases up in Seattle, magnetized by the ability and power of this small nineteen-year-old Chinese kid. Glover was the first to inquire about learning from Bruce. As an African American teen growing up in Seattle, Glover had been brutalized by a drunken police officer. Now in his midtwenties, he was interested in martial arts for the sole purpose of exacting revenge on his attacker, and Jesse approached Bruce already having an accomplished background in judo and boxing.

Not long afterward, James Demile cast a skeptical eye toward Bruce during an Asian heritage festival at Edison Technical School, where they were both completing their high school educations. Demile, of mixed-race ancestry, went from a hard childhood in an orphanage, to a long list of teenage gang fights, to a stint of boxing while in the air force. He joined a crowd of spectators to watch this sharply dressed Chinese student perform a peculiar physical routine. When Demile heard the student bill the demonstration as "deadly" Asian fighting techniques, he was as amused as he was skeptical.

"Bruce looked about as dangerous as Don Knotts," Demile recalls. "It was a beautiful performance, sort of a cross between ballet and mime, but it sure didn't look like fighting."

At one point during the festival demonstration, Bruce feared he was losing the crowd's interest, so he called Demile—the biggest guy in the crowd—forward so that he could demonstrate.

"You look like you can fight," Bruce stated. "Hit me as hard as you can."

Weighing close to one hundred pounds more than Bruce, Demile (who was actually on probation at the time) was half worried he might kill the kid. When he finally obliged, Bruce moved around him in a blur, locking Demile's arms against each other with the Wing Chun trapping technique of *lop sau* (the pulling hand), effectively neutralizing any chance for his much larger opponent to land a blow. As Demile would recount years later: "I felt myself being jolted as he flicked my jab aside, caught my other arm, and in a flowing motion planted both arms crossed on my chest like I was dead. In an act of panic I tried to leap back and away from him. He was like a bad smell, I could not get away. No matter how I moved, backwards or side to side, he stayed with me while maintaining pressure on my locked arms. I finally stopped when I hit the edge of the stage." Finally, just to assert his dominance of the situation, Bruce began tapping on Demile's head like an older sibling torturing a little brother on a lackluster Saturday afternoon, asking, "Hello? Is there anybody home?" Humbled, Demile quickly realized he could learn some things from Bruce.

More students soon followed, like Skip Ellsworth, who grew up as the only white kid on an Indian reservation, fighting Native American youths on a daily basis amid dismal poverty. Another was Taky Kimura, a thirty-six-year-old Japanese American whose self-worth had been adrift since his internment during World War II. These men were among the scrappy bunch of blue-collar street fighters who composed Bruce's first class in the early 1960s. One by one, they had been thunderstruck after witnessing Bruce's abilities.

At nineteen Bruce would never have been allowed to teach back in Hong

Kong. Given that Bruce had only five years' experience and limited mastery of Wing Chun, the very idea would have been laughable to the aging masters who populated the postwar colony. But on the West Coast in 1960, Bruce arrived unaligned with the Chinese martial arts racial-exclusion code that he himself had been a victim of while in his teens. Bruce's younger-generation worldview provided an opportunity for a modern class environment, where the rules could be freely rewritten. The result was the most racially diverse group of students in the history of the Chinese martial arts to that point, another evolutionary step forward from the high-water mark of Geddes and the Choy family (among very few others, such as Sophia Delza). When Ruby Chow, the stern female restaurant owner who provided Bruce with employment and lodging, expressed disdain for his teaching of non-Chinese students, Bruce didn't hesitate to dispute the issue with her.

Bruce was settling nicely into Seattle. He was poised to receive his high school diploma and begin college classes at the University of Washington, where he would study philosophy. Away from school he hoped that his informal martial arts classes (they often practiced in parks, parking structures, and alleyways) could in time develop into a more legitimate business and liberate him from his menial hours bussing tables at Ruby Chow's restaurant (an arrangement that he regarded as a sort of indentured servitude). Yet more than just teaching, Bruce was tangibly benefiting from the situation as well. His class of street-tough Seattle students enabled him to acclimate to an entirely new cross section of opponents. As Glover would later put it, "We were all dummies for Bruce to train on." In this regard his abilities were progressing as much as those of his own students.

Open to drawing on more than just classical Wing Chun, Bruce began to evolve what he was practicing. He did so to adjust to the size of Western opponents and to achieve progress that was no longer available through traditional study with a teacher such as Ip Man. It was an approach—a kind of permanent evolution—that would last the rest of his life, characterize his own art, and eventually help him create a new paradigm in the field itself.

At the moment, however, Bruce's credibility was being called into question. He had been harassed lately—at demonstrations, in the cafeteria, in the hallways—by a Japanese student and karate practitioner named Yoiche

Nakachi, who considered Bruce's abilities a farce. Once the hothead willing to jump at any challenge, Bruce avoided the confrontation, possibly wary of what another expulsion would mean to him at this point in his life. As a result Bruce was suddenly on the flipside of his own Hong Kong reputation, no longer the challenging upstart but instead the wary senior.

Glover knew of Yoiche's street-fighting reputation, and though it would get lost in the shuffle years later, the guy was known for some tough fights around town. Yoiche had been formally trained in karate since the age of twelve while growing up in Japan (he was now twenty-nine), and had a background in judo as well. According to Glover, Yoiche was fast, in good shape, and could attach power to his punches and kicks. Most recently Glover heard a story of how Yoiche had disarmed and defeated a knife-wielding opponent in a heated street brawl.

The origin of their conflict stemmed from one of Bruce's recent demonstrations, in which he drew distinctions between kung fu and karate that Yoiche had found offensive. Bruce often highlighted the softer side of kung fu as a more nuanced approach to fighting and body mechanics. In comparing this to the hard striking techniques found in karate, he drew Yoiche's ire. It would not be the last time that one of Bruce's outspoken demonstrations caused a fight.

Standing in the yard at the YMCA, Bruce waited, businesslike in street clothes, while accompanied by Glover and a few other students. Yoiche surfaced ready to fight wearing a traditional karate gi, a white uniform tied at the middle by a well-worn black belt. Bruce, by contrast, just took off his shirt and shoes. Mindful of consequences, Bruce had one point to clarify with his challenger: "Let's get this straight, you're challenging me, right?"

"Yes, I'm challenging you," his opponent replied confidently.

Bruce appeared content now. "That . . . is all I wanted to know."

Back in San Francisco T. Y. Wong's students were scattered around the room sunk deep into their individual horse stances, as they were inclined to do just prior to class. Like Lau Bun, T.Y. regarded horse-stance training as the cornerstone of a fighter's abilities, and his students would descend the steps before class and set themselves around the room like century-old statues.

T.Y. was reading the newspaper at his desk with his reading glasses on as a young stranger came down the steps of Kin Mon.

"Are you the teacher?"

"Yes, boy." (In his broken English T.Y. called all his juniors "boy"). "I am professor."

"How would you block this?" the young man asked, slowly stretching a high roundhouse punch with his left fist.

T.Y. glanced up, as did his students. These sort of upstart intrusions were rare but not unheard of. Without letting go of his newspaper, T.Y. lifted his right forearm up to the theoretical punch. "I block like this, boy."

Now with the right. "How would you block this?"

T.Y. shifted up his left, seeming bemused, eyes on the newspaper. "Like this, boy, I block like this."

And then, in an instant, the walkup challenger threw it at him full speed. T.Y. countered quickly, catching the left-hand punch and throwing it across into his opponent's own right arm. Letting go T.Y. jabbed stabbing fingers within a half-inch of his challenger's eyes, causing him to whip his head back in retreat.

Kin Mon was quiet as T.Y. caught the loose ends of his newspaper and snapped it back up to reading level. His students still populated the room in their frozen horse stances, slack-jawed as they watched the intruder hustled up the steps, happy to still have his now watering eyes.

Silence.

And then, nonchalantly from behind his newspaper, T.Y. remarked, "That boy know nothing."

There is a notion that often surfaces around kung fu culture about the context of assessing fights: a true master can dispatch his opponent quickly, in just three moves or less, essentially countering any attack and ending the contest in a brief instance of offense. From parables of elder warriors to the ambitions of younger practitioners, that is the pinnacle of victory and the mark of a true master.

In the courtyard of the Seattle YMCA, Bruce set a classic Wing Chun stance, ready to fight, his right palm extended forward and facing skyward.

Yoiche began high and then dipped into a crouch. They held still for a moment, before Bruce's opponent launched the first attack.

Yoiche shot a kick out at knee level, which Bruce quickly anticipated, batting his foot away with his forearm and then—in the words of Glover and other witnesses—"drove his opponent" across the yard with a furious barrage of straight punches to his face, until Yoiche bounced off the courtyard's rear wall and grasped wildly for traction. Bruce sidestepped him, and as his opponent fell to his knees, his white gi already red with blood, Bruce launched a final kick toward his head that caused Glover to yell out in panic, as the impending knockout blow seemed far more like an execution-style kill shot. The kick connected hard to Yoiche's face, leaving the group of spectators to stare at an unconscious heap.

"The man took a long time to regain consciousness," Glover recounted. "I thought he was dead. The left side of his face looked like it had been hit with a series of baseball bats. Later we found out his skull was cracked all around the eye socket."

Over time it would occasionally be referred to as the "eleven-second fight," in which witnesses attest that in addition to the knockout kick, Bruce landed a multitude of punches in a mere eleven seconds. In the high ideal of effective victories, Bruce met a challenge by a formidable opponent and successfully applied his technique to obliterate him in a few short moves. There is scant variation on what transpired.

Bruce's next fight would also be predicated on the contentious nature of one his demonstrations. That fight, however, would be much harder to assess. In fact, half a century later, martial artists would still be arguing about it, debating what they heard from the rumor mill and urban mythology. That showdown was still a few years in the making, during the first few months of Bruce's move back to the Bay Area. It would be a fight that would shape the lives of its participants for years to come. Yet it wouldn't occur in San Francisco but rather eastward, where Bruce would find some of his closest colleagues, on the other side of the Bay.

In re:

LEE JUN FON, alias BRUCE LEE,
native born citizen of the
United States, for citizen's
Return Certificate, Form 430.
(Male)

••••••••••••••••••••••••••••

State of California)
City and County of) ss
San Francisco)

Photo of
LEE JUN FON

Photo of
HO OI YEE

HO OI YEE, being first duly sworn, deposes and states as follows:

That she is a temporary resident of the United States; that she
was duly admitted to the United States by the United States Immigration
Authorities at the Port of San Francisco, California, incident to her arrival
from China, ex SS "President Coolidge", on the 8th day of December, 1939,
No. 39707/8-25;

That she is the mother of LEE JUN FON, alias BRUCE LEE, who is
applying for a citizen's Return Certificate, Form 430, at the Port of San
Francisco, California; that the said LEE JUN FON, alias BRUCE LEE, was born
in the United States;

That affiant has attached her photograph and that of her said son,
LEE JUN FON, alias BRUCE LEE, hereto for the purpose of identification;

That your affiant makes this affidavit for the purpose of aiding
her said son, LEE JUN FON, alias BRUCE LEE, in obtaining a citizen's Return
Certificate, Form 430.

Ho Oi Yee

Subscribed and sworn to before me
this 5th day of March, 1941.

Notary Public in and for the
City and County of San Francisco,
State of California.

1. Lee family immigration documents containing photos of a three-month-old Bruce Lee alongside his mother, Grace, in March 1941. Bruce's parents were meticulous in putting his citizenship papers in proper order before departing home to Hong Kong. Other documents from this file are interesting as well, such as an exit interview in which Grace states that her mother was English and had no Chinese blood. (Courtesy of the National Archives and Records Administration, San Francisco)

2. (*left*) Lau Bun, the patriarch of the early martial arts culture in San Francisco's Chinatown, photographed in his Hung Sing studio in early 1959. Lau Bun had already been formally teaching in the neighborhood for over two decades at the time of this photo and would continue until his death in 1967. (Courtesy of the Kem Lee Archive, University of California, Berkeley)

3. (*above*) Lau Bun, upper left, with his senior students in the Hung Sing's basement studio on Brenham Place (now Walter Lum) across from Portsmouth Square (with student and longtime Chinatown martial arts practitioner Bing Chan, third from left). Lion Dancing was an integral part of Lau Bun's school, and Hung Sing continues to perform around the Bay Area today, over a half-century later. (Courtesy of the Kem Lee Archive, University of California, Berkeley)

4. (*above*) Members of the Hop Sing Tong photographed in front of their headquarters on Waverly Place in the early 1960s. T. Y. Wong is on the far right, while Lau Bun is in the second row wearing glasses directly behind the solo lion dancer in white. (Courtesy of Gilman Wong)

5. (*right*) Wong Tim Yuen, also known as T. Y. Wong, was a core founder of the early martial arts culture in San Francisco's Chinatown dating back to the early 1940s. Wong ran his Kin Mon ("Sturdy Citizen") Chinese Physical Culture Studio in Chinatown for close to thirty years and was among the very first to expose Westerners to the Chinese martial arts. (Courtesy of Gilman Wong)

態神之演表源添黃龍趙足高暨柱天梁軍殿虎國館術國央中
時民國念五羊年冬

6. A photograph from the Central Guoshu Institute's national martial arts demonstration of 1928 in Nanjing, China. T. Y. Wong (then in his twenties) is on the far right in a tai chi pose, while his teacher, Leong Tin Chee, is in the center, with senior student Chew Lung on the far left. (Courtesy of the Kem Lee Archive, University of California, Berkeley)

7. T. Y. Wong, center with butterfly swords, during a San Francisco street parade in the 1940s. (Courtesy of Gilman Wong)

CHINESE KARATE KUNG-FU

ORIGINAL "SIL LUM" SYSTEM

少林內外派

FOR HEALTH & SELF DEFENSE

by PROF. T. Y. WONG
and K. H. LEE

8. (*left*) T. Y. Wong's 1961 book, as published by James Lee, was among the very first works by a Chinese master in English. James Lee's use of the Wade-Giles style of pronunciation, with *kung fu* rather than *gung fu*, would integrate into the English lexicon. The book eventually led to a falling-out between T.Y. and James due to a misunderstanding over publishing costs. (Courtesy of Gilman Wong)

9. (*above*) Tai chi master Choy Kam Man rounded out Chinatown's small group of martial arts teachers at the start of the 1960s. Over twenty years earlier, Choy's father had come to the United States and opened tai chi social clubs in San Francisco, New York, and Los Angeles. Choy Kam Man's martial abilities were greatly affected by his mastery of the soft arts. As one student put it: "Master Choy could bend space and time." (Courtesy of Jack Wada)

10. By the end of the 1960s, Master Choy Kam Man had attracted a diverse array of students to study tai chi with him, often filling the playground at the Chinatown YMCA on Sacramento Street. In time this following earned Choy threats from around the neighborhood for teaching martial arts to non-Chinese students. (Courtesy of Jack Wada)

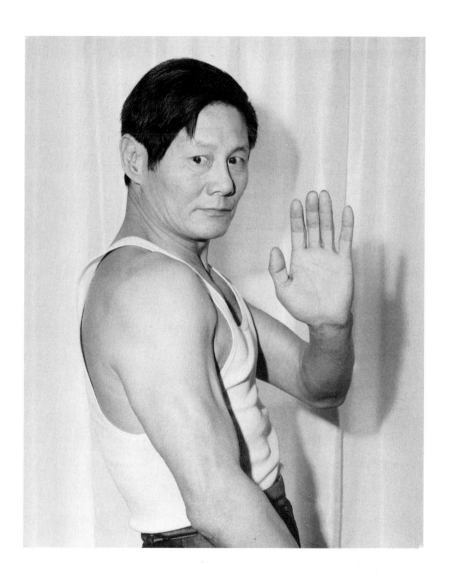

11. Modern martial arts pioneer James Yimm Lee was in his early forties when he first met Bruce Lee. A working-class family man, James ran his own martial arts publishing company and invented one-of-a-kind training equipment in his spare time. Al Tracy calls James Lee "one of the great missing pieces of the martial arts in America." (Courtesy of Greglon Lee)

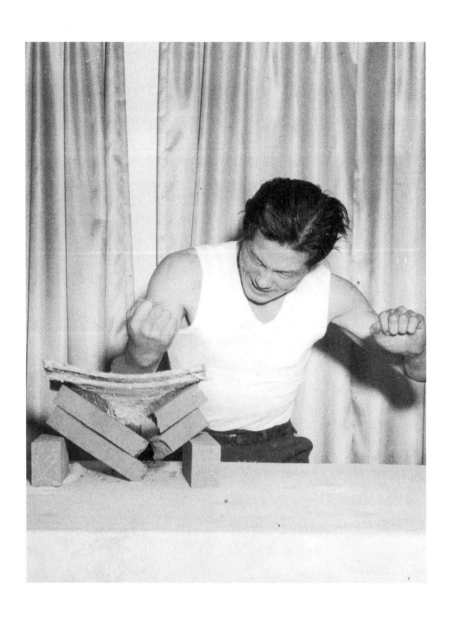

12. An accomplished practitioner of Iron Palm, James Lee was known for his powerful breaking technique. Like his friend Allen Joe, James was heavily influenced by the early fitness culture in the East Bay as pioneered by the likes of Jack LaLanne and Ed Yarick. (Courtesy of Greglon Lee)

13. Although born in San Francisco's Chinatown, Bruce Lee gravitated to Oakland and the martial artists in James Lee's orbit. He opened a school in Oakland during the summer of 1964. (Courtesy of Barney Scollan)

14. Bruce Lee working out on the wooden dummy in James Lee's garage in Oakland. (Courtesy of Barney Scollan)

15. Wally Jay, right, pictured with Professor Henry Okazaki upon being awarded his black belt in 1944. Wally relocated to the San Francisco Bay Area in 1950 and taught at his Island Judo/Jujitsu Club in Alameda for the next sixty years. (Courtesy of Bernice Jay)

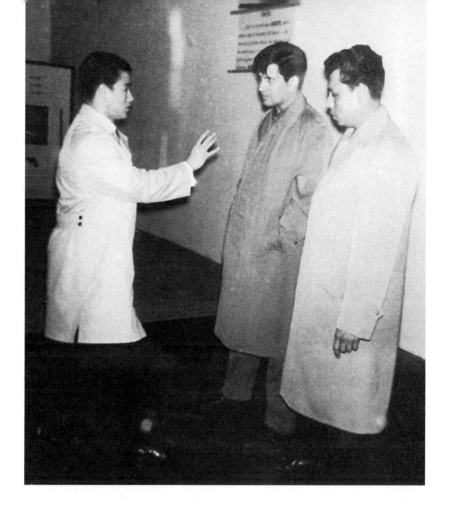

16. (*top left*) A group photo from one of Professor Henry Okazaki's advanced jujitsu seminars at his home in Hawaii, dated February 22, 1948. Wally Jay is in the middle row, far right, while his wife Bernice is in the middle row, third from the left. (Courtesy of Bernice Jay)

17. (*bottom left*) Ed Parker also emerged from the "melting pot" martial arts culture in Hawaii. After opening his first school in Southern California in 1957, Parker quickly became popular with the celebrity crowd in Hollywood, training such well-known figures as Warren Beatty, Gary Cooper, and Elvis Presley. His annual Long Beach International tournaments were a key foundation to martial arts culture in America. (Courtesy of Ed Parker Sr.'s IKKA, Kam IV, Inc.)

18. (*above*) Bruce Lee discussing technique with kenpo practitioners Ralph Castro and Ed Parker at Castro's school on Valencia Street in San Francisco circa 1963. (Courtesy of Greglon Lee)

19. Leo Fong during his semipro boxing days at Hendrix College. After growing up in Arkansas, Fong eventually relocated through his church to Northern California. In time Fong trained in Hung Sing with Lau Bun, Kin Mon with T. Y. Wong, and Oakland with James and Bruce Lee. (Courtesy of Leo Fong)

20. Ed Parker and Bruce Lee with some of the notable figures and participants at the inaugural Long Beach International Karate Championship in 1964. Front row, left to right: J. Pat Burleson, Bruce Lee, Anthony Mirakian, Jhoon Rhee; back row, left to right: Allen Steen, George Mattson, Ed Parker, Tsutomu Ohshima, Robert Trias. (Courtesy of Ed Parker Sr.'s IKKA, Kam IV, Inc.)

21. (*above*) Bruce Lee performing his "closing the gap" demonstration on a volunteer during an impromptu gathering the night before the 1964 Long Beach Tournament. (Courtesy of Barney Scollan)

22. (*right*) Bruce Lee pictured with Diana Chang Chung-Wen, "The Most Beautiful Creature of Free China," the day of the infamous Sun Sing Theater performance. After Bruce's fight with Wong Jack Man, a Hong Kong newspaper ran a sensational story in its celebrity gossip column alleging that Bruce was fighting off Wong Jack Man as an overzealous suitor of Diana. (Courtesy of the Kem Lee Archive, University of California, UC Berkeley)

23. (*left*) An original sketch by Bruce Lee. (Courtesy of Barney Scollan)

24. (*above*) Bruce Lee with Oakland student Barney Scollan outside James Lee's Monticello Avenue home. (Courtesy of Barney Scollan)

25. Al Novak, right, at his home in Fremont, California, with longtime friend Allen Joe in 2011. A World War II veteran who raided Normandy on D-Day, Novak was the first Caucasian to train within the insular martial arts culture of San Francisco's Chinatown. Born and raised in Oakland, Allen Joe took to the early physical fitness scene that surfaced in the East Bay beginning in the late 1930s. Joe would win Mr. California in his height division in 1946, the first Asian American to do so. (Courtesy of the author)

PART 2

Oakland

7 THE INNOVATOR

James Lee's reputation was built on his physicality. His legacy, by contrast, would be based around his intellect.

The brick breaking didn't help to clarify this paradox. Steadying himself in the quiet solitude of his two-car garage, James focused on the short vertical stack of carpenter's bricks that were arranged on the table before him. A seasoned practitioner of Iron Palm technique, James had developed a knack for pulverizing dense objects with his bare hands. It was an impressive sight, though one that probably failed to accurately convey the full extent of his mental acumen.

In an instant he struck down with his left hand, the impact rendering a sound that was percussive and blunt, like the heavy thump of a well-swung sledgehammer. As the broken pieces fell away at their center, James stepped back to catch his breath. His upper body was rugged and muscular beneath a white tank top, with powerful arms that implied an imposing force well beyond his mere five feet seven inches. At forty-two his physique not only belied his age but gave testimony to the achievements of his youth, as a bodybuilder, a gymnast, and a street fighter.

James arranged a new stack of bricks, feeling their friction as they pressed together atop one another. A welder by trade, he had fashioned his own custom "breaking table" of appropriate height and width to handle his Iron Palm practice, just as he had employed the skills of his day job to invent other types of equipment to suit his training needs. These odd-looking devices populated his garage, such as the spring-loaded punching board, the choke-hold training device, and his homemade incline bench. Collectively, these inventions gave the workout space a peculiar air, hints of a mad scientist's laboratory.

James spent a lot of time down there in his garage training studio below his family's home on Monticello Avenue. After dinners with his wife and two children, he'd descend the steps to put in dedicated hours lifting weights and perfecting his fighting techniques. In the process he had a lot of time to think, quiet moments when he got his blood pumping and contemplated his latest plans for new contraptions, training strategies, and books to write.

Though an unlikely candidate to run his own publishing company, James began producing his own titles after realizing that there were scant few martial arts books available to enthusiasts. A few years back he had published his first work, *Modern Kung Fu Karate: Iron, Poison Hand Training; Brick Break in 100 Days.* He advertised it in the classified sections of national men's magazines, such as *Popular Mechanics* and *The Ring.* In short order, packages and envelopes began arriving from all over the country (and the world) with payments for his book, solidifying James's opinion that the obscurity of martial arts in America was poised to give way to a substantial popularity.

While considering a title for his first book, James had done something interesting. He found the term *gung fu* too unwieldy and hidebound for the Western mind. So he tweaked it by applying the Wade-Giles style of pronunciation, effectively anglicizing it slightly to *kung fu*, which resonated more like the term *karate*, a word that Americans interested in the martial arts were beginning to use with some familiarly. He could hardly have known it at the time, but James was playing a key role in bringing the term into the English lexicon. It was one of the many places where he would quietly put his mark on the foundations of martial arts in America.

Born and raised in the city of Oakland, James had attended the city's Technical High School, where he excelled in boxing and gymnastics. At the local YMCA he broke weight-lifting records for his age group and then fell in with a local muscle crowd that pursued bodybuilding with dedicated zeal. Most notable was the reputation James had built for himself as a street fighter, known to be as fast as he was fearless in using his fists. The rumors and urban legends of these brawls, which still persist, put his fight tally north of one hundred.

After school he took a welding apprenticeship in the Pearl Harbor Shipyards in Hawaii. It began on December 1, 1941, a week before the Japanese attack. Over the next few years he learned his trade in the urgent atmosphere of repairing the Pacific fleet. In his free time he studied judo and jujitsu in the islands' thriving martial arts scene. He entered the service toward the end of the war and contracted a case of malaria in the Philippines so grave that the medical staff moved him into a tent housing the bodies of the recently deceased. The same grit that saw him through so many East Bay street fights somehow got him out of that tent as well.

After returning to Oakland following the war, James struck a balance between his hobby and his career, muddling their definitions even as he found near equal time for the two. Between marriage and kids James continued his enthusiastic pursuits of martial arts, studying Sil Lum kung fu under T. Y. Wong in Chinatown. As a star senior student, James eventually proposed a book project to T.Y. Their resulting collaboration, *Chinese Karate Kung-Fu: Original "Sil Lum" System, for Health and Self Defense*, was among the very first books by a Chinese master in English. The project proved both groundbreaking and deal breaking, as James's relationship with T.Y. quickly went sour after a misunderstanding over publishing costs. James abruptly stormed out of Kin Mon and headed back to the East Bay resolved to start his own school.

Talking with his close friend and business partner Al Novak after their split from T.Y., the two of them both seemed to know a lot of guys—cops, bouncers, construction workers—who would be interested in a less traditional martial arts curriculum. With this in mind James figured he would devise a more modern training environment—and would even call it as much: the East Wind Modern Kung Fu Club—essentially applying a boxing-gym setting to martial arts instruction. No months upon months of horse stances or forms. They would work out hard, they would spar, and his students would be able to handle themselves in real-world encounters beyond his school. As James would explain it, what his students would learn that day, they could use that day. After trying to make a dilapidated space in Hayward work as their headquarters, Novak and James retreated back to the two-car garage, where they seemed to be the most comfortable anyhow.

Poising himself now for the new stack of bricks, James took a deep breath. With a shift of weight, he snapped a backfist to the bricks. Again the bludgeon-like thud reverberated through the garage as the bricks fell apart.

James soon returned upstairs. He had a fair amount of mail to open and orders to fulfill. He also had to put in a call to his friend Allen Joe. The two of them had gone to high school together at Oakland Tech and still remained close, sharing interests in both martial arts and bodybuilding. Allen was set to take his family to Seattle for the World's Fair, and James wanted him to look up that Bruce Lee kid and scout him out. Again and again people were mentioning the guy to James. First, his brother, Robert, who took dance lessons with Bruce, and then George Lee, who also caught him a few years back at the Chinese Citizen's Alliance in Oakland. Just recently, his friend Wally Jay had visited Bruce in Seattle while traveling with his judo team and returned with a glowing impression. Wally was a nice guy, but he wouldn't gloss up his assessment of somebody's martial prowess to James.

If a more modern approach was what he was seeking, James figured, then maybe this Bruce Lee guy had something to offer. He picked up the phone and began to dial.

Allen Joe ordered a single malt Scotch and settled in by the bar at Ruby Chow's. The hostess told him that Bruce was off for the night, but was likely to resurface after 11:00 p.m.

Allen had spent the day navigating his family through the colossal crowds of the Science Exhibition and Twenty-First Century Pavilion. The entire city of Seattle was in the midst of world's fair mania, which included long lines, traffic jams, and sold-out hotels. As luck would have it, the hotel Allen had secured for his family was half a block from Ruby Chow's restaurant, where Bruce worked as a busboy. This proved conducive for the scouting mission that James Lee had asked of him.

Allen had grown up with James attending Oakland Tech in the late 1930s. Thinking back on those rambunctious days, Allen remembers gathering in a screaming mob—on numerous occasions, actually—to watch James fistfight after school. The guy was a different kind of tough: not big, just powerful and wholly fearless. His fighting abilities were exhilarating to witness, though fairly unnerving, as well. Little wonder that they elected James to be the student body president.

James and Allen had come of age at an interesting time in Oakland, the two of them swept up in the tide of a burgeoning physical-fitness scene unlike anything else in the country. In 1936 Jack LaLanne opened what is widely considered to be the first modern health club in America, on Fifteenth and Broadway in Oakland. A native of nearby Berkeley (the next town up), LaLanne had suffered acne and mood swings as a junk-food-obsessed teen. Exhausted by his eating habits and erratic behavior, LaLanne's mother took him to a lecture by nutritionist Paul Bragg, who successfully inspired the teen toward a healthy diet and physically fit lifestyle.

After the opening of Jack LaLanne's Physical Culture Studio, criticism arose from the medical community, branding LaLanne a charlatan whose fitness program could (by their assessment) result in such adverse physical side effects as sterility, hemorrhoids, and heart attacks (and that women would suffer a grotesque "musclebound physique"). Later when he began a weekly fitness show on ABC, LaLanne not only had to pay for his own airtime but was derided by critics who gave the program a few weeks at best. Instead, it aired for thirty-four years, and LaLanne was proven a visionary, a fitness icon who changed the American lifestyle.

But for the East Bay around the war years, LaLanne was hardly the lone fitness guru, merely the best know. The "friendly competition" that soon arose in the form of other local gyms produced many other notable figures as a unique (and now, widely forgotten) Northern California "muscle beach" scene began to thrive.

Although Allen would eventually become a close colleague with LaLanne (running the Fremont location of his fitness chain years later), his mentor during this time was Ed Yarick, a six-foot-four, 250-pound longshoreman of Swedish descent who ran a gym on Oakland's Foothill Boulevard for rugged characters interested in serious bodybuilding. Yarick would produce four Mr. America winners out of his space in Oakland—Steve Reeves (later famous for his silver screen role as Hercules), Jack Delinger, Clancy Ross, and Roy Hiligan—not to mention Olympic Gold medalist Tommy Kono.

Outside the gym, they took to the surf and sand, becoming regular fixtures at local swim spots like Sunny Cove and Neptune Beach, where they would pass the time showing off their physiques with gymnastics and other feats of strength (multiple-person vertical balancing acts were the most popular). Allen's Asian heritage never mattered within Oakland's muscle culture. Still outsiders themselves, they welcomed him in his late teens when he was a scrawny kid still shy of one hundred pounds. Later, after his service in World War II, Allen returned to the scene with gusto, winning Mr. Northern California in 1946 within his height division, the first Asian to do so.

Working on a second Scotch there in Seattle, Allen looked up to see the hostess pointing a young, well-dressed, and bespectacled Chinese man in his direction. *That . . . is Bruce Lee?* Allen thought to himself, sizing up the guy's neatly pressed gray flannel suit, *the kid looks like a fashion model.*

Allen introduced himself as Bruce came over to his side of the bar. He sensed that Bruce was suspicious of who was asking for him and quickly tried to put him at ease.

"I was told about you from Robert and Harriet Lee, they took dance lessons from you in Oakland," Allen explained. "They said you are pretty good at Gung Fu."

Bruce's face lit up with excitement. Apparently those were the magic words.

"You practice Gung Fu?" Bruce asked with surprise.

"Yes, with Robert's brother James," Allen explained.

And with that . . . Bruce had made a new friend. "Come on, let's get a bite to eat."

The two of them made their way down the block to a hamburger joint, with Bruce talking excitedly about his life in Seattle. Bruce explained how after completing his high school education at Edison Tech, he had then transferred to the University of Washington, where he was now studying philosophy. He explained the informal martial arts classes he held around town and his plans for opening his own martial arts school, possibly by the end of the year. Bruce also recounted his meeting with Wally Jay, expressing admiration for the jujitsu master.

From there Allen clued Bruce into their scene in Oakland, explaining that James Lee was a serious practitioner who ran his own school, built his own equipment, and even published his own martial arts books. In the meager martial arts landscape in America, these credentials were impressive to Bruce, and the two of them began hashing out the possibilities of a meeting.

Walking up to the burger place, Bruce stopped Allen on the sidewalk.

"Before we go in," Bruce told him, "I want you to try to hit me as hard as you can."

A mile east across San Francisco Bay, happily withdrawn from the Pacific fog, the city of Oakland takes up the opposite shore with low-key moxie. Historically built and populated around opportunities of industry, Oakland—like Chicago or Seattle—is entirely unapologetic in its core identity as a working-class city, particularly as its peacock of an older sister across the Bay aspires to be America's self-styled version of Paris. There's a tidy balance to this, to the two cities teetering on fault lines along either side of the Bay: Oakland and San Francisco; small to large, humble and glamorous, east and west.

Driving his black Ford Fairlane "police car" south along 580, Bruce was in the final stretch of the twelve-hour drive from Seattle. Although born in the heart of San Francisco, Bruce Lee was poised to discover his kindred spirits in the city of Oakland.

Allen Joe had returned from his family vacation in the Pacific Northwest and reported his assessment of Bruce to James Lee. He kept it short and simple: "James, the kid is amazing." Bruce and Allen had stayed up late into the night back in Seattle, exchanging techniques and talking fitness and philosophy. Back in the Bay Area Allen had successfully connected Bruce and James, who talked via phone. James invited Bruce to stay at his house in Oakland the next time he was down to visit. Now, with San Francisco Bay on his right, Bruce drove south as the East Bay hills rose on his left.

Two hundred years earlier those hills had been occupied by towering old-growth coastal redwoods. The tallest species of tree on planet Earth, the redwoods populating the eastern hills of the Bay were so large they were used as navigation markers by Spanish explorers during their Pacific excursions from Mexico in the eighteenth century. By the pre-gold rush days, just as the settlement of Yerba Buena was transitioning to becoming the city of San Francisco, those same redwoods would begin falling at the hands of squatters, deserters, and frontier opportunists who rowed across the water to pounce on the local market for lumber.

As San Francisco blossomed overnight in the wake of the gold rush, the price of lumber surged with it. Many workers who had initially deserted the lumber camps for the gold fields soon returned, realizing that a more dependable fortune could be made closer to the Bay. Logging camps evolved into sawmills, and by 1860 the redwoods that had lined the hills were cut clean; only the massive stumps of the old growths provided any proof of their existence. As the trees had rapidly fallen, the city of Oakland slowly rose.

Oblivious to the ghosts of ancient trees, Bruce continued south, anxious to reach his destination after so many hours behind the wheel. In the near distance, beyond the Bay Bridge, the Oakland shipyards broadcast an industrial identity. Oakland had grown with San Francisco over the years, maturing in an age of steel and transportation. In 1868 Oakland was chosen to be the western terminus of the transcontinental railroad, a key designation as the nation continued to revise its spatial boundaries. (At the time there was talk of incorporating Oakland into San Francisco as one large and unified Bay Area entity, yet the water between them ultimately enforced a permanent separation.)

With the turn of the century, the city's population doubled in size as refugees from the 1906 earthquake departed the San Francisco peninsula. As Oakland historian Beth Bagwell explains: "There were those who thought San Francisco was finished, that Oakland would become the main Bay Area city. . . . San Francisco, of course, survived. Before a month passed, there were jubilant plans for resurrection. But not everyone wanted to go back. Whatever their reasons, tens of thousands decided to stay in Oakland. Businesses came, too; their temporary emergency quarters in Oakland became permanent. The U.S. Census figures tell the story. Oakland's population grew from 67,000 in 1900 to 150,000 in 1910."

With the opening of the Panama Canal in 1915, the port of Oakland thrived, becoming a major West Coast hub for heavy shipping and ship-building. Aeronautics soon followed, and the Oakland Municipal Airport was constructed to feature the largest runway in the world. (Amelia Earhart operated numerous expeditions in and out of Oakland and held an office downtown at the Leamington Hotel.) By the 1920s the city was being dubbed the "Detroit of the West" as the automotive sector established satellite plants in Oakland. The industry and job opportunities brought by World War II brought a new gold rush to California, with Oakland benefiting the most. The shipyards thrived in this era (at times, running twenty-four hours a day), and many Americans migrated to Oakland for the work. The sum total of this industrial arc not only distinguished Oakland from San Francisco but also impressed upon the city some long-term and very distinguishing features in the form of a highly diverse and multiracial population, as well as a middle-class blue-collar identity.

For Bruce the view from the eastern shores of the Bay out toward the skyline of San Francisco inevitably stoked memories of his childhood in Kowloon, looking out toward Hong Kong Island. It was a subtle and nearly subconscious affiliation, but one more reason for his comfort in the city of Oakland.

If James Lee was searching for a modern take on the Chinese martial arts, it was now standing on his doorstep with a nervous smile. Bruce stood there a full two decades younger than James, a college student settling into adulthood greeting a family man years into a nine-to-five career. Even still, it was a fateful meeting and the beginning of a fraternal relationship that would mark the remainder of both of their lives.

For Bruce the trip down to the Bay Area was not entirely just martial arts whimsy. Juggling a variety of employment—Ruby Chow's, his own fledgling martial arts school (still without a physical location), and a monotonous gig stuffing inserts into the *Seattle Times*—Bruce also had standing work offers in the Bay Area to teach dance lessons, including a fairly lucrative one that had developed with the renowned Arthur Murray Dance Company. He was planning a trip back to Hong Kong in the coming year (his first return since he had left on that ocean liner in the spring of 1959), and he intended to return home with gifts for his parents and money for his siblings, a Chinese tradition that would assert his maturation and independent success. In this sense the rich kid who grew up attended to by family servants and couldn't hold the restaurant job his godfather had gotten him years earlier had developed an admirable work ethic in his early adulthood.

All that aside, Bruce was anxious to meet James Lee. Allen Joe had painted Bruce a vivid picture of their Oakland martial arts scene, with stories of bodybuilding, book publishing, and one-of-a-kind training equipment. Collectively, it resonated as the sort of martial arts future that Bruce himself had already been envisioning.

On Monticello Avenue he was greeted with warmth and enthusiasm, and it wasn't long after meeting James's wife and children over tea in the living room that Bruce was standing in the garage in front of the spring-loading punching board with mischievous intention. "So," he asked with boyish zeal, "how does this thing work?"

As the entire house began to reverberate from the drum-like bursts of Bruce and James assaulting the various contraptions in the garage, not only was a long-term friendship taking shape but a new and formative chapter in Bruce's life as well.

James Lee and his colleagues in the Bay Area represented a fresh opportunity for him. Already critical of the traditional masters, yet anxious to learn from experienced practitioners, Bruce discovered the next logical step in his martial arts evolution.

Having spent his teen years within Hong Kong's rooftop fighting culture while also studying under Ip Man, Bruce then honed his skills by practicing against the raw toughness of Seattle street fighters. The colleagues Bruce was now discovering in Oakland via James Lee represented an entirely new dynamic. In addition to being older and formally accomplished, the East Bay camp embodied the kind of modern martial arts mindset that Bruce was seeking.

"Bruce was smart," says James Lee's son Greglon. "When he's in his twenties he's hanging out with guys in their forties, so he can gain their experience."

Yet they would regard Bruce not as a student but as an equal and a colleague. Collectively, they would immerse themselves in an exchange of ideas that looked more to the future of martial arts, than to its past.

The following morning James Lee put in a call to his friend Allen Joe, anxious to report back to him on his time with Bruce. James kept his assessment short and simple: "Allen, the kid is amazing."

8 THE HAWAIIAN CONNECTION (PART ONE)

It was getting late on Eagle Avenue, but the conversation only grew more animated with the hour. Wally Jay was hosting a lively bunch, and the domestic setting of his living room was at times challenged to contain the company.

Bruce Lee jumped off his chair eager to exhibit some Northern Shaolin technique, shortly after James Lee had held the floor reexamining the perils of a past street fight. Al Novak was also in attendance, his size and energy akin to a grizzly bear politely attending a cocktail party.

Bruce was down from Seattle again. His trips to the Bay Area had become more frequent as his friendship with James Lee grew and the two of them began to collaborate on a new book project together. They arrived at the Jay household with Novak earlier in the evening, and after dinner the conversation zigzagged in many directions, though always keeping a wide-net approach to the topic of martial arts. The talk came packaged with demonstrations, which not only gave the room a hands-on think-tank type of atmosphere but increasingly resulted in the furniture getting pushed further and further to the corners of the house (despite the polite suggestions of Wally's wife, Bernice, urging them to "all just go out back").

On the topic of kung fu styles, the group observed how the Bay Area only showcased southern Chinese fighting systems: Lau Bun with Choy Li Fut and T. Y. Wong with his brand of Sil Lum Fut Gar (like many others, they were unaware that Master Choy was extensively skilled in Southern

Mantis). James remarked how there had also been a Hung Gar teacher in Chinatown named Chan Heung, who taught that particular southern style at a small school on Ross Alley, but he had passed recently.

On his feet now Bruce offered to give everyone a glimpse of northern China. He related how during his late teens in Hong Kong he had traded cha-cha lessons for instruction with a Northern Shaolin master, a worthwhile arrangement, since Bruce picked up the fighting style much faster than his counterpart could improve at dancing. (Bruce's buddy Hawkins Cheung had come with him for lessons, but the master's dog barked at him incessantly, wearing Hawkins out after just a couple of sessions.) Bruce explained how the acrobatic nature of the Northern Shaolin style provided some visual flash for his kung fu demonstrations, particularly when performing for the uninitiated.

Whereas Bruce's Wing Chun was short and direct, with explosive bursts of punches, he demonstrated how Northern Shaolin style was more expansive in nature, with particular emphasis on far-reaching kicks. In this regard it was poorly suited for a nicely furnished living room. Bruce snapped the kicks high and wide, as if he were trying to dislodge the overhead light fixtures. In time Bruce would exhibit Northern Shaolin technique not for its flare but rather as a launching point into his criticisms of overly extravagant fighting styles.

The conversations continued on to many other topics, everything from Novak's combat experience to the closing techniques of fencing practitioners. On the subject of American boxing, Bruce expressed a great admiration for Jack Dempsey and Sugar Ray Robinson. "Dempsey was out for the kill," Bruce declared. "He was a stalking tiger." This reference led to an analysis of boxing footwork—much to Bruce's considerable interest—which now spurred Wally forward to demonstrate. Prior to his jujitsu training in Hawaii, Wally had also spent his teen years training as a boxer, first in high school and then later in college.

Inevitably then, the topic steered to the kid Cassius Clay, and everyone seemed to have a take on the upcoming title fight between him and Sonny Liston. As egotistical as he was dynamic, with a stunning penchant for trash talking, Clay was a polarizing figure who elicited strong opinions.

Unsurprisingly perhaps, Bruce expressed a real affinity for the young challenger.

All debate and differences over Cassius Clay aside, Bruce held the present company on Eagle Avenue in very high regard, respectful of both their real-world fighting capabilities and their forward-thinking approach to the martial arts. Novak would have fit in well up in Seattle, with the likes of Jesse Glover and James Demile, who shared his sense of street-fighter grit and instinct. If Novak's size and abilities weren't impressive enough, the stories of his background were like something out of a military adventure novel. Having been stationed in Pearl Harbor during the Japanese attack, Novak soon trained alongside a young John F. Kennedy on the swift boats and was deployed to the Atlantic (Kennedy went to the Pacific), where he helped invade Normandy on D-Day. Later, he was in the Pacific theater when the atomic bombs were dropped on Japan at the end of the war.

Bruce was also becoming close with Wally Jay and made a point of visiting him with each trip to the Bay Area. Bruce relished the fact that Wally was a Chinese practitioner who not only had mastered a Japanese martial art but was beating Japanese fighters at it in competitions on a regular basis.

More notably though, Bruce felt that he had found another like-minded peer (similar to James Lee) in the way that Wally was always reevaluating his art, constantly pushing for it to evolve beyond its current incarnation. In fact, when Wally's son returned home from college, the family's jujitsu system had evolved so much that it appeared foreign to him.

As Bruce was becoming an increasingly vocal critic of what he saw as the static and ineffective nature of traditional martial arts, these Oakland practitioners appealed to him as the antidote: tangible examples of how innovative and modern approaches could be effectively applied as real-world fighting principles. Conversely, they saw something special in Bruce, not merely in the sense of a talented colleague, but something far greater, a sort of profound potential that might just render a one-in-a-billion trajectory.

Often over the course of the evening, the conversation would shift back to Hawaii. It was where Wally was born and raised, and where James and

Novak had spent time in their twenties. The three of them had all studied martial arts there. And just as the names of Lau Bun and T. Y. Wong constantly surfaced around the topic of San Francisco's Chinatown, there were certain figures who came up whenever Bruce's colleagues spoke about the martial arts culture in Hawaii, names like Mitose, Okazaki, Emperado, Chow. These practitioners, and the stories that surrounded them, impressed upon Bruce the sizable but little-known role of Hawaii as a unique martial arts proving ground.

In 1922 British heavyweight boxer Carl "KO" Morris arrived in the Hawaiian Islands and extended an open invitation to Asian martial artists to test their mettle against him in the ring. Morris had a reputation for being openly condescending toward the Asian fighting arts, and his challenge was quickly considered a standing insult to the islands' large Japanese immigrant community.

Starting in the mid-nineteenth century, the vast employment opportunities offered by the Hawaiian sugar plantations drew large waves of Asian immigrants, even though the work itself was particularly harsh and the labor contracts that organized it all amounted to indentured servitude. The Chinese came first, during the 1850s, and similar to those who flocked to the San Francisco gold rush, they mainly arrived from Guangdong Province in southern China. The American exclusion laws at the end of the century curbed Chinese migration to the islands (just as it had done on the mainland), thus beginning a similar process with the Japanese.

In the social turbulence of modernization in Japan during the late 1800s, many of its citizens ventured further out into the Pacific to seek employment in the Hawaiian cane fields. In fact, by the early 1920s the Japanese would compose some 40 percent of Hawaii's population, just before a new federal act in 1924 significantly restricted immigration into the United States. Signed into law by President Coolidge with little congressional opposition, the Immigration Act of 1924 (also known as the Johnson-Reed Act) was a heavy-handed and far-reaching piece of legislation that severely reduced immigration into the United States for the next four decades, in an effort to "preserve the ideal of American homogeneity."

Filipinos, who were exempt from the new restrictions as citizens of a U.S. colony, rounded out the last major wave of Asian immigrants into Hawaii, coming on the heels of the earlier Japanese influx. All these migrant groups maintained strong ties to their native lands, bringing their customs, cuisine, and martial arts with them.

"Hawaii was the first great melting pot of Asian martial arts," explains Dan Inosanto, an eclectic martial arts master who would become one of Bruce Lee's closest friends. "It's where Chinese trained Japanese, Japanese trained Chinese, Chinese trained Philipino, and then Hawaiians themselves got involved in all those arts, too."

By the time that Morris made his dismissive challenge in 1922, Hawaii already had a diverse and thriving martial arts culture unlike anywhere else in the world.

In seeking out a practitioner to represent their nation in the ring, the Japanese community in Hawaii appealed to a local martial artist who fully embodied the multifaceted nature of the local fight culture. At thirty-two Seishiro Okazaki was the fourth son in a long family line of samurai, the military aristocracy of Japan for many centuries. Okazaki was born, however, after the sun had set on the samurai class. During the late nineteenth century, the emperor of Japan abolished the long-held caste system in an effort toward modernization, which (among other things) resulted in the disenfranchisement of the samurai. They were stripped of their social entitlements and could no longer carry swords. Okazaki's father was one of many samurai who were unsuccessful at making the transition to more domesticated business pursuits.

During family financial turmoil, Okazaki set out for the Hawaiian sugar cane fields in his late teens. He suffered severe health problems (and related depression) at the age of nineteen and found his way to jujitsu through a Japanese doctor who advised it as a way to invigorate his physical well-being. This proved to be a successful approach, returning Okazaki to health and inspiring him toward a lifelong pursuit of both martial arts and healing practices.

Living in the Hilo region of the big island, Okazaki spent the next twelve years of his life practicing not just jujitsu (of which he mastered three different styles) but any martial arts that he could seek out on the islands: kung fu with a seventy-eight-year-old Chinese master in Kohala, karate from an Okinawan, Filipino knife fighting, Western wrestling, and the native Hawaiian martial art of lua. He also spent considerable time studying restorative medicine and massage.

If there was a fighter who could beat the English boxer, the Japanese community reasoned, surely it was Okazaki. Upon hearing their request, however, he quickly turned them down. When a Japanese black belt named Takahashi finally did step into the ring against Morris, the British pugilist made quick work of him with a first-round knockout. Again, the Japanese community appealed to Okazaki. After all, it was now, more than ever, a matter of national pride. This time he relented.

The fighting method of jujitsu is believed to have emerged from samurai combat techniques around the sixteenth century in feudal Japan. Translated to mean "the art of gaining victory by pliancy," the term jujitsu was eventually employed to describe a wide range of grappling techniques, in which the practitioner uses throws, chokes, and locks to gain advantage over an opponent. These methods, with their grappling-style emphasis, were originally devised for use against heavily armed and armored opponents on the battlefield, in which open-hand strikes would be ineffective. Over time, particularly during long bouts of peace in Japan, jujitsu evolved into a more focused unarmed fighting system.

Later, in an effort to create an avenue of competition and sparring that didn't leave participants with broken bones and other serious injuries, the art of judo was developed in the late nineteenth century by Jigoro Kano as a competitive sport, and really a less lethal form of jujitsu (as one of Wally Jay's students explains it, "they took all the nasty bits out").

Whereas the Chinese martial arts remained remarkably insular, judo had spread well beyond Japan by the beginning of the twentieth century, so much so that President Theodore Roosevelt took lessons from a Japanese judo instructor for a time at the White House. (Roosevelt, in his more overzealous moments, would often demonstrate judo techniques on young men visiting the Oval Office.) More so than even the Okinawan art of karate (which remained obscure prior to World War II), judo was really the first Asian martial art to cross borders in the West.

In preparing for the Morris fight, Okazaki was saddled with the challenge of how to successfully apply his jujitsu training and wider martial arts knowledge to defeat a formidable Western boxer. He spent the weeks leading up to the fight analyzing boxing technique in an attempt to find an approach that would fare better than that of his vanquished predecessor Takahashi. As a result Okazaki developed an especially low fighting crouch, with the reasoning that boxers had little practice punching downward.

On May 19, 1922, Okazaki met Morris in the ring for a wild bout. Okazaki quickly had his nose broken in the first round but managed to throw Morris out of the ring twice. Seeing the boxer hang his jab too long, Okazaki drove under his arm and threw him to the mat in a move that appeared to break Morris's arm on the spot, much to the manic delight of the Japanese spectators in attendance. Humble in his victory, Okazaki visited Morris in the hospital and treated his arm (which wasn't broken but badly injured) with his own method of massage. Later Morris would study jujitsu in Okazaki's class during the remainder of his stay in Hawaii.

In 1926 Okazaki returned to Japan, and used his time to seek out more martial artists. He traveled to numerous schools around the country, adding a variety of different techniques to his repertoire. When he returned to Hawaii, he developed his own particular system of jujitsu, an eclectic approach that incorporated elements of kung fu, karate, and many of the other styles he had been exposed to over the years. He called his particular brand of jujitsu Danzan Ryu, which translates as "Cedar Mountain Style," a reference to the Chinese term for the Hawaiian Islands (as well as an acknowledgment to honor his Chinese kung fu teacher).

Photos of his students in the years prior to World War II depict classes with very large enrollment, including what would add up to thousands of American servicemen taught over the years at the Honolulu YMCA. Although the local Japanese community had embraced him for the Morris fight—awarding him a gold watch for his victory—they had long-running tensions with Okazaki over his willingness to teach Japanese martial arts to Caucasians (much in the style of the old Chinese tong code surrounding kung fu). Through many confrontations Okazaki always maintained that if Hawaii was a part of America, then he would continue to freely teach Americans.

With the Japanese attack on Pearl Harbor on the morning of December 7, 1941, Okazaki grabbed his family's samurai sword and raced into the streets ready to fight a land invasion that never came. In the aftermath Okazaki was put into an internment camp by American authorities. He spent three months at the facility in Ewa, before local police, politicians, and journalists successfully advocated for his release.

Born to Chinese immigrants on the Hawaiian Islands, Wally Jay started his martial arts training with boxing, before he began studying jujitsu at Okazaki's school in the late 1930s. He trained under senior instructor Juan Gomez and worked his way up to a black belt in 1944. In the years that followed, Wally became close with Okazaki, learning his healing methods and helping him in personal affairs.

Intent on furthering his skills, Wally also studied judo for a time with Ken Kawachi. As the Hawaiian judo champion for many years, Kawachi was a physically small man who often dominated opponents twice his size. Wally marveled at this, and eventually his studies with Kawachi would become a core component of his martial arts approach.

In 1950 Wally moved his family to the Bay Area, where he soon built a small gym behind his home in Alameda and formed the Island Judo Jujitsu Club, which would host thousands of students over the course of the next six decades. However, Wally's evolution as a martial artist was heavily influenced by an early failure, when during a hefty loss at a competition in San Francisco, his coaching abilities and his team's skills were publicly ridiculed by Mits Kimura, the highest ranking judo practitioner in America at the time.

The disparaging remarks weighed heavily on Wally and sparked a period of introspection and reevaluation. Thinking back to Ken Kawachi's ability to dominate, Wally reexamined what he had learned during his time with Kawachi and soon developed the Small Circle Theory. He integrated Kawachi's emphasis on superior leverage through a nuanced approach to commanding wrist action. For Wally and his students, this would be the key to their future success.

"When we first came out here to the U.S., we got wiped out," explains Wally's son Alan. "But the generations after me became much better. As my dad improved, the entire team improved. Soon he had national champions on his squad."

Wally became a popular and well-known figure around the United States, as a result of driving his judo team (on funds generated from his twice-a-year luau parties) around the country to compete. His openness and positive disposition made him into a sort of early ambassador of the fledgling martial arts culture in America. However, in the years after Okazaki's passing, Wally would field criticism from quarters of Danzan Ryu for deviating too far from their professor's model. Knowing that Okazaki was at heart a modernist and an innovator, Wally stood firm in maintaining that his professor would have encouraged him to continue evolving. This theme—of seeking innovation over static interpretation—would be a key feature of Wally Jay's career and a point of connection with Bruce Lee's own evolution.

"There was a kind of two-way admiration between them," says Dan Inosanto. "Wally had a very high respect for Bruce Lee, and like most people, Bruce admired Wally Jay. In time, Bruce adapted a lot tactics that came from Professor Jay."

Yet Wally Jay was not the only influence out of Hawaii that would shape Bruce Lee's career in the days to come.

9 THE HAWAIIAN CONNECTION (PART TWO)

Bruce shifted his weight with a bounce, poised to advance, "Are you ready?"

"Ready when you are Bruce."

Ralph Castro steadied himself for Bruce's strike, while James Lee and Ed Parker looked on, half amused and half curious. The four of them stood inside Castro's martial arts school on Valencia Street in San Francisco's Mission District, and much like the late night think-tank sessions at Wally Jay's home on Eagle Avenue, they were deep into discussing and demonstrating a wide range of martial arts matters. At the moment Bruce was ready to show off the speed of his lead-hand backfist, charging Castro with the task of blocking it.

Parker and Castro had just been introduced to Bruce earlier that evening. He was staying at James Lee's house while down from Seattle. Parker was staying with Castro while up from Los Angeles. As he often did with other martial artists in his circle, James arranged for everyone to meet. After dinner in Oakland, the group all put on long beige trench coats (at the moment they collectively looked like a bunch of FBI agents) and braved the inclement weather to travel over the Bay Bridge to visit Castro's school on Valencia.

As the conversation surged forward about styles, technique, and fighting mechanics, Parker began to warm up to Bruce. At first the kid was coming across as too cocksure for his liking, but the more they talked, and the more he demonstrated, the more Parker could see that Bruce could back up his attitude. Castro was also impressed with the kid, though at the moment he was confident he could block the impending backfist.

Parker and Castro were both natives of Hawaii. The two had known each other for a decade now, having spent Coast Guard training together at the nearby Alameda naval base. Later, on a trip back to the islands, Castro learned that Parker had studied kenpo under the same teacher as he had. These days they were close colleagues, operating their kenpo schools in a tight-knit orbit.

Castro had a tough reputation dating back to his high school days in Hawaii. In California his students were an intimidating presence at tournaments and martial arts gatherings. As a Bay Area resident, Castro would soon become a regular at those late-night martial arts sessions, exchanging ideas and techniques into the early hours of the morning with Bruce, James Lee, Al Novak, Wally Jay, and Allen Joe.

Parker too would fit right into the mix whenever he was in town from Southern California, and in time he would play a much larger role in the long-term trajectory of Bruce's career.

Bruce was ready now with his move and in an instant stood still in disbelief. Castro had blocked his backfist clean. Again, the Hawaiians were surfacing on Bruce's radar.

The word *kenpo* translates as "fist law," or rather "the method of the fist." It is a broad term—like "martial arts" or "self-defense"—that carries a complex and colorful history: it can be described as a Japanese word for a Chinese concept that was heavily influenced by the Okinawans, and uniquely interpreted by the Hawaiians. Better yet, kenpo would also be integral to the rise of martial arts culture in America.

Kenpo's origins in Hawaii are often linked to James Mitose, a highly polarizing figure who is still controversial for many martial artists decades after his passing, having spent the last seven years of his life in Folsom Prison serving a sentence for murder and extortion (charges he denied to his death). Born in Hawaii, Mitose was relocated as a child to live with his mother's family in Japan, where he learned his family's art of kenpo, which contained techniques that bore similarities to jujitsu and Okinawan karate. He returned to Hawaii in 1935 while still in his early twenties and soon began teaching his family's style around Honolulu.

Parker and Castro learned kenpo in Hawaii years later from William Chow, a small, gruff man of pure muscle who at five feet two went by the nickname "Thunderbolt." He was known to be a volatile character who was rumored to have often tangled with U.S. servicemen around Honolulu. Chow worked with Mitose for a time (whether as a student or a colleague is a matter of debate) before running his own school, where he taught a style that was more heavily influenced by his Chinese heritage, conducting classes that were notorious for their stark physicality. In reflecting on Chow's teaching style, one student recalled, "He was into full-on fighting in the classroom rather than sparring. I used to get broken ribs. It was bad. That's how we learned it."

Born into the Mormon faith, Parker was raised in the multiethnic working-class Kahili district of Honolulu, a rough immigrant neighborhood that boasted its fair share of street violence. In his late teens he studied under Chow for a relatively short period of time before attending college at Brigham Young University in the mid-1950s.

Accustomed to the thriving martial arts environment he had grown up around in Hawaii, Parker arrived on the mainland to realize that there were only a scant few martial arts schools in America. During the halftime of a Brigham Young–UCLA basketball game in 1955, Parker gave a kenpo demonstration and was subsequently met with a huge wave of interest from both students and local law enforcement.

He corresponded with Professor Chow and gained permission to open a school on the mainland. Relocating to Pasadena California in 1956, Parker soon opened his first location and quickly began attracting interest from the Hollywood crowd. Elvis Presley watched one of Parker's demonstrations at the Beverly Wilshire Hotel in 1960, and the two became close friends and colleagues until Presley's death years later. By 1961 Parker had been profiled in *Time* magazine as the "High Priest of Hollywood's Karate Sect." Two years later Parker appeared in an episode of *The Lucy Show* in which he taught judo to Lucille Ball. Over time his celebrity students would include the likes of Warren Beatty, Gary Cooper, and Blake Edwards (who cast Parker in two of his *Pink Panther* films).

Without many years of extensive training experience, Parker proved tireless in researching and interpreting a wide range of styles, developing his own modified system, and terming it American Kenpo Karate. By the time of his meeting with Bruce Lee, while the Asian martial arts were still scarcely known in America, Parker was really just getting started. He already had a small network of schools in place on the West Coast and possessed a much greater vision for numerous locations around the entire country. More notable still was an event that Parker was planning in the coming year, which would draw an unprecedented gathering of martial artists together, and become a cornerstone of martial arts culture in America.

10 WAY OF THE INTEGRATED FIST

Leo Fong worked the heavy bag in James Lee's garage on a Friday night, still trying to chase down the "the ultimate." Or at least, that's how he liked to phrase it. Even with his extensive background in American boxing, Fong had spent the past few years making the drive to study at martial arts schools around the San Francisco Bay, looking to expand his repertoire and cobble together some kind of uniquely sublime fighting style.

He studied at Hung Sing with Lau Bun, with T. Y. Wong down in Kin Mon, and now with Jimmy Lee in his garage on Monticello Avenue in North Oakland. Like a small but ever-increasing number of young American men in those days, Fong was compelled by the allure of Asian martial arts, surmising that there were some superior fighting secrets to be unearthed. As a result he was contemplating a "radical overhaul" of his martial arts focus, despite his success as a boxer. So in addition to his Bay Area training, Fong had even clocked time studying tae kwon do and jujitsu in recent years, as well.

Fong practiced his main boxing combo to keep it in tune: drop down for a fake to the body with the right, then lights out up high with a left hook to the jaw. Jimmy's garage now echoed with a sharp "pah-pah . . . pah-pah," as Fong delivered the technique repeatedly to the bag. He had racked up eighteen knockouts with that particular move in his college days, and he could still throw it with devastating effectiveness.

Currently assigned to a church in Vallejo, Fong's parish duties as a

Methodist minister left him with little free time, making Friday nights one of the few parts of his week that he could dedicate to martial arts. These odd hours rendered him an outsider to the typical class structure, leaving him to work out in quiet, scarcely populated sessions while the main class members and senior students were busy with extracurricular weekend pursuits. This suited Fong just fine, who had spent the majority of his life as an outlier to the groups around him.

So with little company beyond the unique contraptions that populated Jimmy's garage, Fong worked the heavy bag. *Pah-pah . . . pah-pah.* Another Friday night chasing the ultimate. It was the same story throughout Fong's entire life: always in the ring but forever outside the box.

At the age of fifteen, Leo Fong's first "smoker" fight was against the high school's varsity quarterback, a kid named Dave Hodge. As soon as he had been approached with the opportunity to fight, Fong knew that he was clearly outweighed in the match-up (118 pounds to Hodge's 175), but the guys setting up the fights minimized the concern and scheduled him anyhow. In boxing terminology Fong was being set up as a "tomato can," a fighter who is being put in the ring just to fill out the card and lose to a superior opponent.

The match was held in an abandoned schoolhouse in the town of Widener, Arkansas. About fifty local men were in attendance, drinking and smoking (hence the "smoker" slang), and betting twenty-five cents a fight. The ring was merely a loosely hung rope along three sides. The fourth side was the schoolhouse wall.

When the bell (or whatever makeshift apparatus) had rung, Fong aggressively raced over to attack Hodge and was met with a few stiff jabs before getting his head bounced off that schoolhouse wall. The fight lasted a few more lopsided rounds before the organizers realized they were obligated to intervene. Fong walked home depressed, wondering why he had lost so badly.

The residents of Widener had never known what to make of Fong. They assumed he was Mexican or Native American or maybe African. The sign out front of town read "Population 92"—even though in reality there were close to four thousand African Americans residing there—and few locals had ever actually encountered a Chinese person before. The kids at school, however, understood where he was from, and on his first day of school, in 1934, they heckled him with a "Ching Chong Chinaman-kinda chant." Later that day Fong related the incident to his dad, thinking the boys were praising him. His father had to explain that it was actually ridicule.

Starting the very next morning, Fong got into a lot of schoolyard fights, responding to taunts by hitting kids quickly before they even knew what was happening. This typically resulted in the principal taking a paddle to Fong for his actions, but it made little difference. Certain slurs were simply fighting words, paddle or not, and before long his childhood was riddled with these types of incidents.

Fong and his family were the only Chinese for miles, running a local grocery in the hostile atmosphere of pre–civil rights Arkansas. ("The racism was so deep," explains Fong, "you would not believe it.") In addition to the regular schoolyard fights, two other events would shape the remainder of his life. First, he suffered a horrible fever around the age of eleven, which lasted for close to two weeks. It was so severe that it prompted Fong to promise God that he would become a minister if restored to health. He was, and he eventually did. Next, he found the book *Fundamentals of Boxing* by former world champion Barney Ross. For a kid who already had a way with his fists, Fong's formal interest in boxing grew with each page, and his fighting abilities were bolstered by the book's detailed instruction. He would hang a pillow up in his room and work on the punch combinations each night as detailed by Ross.

So walking home after that first smoker fight, the teenage Fong had to wonder where he had gone wrong. Regardless of his opponent's superior size, the loss had taken him unexpectedly. His mistake—namely, his impatience in the ring—finally dawned on him late that night.

Fong sought out the smoker organizers the next day and requested another fight, much to their surprise. This time around he slowed the pace down, hanging back and hanging back and waiting for his opponent to show a flaw. When he did, Fong lit him up with a one-two straight out of the Barney Ross manual, securing the first knockout of his career. He felt right walking home that evening.

From there he began fighting in the smokers regularly. He would slip around his parents on Saturday nights and fight in all kinds of underground venues, rickety barns and weed-infested backyards. Sometimes the fights would be heavily attended; other times he would fight in front of ten people in someone's garage. He was matched against local kids who didn't have formal training but who were "raw bone strong," conditioned tough from years of bailing hay and herding cows. Having at one time regarded him as a "tomato can," the organizers soon had trouble finding Fong a willing opponent.

Fong pursued boxing formally in college, training under Kirby "KO" Donohoe—the school's scrappy-minded coach. Once, after getting battered by an opponent throughout the first few rounds, Fong asked his coach to throw in the towel, but instead Donohoe just pushed him back out for another round. Fong won that fight by knockout in the next minute while on the ropes, learning the lesson of "a sliding right" maneuver against an advancing opponent, shifting his right foot backward even as he threw a punch forward with his right hand. Yet even with a record of 22-3, his losses in the ring contributed as much to his evolution as his many victories, not unlike his experience with the smoker fights.

Later the Methodist Church assigned him to a parish along skid row in Sacramento (one of the few congregations that would take a Chinese minister), relocating him out of the American South and over to California in 1954, when he was still in his twenties. It was around this time that Fong gained exposure to other types of martial arts and fighting styles, causing him to wonder if there was a better approach than boxing. After training at various schools with numerous teachers, Fong walked out of Kin Mon with James Lee in 1962 during the fallout with T. Y. Wong.

Now in Oakland, Fong found common cause with James in trying to distinguish what worked, what was real, and what was just hype. Fong's recent training experiences had already provided him with some evidence, even if he struggled to glean what it actually implied. While Fong sparred with his prior kung fu classmates, his boxing instincts immediately picked up on easy openings in his opponent's defense, and he tagged them up with little difficulty. But he never chalked it up to the merits of his boxing abilities. Instead Fong figured that they were just going easy on him.

It was actually Bruce Lee, in the coming year, who would urge Fong to differentiate between martial arts fact and fiction.

There were two notable martial arts books published in 1963. They were extremely different from each other but equally significant in their own way. One would gain momentum over time and eventually be reprinted for decades to come, while the other would enjoy an initial popularity before slowly falling into obscurity.

After months of enthusiastic collaboration, James Lee published Bruce Lee's first book, *Chinese Gung Fu: The Philosophical Art of Self-Defense*. Similar to T. Y. Wong's book a few years earlier, it was among the very first titles published in English on the Chinese martial arts. Somewhat uncharacteristically, Bruce played it safe, publishing more of a primer for beginners than something that better reflected his far more modern and nuanced outlook. The book opened with short author testimonials from James Lee, Ed Parker, and Wally Jay. In addition to the illustrated instructions (both drawings and photographs), Bruce committed space to his philosophical perspective, emphasizing the concept of yin and yang in the execution of the techniques. He not only showcased some basic styles and technique apart from Wing Chun but also included some of the "classical" approaches that he was becoming so openly critical of in that period. Compared to the increasingly confrontational content of Bruce's demonstrations at the time, the book itself was straightforward and fairly innocuous.

Conversely, *Secret Fighting Arts of the World,* by John F. Gilbey, was billed as "a book crammed full of secret fighting techniques never before divulged in print." Gilbey's book hopped around the globe from chapter to chapter, detailing all kinds of highly unusual fighting styles, such as the "The Liverpool Nutter" (profiling a British master of the head butt) and the "Ganges Groin Gouge" (fairly self-explanatory). A chapter about "The MVD Special" explains how a former Soviet secret service agent (kicked out twice for "over-zealousness") had perfected an open-hand slap more powerful than a well-thrown fist. In the realm of the Chinese arts, Gilbey chronicles the oft-rumored technique of *Dim Mak*, "the Delayed Death Touch," in which a master could merely tap an opponent at a certain point on the body during a certain hour to ensure his demise days or even weeks later. The "About the Author" section explains how Gilbey was "an heir to a textile fortune" who "knows self defense like no other man."

If it all sounds a bit ridiculous, it's because it was—the book was a hoax. Gilbey was the farcical pen name of Robert W. Smith, a unique figure and prolific writer in the early days of martial arts in America. Like Gerda Geddes (and at about the same time), Smith was one of those rare Westerners who through special circumstances became an early student of the Chinese martial arts.

A World War II veteran with a degree in history, Smith spent time in the Red Cross before joining the U.S. intelligence services. In 1959 he was stationed in Taiwan, as a liaison to Chiang Kai-shek's nationalist government. With a background in boxing and judo, Smith spent his free time during his Taiwan assignment seeking out local Chinese martial artists. Most notably, he studied tai chi under Chen Man Ching (who like Geddes's teacher, Choy Hak Pang, was a student of renowned Yang-style master Yang Cheng Fu). When Smith returned to the United States, he began a long teaching tenure as one of the early tai chi instructors in America and would publish numerous books on the martial arts for many years to come.

In its simplest form Smith's *Secret Fighting Arts of the World* was the result of a vivid mind and incredibly wry sense of humor. But the parody of it all was actually quite significant. Smith wrote the book as a way of illustrating the many far-fetched and outlandish tales that populate the martial art landscape, as well as the pervasive inclination for Westerners to wholeheartedly believe them. Unsurprisingly perhaps, a great number of readers took the contents of *Secret Fighting Arts* . . . quite seriously. For years to come Smith would receive letters addressed to Gilbey on all manner of peculiar topics seemingly related to his book.

Anthropologist and martial arts historian Thomas Green remembers encountering Smith's book as a college student not long after it was first published: "What we were reading in that book was exactly what we all wanted to have. What young man doesn't want to be invulnerable? And here are all these fantastic secret arts. The book contains such a mix of things that appear to be accurate, alongside things that are just absolute fantasy, that it keeps you guessing. I really wanted it to be true, as did my friends . . . and for a while I ran into it everywhere I went." Whereas a few decades earlier Tang Hao had tackled the same issues of folklore and hyperbole in the martial arts, Smith had taken a sly approach, applying a Mark Twain sense of satire to the issue (and as a result, evading blowback from the community).

Yet while these two books from 1963 differed in a variety of ways, the authors shared common ground in that they would both dedicate themselves to the same sort of reformist efforts as Tang Hao had years earlier, by conveying candid and often unpopular assessments of trends within the world of the martial arts. As Smith would later write in his memoir: "So much of what passes for the fighting arts in America and Asia is bogus. Except for judo, which has fairly consistent standards, one is lucky to get the authentic in a sea of chicanery. Always and everywhere it is hard to distinguish the thing from the version of thing." In the days to come, Bruce would prove unflinching in voicing these sentiments not only to colleagues like Fong but to a very wide cross section of the martial arts community.

At the end of the year, Bruce made the drive from Seattle to Oakland with his girlfriend Linda Emery shortly after the Christmas holiday. Emery was a freshman at the University of Washington who had begun taking lessons with Bruce in Seattle earlier in the year, and while on break, they planned to travel down to Pasadena to watch the Huskies in the Rose Bowl (though really, Bruce just wanted to visit Ed Parker). Upon their arrival in Oakland, James presented Bruce with a finished copy of his book for the first time. It marked the end of an eventful year.

In numerous ways 1963 had been good for Bruce. He had found a location for his school in Seattle and given it the eponymous title, The Jun Fan Institute of Gung Fu. The business had enabled him to finally step away from the menial work of waiting tables and stuffing inserts into newspapers. Over the summer Bruce had traveled to Hong Kong for the first time since he boarded an ocean liner in virtual exile four years earlier. It was a triumphant homecoming. Having left beneath a cloud of teenage trouble, Bruce returned a university student and a business owner, with gifts and money for his family. They marveled at how mature he had become and, most importantly, Bruce's father beamed with pride at his son's growth into adulthood.

Now, at the year's end, Bruce had also become a published author, with testimonial support from a reputable array of modern martial artists. Perhaps it was the sum total of these successes that would shape Bruce's tone in the year to come, when he would so openly air his criticisms of what he saw as the static and ineffective nature of the martial arts in America.

With James Lee, Allen Joe, and Linda in Oakland, by the lights of the Christmas tree, Bruce toasted to the year ahead—to the Year of the Dragon. It would be one of the most eventful and pivotal years of his life.

PART 3

1964

11 YEAR OF THE GREEN DRAGON

The Year of the Dragon arrived in San Francisco's Chinatown with epic and unprecedented fanfare. Three weeks of New Year's celebrations had built up in the neighborhood throughout the month, as the days of the Black Water Rabbit had given way to the Green Wood Dragon with the Lunar New Year on February 13. Just over a week later, the celebrations collectively climaxed with the city's annual Chinese New Year parade. It was the largest that San Francisco had ever seen.

City coordinators and police brass were befuddled managing the roughly three hundred thousand spectators who packed the downtown sidewalks along the parade route for blocks on end, from Chinatown straight through the financial district. By 6:00 p.m., the crowd had grown so large that the rest of the city had devolved into a "monumental" traffic jam. Both the Golden Gate and the Bay Bridge were at a standstill, and to the south, the highway was backed up for miles down to the city of San Bruno.

In Chinatown police barricades were overrun as revelers seeking a closer vantage point had narrowed the actual parade route to a mere ten feet across. Above the street level, spectators peered from atop marquees and out of open windows, while others clung to lampposts, treetops, and fire escapes. SFPD patrolman William Goodwin, who had worked the event for the past decade, remarked that he had never seen anything like it.

The parade itself was the largest ever assembled in the holiday's history, with more than two hundred eclectic groups of participants, from high school marching bands to dance troupes to the many elaborately decorated motorized floats. Mayor John Shelley waved from a vehicle in the parade's vanguard, while a team of bagpipe players followed close behind. One reporter deemed the procession "a combination of marvelous incongruities."

Lau Bun's Lion Dance team from Hung Sing made their way down Grant Avenue just as T. Y. Wong and his squad from Kin Mon roved the parade route further behind. Adorned in their best uniforms, the two teams had been a near-constant presence around Chinatown throughout the month, performing at numerous banquets, parties, and street celebrations. They now made their way mindfully, careful to conduct their lions with skill, spirit, and proper etiquette.

As expected, the Forbidden City float gained considerable attention, though for unexpected reasons. Coby Yee, the star dancer who had recently purchased the legendary nightclub from longtime owner Charlie Low, had generated some buzz earlier in the week with the float's theme: "A flower boat with singing girls comes drifting down the stream." It was a line from the popular musical *Flower Drum Song*, and a concept expected to be manifested to great effect by the club's stunning female dancers. However, the float briefly caught fire at the start of the procession and later completely broke down at the intersection of Sutter and Grant, leaving "ten saddened beauties" stranded in the street while the impaired vehicle was frantically pushed away from obstructing the parade route.

The loss of the Forbidden City dancers was tempered by the steady stream of Miss Chinatown winners, past and present. One by one they appeared, waving from open-top convertibles, immaculately dressed and radiant with smiles. The current winner, Shirley Fong of Hawaii, appeared toward the end of the procession, waving from atop an elaborate float that carried a large pagoda made entirely of flowers.

Amid Chinatown's neon signs and hanging lanterns, the star of the festivities finally emerged into view amid the pop and bang of mischievously hurled firecrackers and well-struck gongs. The 125-foot Gum Loong, the Golden Dragon, flashed with bright lights and roved the narrow parade route atop the shoulders of sixty youths who tirelessly animated the silk and bamboo creature to full glory, much to the delight of the diverse crowd of densely packed spectators. All timetables for what was meant to be a two-hour parade had been abandoned. The celebration had taken on a life of its own, as if Gum Loong was savoring the adulation of its admirers and proceeding through Chinatown at its own leisure.

The next morning the *San Francisco Examiner* reported, "Parade officials didn't know whether to boast or weep when it was all over. The crowd, biggest in the celebration's history, exceeded all expectations." The paper succinctly summed it all up with the headline: "Chinatown's Greatest Night."

And so began the Year of the Dragon.

Earlier in the month, the *San Francisco Chronicle*'s much-beloved columnist Herb Caen wrote, "In Chinatown, it's the Year of the Dragon, elsewhere it's the Year of the Beatle." On February 9 the Beatles triumphantly appeared on *The Ed Sullivan Show* (for the first of three broadcasts), and youth culture appeared to shift almost overnight, a glimpse of the days and the decade to come. Bob Dylan had already asserted as much just a month earlier, with the title of his third album, *The Times They Are A-Changin'*. Andy Warhol, the eccentric genius of the New York art scene, would characterize it by asserting that 1964 was "the year that everything went young."

Many historians agree with Warhol in this regard. For all of JFK's youthfulness, his presidency is typically lumped by academics into the same period of postwar prosperity as that of Eisenhower. It was Kennedy's assassination that marked a new era in America, and the turbulence and change of what would be known of as "the sixties" was already surfacing in early 1964.

Interestingly enough, one of the year's (and really, the decade's) bellwether moments occurred just two days after Chinatown's grand New Year celebration, within a boxing ring in Miami, Florida. On February 25 Cassius Clay stepped into the ring against heavyweight champion Sonny Liston for what would be one of the most famous bouts in boxing history. For weeks Clay had been muddling the fight's narrative with brash behavior and a seemingly unstoppable outpouring of trash talking. Liston had long been deemed a villain. His boxing career had begun in a Missouri penitentiary, where he was serving time for armed robbery (later he would be incarcerated again for assaulting a police officer). Armed with massive fists "like cannonballs," he hit with stunning power and quickly found his way to defeating Floyd Patterson in a first-round knockout for the heavyweight title. Handsome and reserved, Patterson had been a popular champion, a figure greatly preferred to the glowering ex-convict Liston. As LeRoi Jones (later known as Amiri Baraka) would peg it, Liston represented something menacing to mainstream America, calling him "the big Negro in every white man's hallway, waiting to do him in, deal him under, for all the hurts white men have been able to inflict on his world."

Somehow, Cassius Clay managed to make himself even more disliked than Liston. Defiantly outspoken and egotistical, the twenty-two-year-old Clay spent the weeks leading to the fight trumping up his superiority over Liston with a loudmouth barrage of schoolyard-style taunts. Then, just prior to the fight, it had been reported that he was meeting regularly with Nation of Islam firebrand Malcolm X and was rumored to be on the verge of converting to the Muslim faith. Between his mouth and his affiliations, Clay soon presented a much greater dilemma for white America.

Even though Liston was an 8 to 1 favorite by the night of the fight, Clay defeated him in six rounds, stunning the world. Two days later Clay announced that he was joining the Nation of Islam and changing his name to Muhammad Ali. Defending himself before the media (who, with the exception of Howard Cosell and just a few others, continued to call him Cassius Clay) he asserted: "I don't have to be who you want me to be. I'm free to be who I want." It was a sentiment that would speak volumes about the younger generation in America in the days to come.

Like the change destined to affect America throughout the decade, San Francisco's Chinatown was on the verge of a new era as well. The long-established social exclusion, both in policy and perceptions, had begun to dissolve in very tangible ways. At the time of the New Year's celebrations, Herb Caen voiced staunch support for the Chinese as integral members of the Bay Area community. For a writer known for droll metaphors and endless double meanings, Caen penned a column that was unusually earnest and straightforward: "It is unthinkable that anyone would discriminate against the Chinese in San Francisco; no other group is so much a part of the city's history. They have contributed in every way possible, even to the point of letting themselves become a Tourist Attraction by remaining, for the most part, in a section that has largely remained a ghetto. The suffering they underwent at the hands of the white supremacists decades ago is part of the city's shame." Within a year the federal government would rescind the long-standing restrictions that prevented greater immigration from China. While the 1902 Exclusion Act was repealed by FDR in the wake of Madame Chiang's trip to the United States in 1943, it was actually the repeal of the 1924 act that finally opened immigration in a full and robust way. This not only brought a new wave of people (and martial artists) to Chinatown but would inflame some tensions as well. The rise of Chinatown youth gangs began to surface along lines of immigration and native identity. By the late 1960s and early 1970s, the Chinatown gangs would engage in a stunning level of neighborhood violence that harkened back to the Tong Wars of the late nineteenth century and would have a considerable effect on Chinatown's economy. Furthermore, a series of new laws throughout the decade began to establish much-needed rules against discrimination in housing. Soon, as new residential opportunities finally became available for Chinese residents in other parts of the city, many of the wealthier residents of the tightly bound neighborhood opted to relocate to more spacious quarters.

The culture began to change as well. As spirited as Coby Yee's ownership of Forbidden City would be, her tenure came as the neighborhood's nightclubs were already in decline. Matters were then compounded further when just a few blocks away, up on Broadway, local dancer Carol Doda made national headlines after she engaged in the unprecedented act of performing topless at the Condor Club in neighboring North Beach in June 1964. Soon, topless dancing was featured at the clubs all along Broadway Avenue (and were heavily attended when the city hosted the Republican National Convention in July). It wasn't long before the elaborate Forbidden City floorshows seemed like a thing of the past.

The old model of Chinatown's martial arts community was set to change as well. Lau Bun and T. Y. Wong, along with the soft arts masters of the Gee Yah Sau, had presided over the neighborhood for a quarter of a century, and now, with the growing popularity of martial arts in America, the landscape was ready to expand.

Bing Chan opened his own school on Jackson Street in 1964. As a well-respected practitioner on the scene for years—first with Chan Heung (the little known Hung Gar master on Ross Alley) and then as one of Lau Bun's senior students—Bing immediately began accepting both non-Chinese and female students. The timing was right for an evolution beyond the old tong code, and it was reflected in the softening of attitudes within the old guard. T.Y. had taken on Irish teenager Noel O'Brien. At Hung Sing, Lau Bun was teaching Hawaiian Clifford Kamaga and not showing open opposition to any of Bing Chan's students.

There was also a notable newcomer on the scene. Wong Jack Man arrived from Hong Kong, a dynamic twenty-three-year-old practitioner of Northern Shaolin style. Clean cut, with a disciplined expression that suited his low-key demeanor, Wong Jack Man's performances and demonstrations of the northern arts quickly impressed the local community. Not only was his style visibly different, but he proved "elegantly athletic" in rendering it. He frequented the Gee Yau Seah and worked as a waiter at the popular Jackson Street Café. Quickly but quietly, he settled in as a new, young, and captivating martial artist in Chinatown.

At the same time, in a sort of mirror image, another twenty-three-year-old from Hong Kong was dazzling people with his performances, but on the other side of the Bay.

Bruce had something new to show off. He called it "the one-inch punch."

James Lee had put a meeting together at his home on the Monday night after Wally Jay's luau. He assembled many of his current students along with others who might be interested in studying with Bruce: Al Novak, Leo Fong, George Lee, and a few others, including a new student from Stockton named Bob Baker.

With Bruce's contentious showing at Wally's luau a couple of days earlier fresh on his mind, Fong was still uncertain what to make of the young kid from Seattle. George Lee, who had been sold on Bruce's abilities since his demonstration at the Citizen's Alliance dance way back in 1959, was thrilled to see him resurface again in the Bay Area.

First, James announced to everyone that Bruce was going to be moving down from Seattle and that the two of them would be going into business on a new school. They had a location scouted on Broadway Avenue along Oakland's "Auto Row" and hoped to open in about a month.

In deciding to move to Oakland (where he would reside with James and his family on Monticello Avenue), Bruce had chosen to drop out of the University of Washington and concentrate more on his martial arts business pursuits. (Initially James considered the idea of moving his family up to Seattle, but the matter for Bruce to move to Oakland was settled on the reasoning that the martial arts culture in the Bay Area was far more robust than in the Pacific Northwest.) Taking a cue from Ed Parker's kenpo school model, Bruce was now expanding his operation to a second location.

Standing in the center of the living room, Bruce talked for a bit about his philosophy of martial arts. As he had done at Wally's luau a couple of days earlier, Bruce threw around the term "classical mess," once again being outwardly critical of what he saw as the ineffectiveness of what other Chinese teachers were practicing. In contrast he stressed that his school curriculum with James would emphasis simplicity and practicality. He then made clear that they were talking about actual street-fighting skills. When he began speaking on the concept of "explosive power," he opted to demonstrate.

Bruce moved the coffee table to the side of the room and then grabbed the hefty Oakland phone book and handed it to Bob Baker, one of the taller men in the room. Bruce had Baker stand in front of the couch and then positioned the phone book over his chest. Readying himself, he put a straight hand out, just touching the front of the phone book with his middle finger, and then curled his hand into a fist, still in close proximity to his target. The room was quiet, and then with a snap that seemed to reverberate from his hip through his wrist Bruce sent Baker over the couch.

Fong and the other spectators were startled. "Bruce knocked him into the couch," explains Fong, "and Baker's legs went straight up and over. I thought he'd go through the living room window."

As everyone settled down, Bruce explained that the purpose of the demonstration was to illustrate how the power of a punch should come not just from the arms and the shoulder but from a much greater portion of the body. The more the muscles relaxed, he said, the more power they could generate. (It was a point that many of those in attendance had heard James Lee make on the topic of his own brick-breaking abilities.) Gung fu contrasted with harder styles like karate in this regard, Bruce concluded, by emphasizing notions of softness as integral to the power within a technique.

As the point hung in the room, James smiled and gave everyone an update on how things would proceed. "Until the new school is ready, we'll continue practicing in the garage," he explained. "Classes resume tomorrow."

The Oakland school would quickly take shape. The few people in attendance were impressed, not just with the demonstration but with Bruce's perspective and his manner of articulating it. The guy was a salesman. Now, with his second school under way, Bruce was set to take the message and the demonstration to a much larger audience.

12 LONG BEACH

At the 1964 Summer Olympics, judo was accepted into competition for the first time in the history of the games, a milestone for martial arts around the world. Later that summer, Ed Parker sought to expand even further the credibility of martial arts as a legitimate athletic endeavor with his Long Beach International Karate Championships during the first week of August.

There had been a few previous efforts to hold a national martial arts event: Arizona in 1955, and then Chicago and Washington DC in 1963 and 1964 respectively. These two more-recent competitions in particular were hampered by widespread disorganization. ("Chicago was a real mess," recalled tournament official George Mattson.) This left Parker striving to pull off a well-run and tightly organized event that could successfully draw together martial artists of myriad styles from around the world, while also conveying a sense of athletic legitimacy.

Having watched so many of Bruce Lee's demonstrations, Parker invited him down to perform. He was well aware of how potentially antagonistic Bruce's perspective could be, but welcomed it all the same: "He (Bruce) was very broad-minded about things—very anti-classical kung fu: he felt that they were all robots. So I told him that if he were to come down to the tournament and demonstrate, people would have a better cross section of the martial arts world."

Bruce was entirely disdainful of the light-contact point-based competitions like the one that would be occurring in Long Beach, where judges assessed the quality of the maneuvers. (In fact, Bruce was known to refer to these types of competitions as "organized despair.") But the opportunity to demonstrate and voice his martial arts worldview to such an eclectic group of practitioners was an opportunity he could not pass up.

When Bruce arrived at Long Beach, Parker assigned Dan Inosanto, one of his kenpo students, to drive Bruce around while in town. At the age of twenty-eight, Inosanto already possessed an extensive and fascinating martial arts background, having studied with an array of notable teachers. As a child Inosanto began his martial arts career learning karate (as well as some judo and jujitsu) from his uncle. Later, when he joined the service in the late 1950s, he studied as a paratrooper under Sergeant Henry Slomanski. In many ways Slomanski had brought a Qi Jiquan-like effect to the U.S. Armed Services, instituting a new emphasis on unarmed combat training. A big and imposing figure who studied karate as a noncommissioned army officer in Japan, Slomanski ran rugged training sessions that became notorious throughout the ranks for their no-nonsense physicality.

After emerging from the service in 1961, Inosanto studied for a time with kung fu master Ark Wong in Los Angeles. Like his Hop Sing Tong peers, Lau Bun and T. Y. Wong up in San Francisco, Ark Wong was among the very first Chinese masters to teach in America and was ahead of the integration curve when he took non-Chinese student Jim Anastasi as early as 1959. From there Inosanto not only clocked time learning jujitsu from Wally Jay but soon began studying kenpo with Ed Parker as well. Much like Leo Fong or even Bruce himself, Inosanto had a voracious interest in all things martial arts.

Inevitably, as Bruce and Inosanto got to talking, the two of them began to exchange some techniques. Inosanto was shocked by the results: "I was completely flabbergasted! He controlled me like a baby—I couldn't do anything with him at all. He didn't really have to use much force either—he just sort of body-controlled me. I'd lost to other people before but not in the way that I lost to him: he was dominating the action completely, calling all the shots like it was a game. I couldn't sleep that night. It seemed as though everything I'd done in the past was obsolete." Just as with Taky

Kimura in Seattle and James Lee in Oakland, Bruce would soon develop a long-term friendship and business relationship with Inosanto.

The night before the tournament, many of Parker's students and colleagues gathered in a vacant ballroom at their hotel for some impromptu demonstrations. Dressed in a black leather jacket and jeans, Bruce exuded a sort of movie star cool by his appearance alone.

Taking the floor to demonstrate, he spared everyone the lecture that evening and just got down to business, performing his closing-the-gap routine and a colorful array of Wing Chun techniques, injecting brief ideas on speed and simplicity.

In doing so he quickly commanded the attention of those in attendance. As pioneering karate master Tsutomu Ohshima observed the gathering that evening, he gestured toward Bruce and told a colleague, "That one . . . is the only one here that can do anything."

Like Ohshima, many observers in the room marked Bruce as someone special to watch at the official event the following afternoon. And indeed, the inaugural Long Beach International would be a seminal moment for Bruce, for Ed Parker, and for martial arts in America.

The turnout at the Long Beach Municipal Auditorium on August 2, 1964, was enthusiastic, diverse, and very large. Dave Hebler, one of Parker's early students and a key organizer for the event, asserts that the competition alone drew a few thousand participants, an unprecedented turnout for a martial arts gathering in America.

"It truly was international; we got people from all styles and all systems together," Hebler explains. "In addition to being the largest tournament ever, it was a social event, where martial artists could meet and form new relationships. We had people from all different styles giving demos. Bruce Lee was one of the minor presenters. He wasn't even the headliner."

Bruce's demonstration was slated later in the day during an unprecedented multicultural showcase of reputable martial artists, which included Jhoon Ree ("the Father of American Tae Kwon Do"), karate masters Robert Trias and Tak Kubota (who had spent much of 1964 training CIA officers in self-defense), and Filipino Kali master Ben Largusa (who would give what was likely the first public demonstration in America of the Kali arts).

"My dad started the internationals to showcase all of the martial arts together," explains Darlene Parker. "He had reached out to everybody, because he had so much respect for all of them. The event opened a door into the martial arts for the rest of the world to see."

There in Long Beach, Ed Parker had made history by successfully orchestrating his martial arts congress, essentially applying the Hawaiian melting pot dynamic to the culture as a whole. The event would run for the next half century and marked Parker's legacy as a visionary architect of martial arts culture in America.

Bruce took the floor in the center of the auditorium during a sluggish part of the afternoon. The air conditioner in the arena was down, and the day was growing long after hours of competitions had played out.

Dressed in a black *jing-mo*, Bruce was notably younger than the other demonstrators. After Parker introduced him as a practitioner of the little-known Chinese art of gung fu, Bruce emerged with Taky Kimura as an assistant. Unlike his succinct performance the night before, Bruce showed up with a big lecture in mind and integrated it into a dazzling array of performances. "Bruce was absolutely electric when he gave a demonstration," explains Linda Lee. And Long Beach appeared to be no exception.

"I had seen it all until I saw Bruce perform with his philosophies, his concepts of martial arts and his speed and power," recalls Richard Bustillo, a twenty-two-year-old boxer in the crowd that afternoon who would later become one of Bruce's longtime students. "I said . . . 'This is real martial arts.'"

Bruce performed the Wing Chun hand-sensitivity drill *chi sao* to a flawless and impenetrable effect against Taky Kimura while also lecturing in the process. Then, after sending a volunteer from the audience flying with the one-inch punch, Bruce got down on the floor to execute two-finger pushups on each hand.

These performances were immediate crowd-pleasers, enthralling many of those in attendance. In time, however, these demonstrations would be retold as if they encompassed the entirety of Bruce's showing at Long Beach. But as one of his biographer's points out, Bruce was not just performing stand-alone stunts: "Although they were impressive, Bruce was against simply doing "tricks" . . . if they had no real point to them. The real purpose of the inch-punch was to show that there is a far more powerful way of striking someone than simply by using the strength of the arm and shoulder muscles." In this regard the content of Bruce's lecture at Long Beach was every bit as important as the demonstrations he employed to convey it. Like his contentious showing at Wally Jay's luau, he took the floor to air his criticisms of what he saw as ineffective and unrealistic approaches to fighting, and he intertwined those opinions with his own blazing displays of speed and ability. The sum total of his cocksure attitude, young age, and emphatic analysis didn't jibe with the culture's code of conduct. So once again, Bruce insulted a lot of the established martial artists in attendance that day.

"The prevailing attitude that I was aware of at that time," says Dave Hebler, "was Bruce was kind of considered to be a bit of an arrogant prick. But he had the right ideas: simple and effective material that works . . . and if it doesn't work . . . don't do it."

Barney Scollan, an eighteen-year-old competitor in the tournament that morning (disqualified for "kicking a guy in the nuts"), was immediately compelled by what Bruce was saying. "He got up there and began to flawlessly imitate all these other styles," Scollan explains, "and then one-by-one he began to dissect them and explain why they wouldn't work. And the things he was saying made a lot of sense. He even made an absolute mockery of the horse stance."

With this point in particular, Bruce wasn't just airing criticisms, he was going for the jugular. The horse stance is a foundational aspect of numerous Asian fighting styles (from kung fu to karate to tae kwon do) and is drilled into students through long hours of practice, often from day one. Now, in front of an international array of teachers (many of whom were in attendance with their students), Bruce was ridiculing one of the core practices of their martial arts training as just one more bit "of the classical mess." He deemed the horse stance as entirely immobilizing for a fighter and a hindrance to generating greater punching power. As he put it, "There's stability, but zero mobility." By contrast he then demonstrated his own more fluid stance and the lightning fast punches he could deliver from it. Yet perhaps more than issues of mechanics were the big-picture concepts that Bruce had conveyed, and which, in time, would mark his martial art's legacy.

"He said the individual was more important than any style or system," Bustillo asserts. "That's when I said, 'I need to train with a man like this.'"

On this point Bruce was inverting the equation of the martial arts status quo. "He was heavily into personalizing the system," explains Dan Inosanto, "and most instructors never personalized their systems. If a technique was done a certain way in Japan, then it was expected that everyone would do it that way. And Bruce saw this as robotic: all the practitioners had the same look."

This was a popular point of discussion at those late-night sessions back in Oakland, and a consensus had formed there that the balance needed to shift away from the system dictating the individual's martial arts identity. As Leo Fong explains it, "Back then, it was 'I'm Okinawan style. I'm kung fu this style or kung fu that style," and that was it. You didn't dare deviate or go outside the box, because if you did, your teacher would say, 'What the hell are you doing?'"

There in Long Beach, before an international audience of martial arts practitioners, Bruce advocated for deviating way outside the box. "Teachers should never impose their favorite patterns on their students," he reasoned. "They should be finding out what works for them, and what does not work for them. The individual is more important than the style."

As seemed to always be the case, opinions were split on Bruce and the perspective he was putting forward.

Dan Inosanto, still having only just met Bruce, remembers the polarized atmosphere in the crowd. "There was a high percentage of people who were just in awe of him," he explains, "but then there is another group who was just really upset."

Clarence Lee, a longtime and well-respected karate teacher from San

Francisco, had been a judge during the competitions earlier in the day, and he remembers that Bruce's attitude and his demonstration didn't sit so well with many of the martial artists in attendance: "Guys were practically lining up to fight Bruce Lee after his performance at Long Beach."

For others, though, like Scollan and Bustillo, Bruce's viewpoint resonated in a profound way. Months earlier Scollan had gotten into a street fight only to find himself hamstrung by his own horse stance, unable to evade the blows of his opponent and dumbstruck as to why the art of karate wasn't proving superior. So while some martial artists at Long Beach were offended by Bruce's criticism of the horse stance, practitioners such as Scollan saw it as a revelation, an assessment that addressed what he had experienced in a real-world fight situation.

"Bruce made a number of enemies that night," says Scollan, "as well as a number of followers."

Jay Sebring was the hair stylist to the stars. Through his men's hair salon on Fairfax Avenue in West Hollywood, Sebring would almost single-handedly revolutionize the industry, spurring an evolution from white-coat male barbers to fashionable stylists. Over the course of his career, his clients would include figures such as Frank Sinatra, Marlon Brando, Jim Morrison, and Dennis Hopper. In time he would have salons around the world, in New York, London, and San Francisco. At Long Beach, Sebring had been one of the many spectators in the crowd at the Civic Auditorium who was enthralled by Bruce's demonstration.

Sebring's life was fated to a tragic end in the coming decade. In two months' time he would meet and fall in love with Sharon Tate. In five years he would perish with her at the hands of the Manson family. For now in 1964, however, he was a unique Hollywood insider, racing cars on weekends with Paul Newman and hanging out with the likes of Steve McQueen. His position as Hollywood's premiere hair stylist brought him into an inner ring of show business.

Not long after Parker's demo, Sebring was cutting the hair of William Dozier, an established Hollywood producer who had supervised shows such as *Perry Mason*, *The Twilight Zone*, and *Gunsmoke*. Dozier was poised to achieve his biggest career success with the campy *Batman* television series. (Not only was it Dozier's idea for the show to take such a slappy tone, but he would be the uncredited narrator that audiences would remember for saying, "Same Bat-time, same Bat-channel.")

During haircutting chitchat Dozier explained to Sebring that he was currently looking to cast his latest project at Twentieth Century Fox: a new Charlie Chan vehicle titled *Number One Son*. Sebring, still fresh from Long Beach, had Bruce Lee come to mind . . . and made a suggestion.

13 INCIDENT AT THE SUN SING THEATER

Barney Scollan couldn't sign up fast enough for Bruce Lee's school in Oakland. Not long after witnessing Bruce's demonstrations at Long Beach, Scollan relocated from Sacramento to Berkeley, where he began his freshman year at the University of California in the fall of 1964. He was thrilled to learn that Bruce's new school was practically down the block.

Through vivid retellings of what he had witnessed down in Long Beach, Scollan convinced two of his college roommates, Dick Miller and Bob Saunders, to attend the school with him, and together they made the short drive over to Broadway Avenue to enroll. The three young college students arrived at the Oakland branch of the Jun Fan Institute and waited patiently for Bruce to finish an earlier class before speaking with him.

"So, Bruce," Saunders asked, after introductions, "why is your approach to martial arts so special?"

Bruce raised an eyebrow, and then in a flash Saunders's eyeglasses were on the other side of the room. Without ever touching him, Bruce had kicked the glasses off of his face.

"That is why," he replied, with a smirk.

Like Bruce's peers up in Seattle, Scollan and his Berkeley roommates were part of a generation that existed in an ever-present American street-fighting culture. "I would get into fights all the time," explains Scollan, "which was just really stupid, but that's how it was. If you went out to a dance or a movie, the odds were pretty good that you might tangle with some other guys by the end of the night."

In this sense the growing national interest in the Asian martial arts was likely due in some part to their appeal as a means for young men to better navigate street fights. Yet a large portion of that appeal appears to have been predicated on the romantic allure of the Eastern world and the notion that the skills were in fact esoteric fighting arts that contained exotic methods and secret techniques.

"There will always be the macho thing of needing a better way of beating up the guy down the street and proving yourself," says historian Thomas A. Green, "but in this case you're proving yourself with secrets. And it's not doing push-ups or working the bag, it's a secret technique that you have."

By 1964 Bruce was attempting to tackle the mythology of the martial arts head on, much like the Chinese historian Tang Hao had done decades earlier, by "emphasizing practicality and renouncing embellishment." Paradoxically, Bruce was pushing for realism even as he was also constantly stoking the imaginations of observers toward the unrealistic. In this sense—of kicking the eyeglasses cleanly off someone's face—his feats of speed and agility were not only drawing students to his business but were also weaving their own mythology in the process. Bruce's students would increasingly attest to how he had become virtually "untouchable" in sparring sessions. George Lee remembers how Bruce could snatch a quarter out of someone's palm and leave a dime in exchange before the person could even close his hand. Bob Cook, a well-traveled martial artist like Fong and Inosanto, allowed Bruce to perform the one-inch punch on him and said it felt like "a hand-grenade" going off in his chest. Like his demonstrations in Long Beach, Bruce's seemingly uncanny abilities would resonate heavily with young men compelled toward the martial arts, particularly when presented with Bruce's emphasis on practicality. Even still, it made for a curious mismatch of perceptions.

More notably perhaps, was that Bruce tied his approach together by interweaving his own sense of philosophy, a blend of classic wisdom he had learned during his studies at the University of Washington and insights he gleaned from the wide range of books he was always consuming, including many self-help books of the era. Bruce thought that the martial arts, when combined with these influences, became a means of personal cultivation, a way for the individual to reach his or her best potential. It is a perspective that has long been debated in martial arts circles: are the fighting arts just that—specifically for fighting? Or are they a gateway to an individual's improvement and evolution, or—as it is commonly termed in the debate—self-actualization. In this regard Bruce differed from Tang Hao in that he genuinely embraced the philosophical (and almost spiritual) side of the field. And it was with this very point of philosophical emphasis on the potential of the individual that Bruce would inspire many of those around him (and later, many others). Leo Fong, for instance, is just one of many students who attest to Bruce having a profound impact on his life.

By the summer of 1964, Fong's Friday-night practice session had consistently turned into one of those long discussions of all things martial arts that had become so popular with the Oakland camp since Bruce's arrival. What had once been quiet sessions between James and Fong now took on new dimensions as Bruce contributed his high energy 24/7 approach to those evenings.

Fong was still trying to figure out where to land with his martial arts focus. He had a remarkable background in boxing, but in the face of the elaborate stories he heard about various Eastern styles and methods, Fong was questioning the worth of his pugilism. During a Friday-night workout session, Fong related to Bruce his own experiences sparring with other kung fu practitioners, and how he figured his success resulted from them going easy on him.

Bruce laughed it off. "Leo, are you serious, man? They just don't know how to handle your boxing skills." Finally adding up Fong's habits, Bruce asked, "Is that why you have been practicing so many different styles?"

"Yeah, Bruce, I'm looking for the ultimate," Fong replied.

"No, Leo," Bruce said, putting his hand on Fong's chest over his heart, "the ultimate is in here. Stick with your boxing Leo, your boxing is real."

A lot had happened in Bruce Lee's life after the Long Beach Tournament. Bruce had been apart from Linda Emery since he cut short his enrollment at the University of Washington at the conclusion of the spring semester. Anxious to make something of himself and expand his business into a new region, Bruce had moved south to Oakland to open his second school. By August he had returned to Seattle with a wedding ring lent to him by James Lee's wife, Katherine.

Linda's family caught wind that that she and Bruce were poised to elope and pulled them in for a tense family meeting to register their protests. Their mixed ethnicities were brought up as a major point of contention, in addition to the normal family concerns about a young couple set on marrying. Bruce's family, with their long history of interracial marriage, seemed to mildly prefer that he marry a Chinese woman but otherwise expressed little opposition. On the seventeenth of August, the two married in Seattle and quickly relocated to live with James and his family at his Monticello Street home in Oakland, where they were soon expecting their first child. In the coming weeks James's wife, Katherine, tragically passed from cancer. Now, living together and supporting each other through their personal battles, Bruce and James became closer than ever.

In the wake of his Long Beach performance, Bruce returned home in Oakland one day to find a message waiting for him. "This guy," Linda said, "this producer from Hollywood, called you and wants to talk with you." Bruce got on the phone and spoke with William Dozier, who explained to him that he was producing a new Charlie Chan show and that he wanted Bruce to audition for one of the key roles. ("We were both very excited," Linda recalls.)

In the meantime, Bruce went back out on the road for a different bit of show business, hired to take the stage with the leading lady of Hong Kong, Diana Chang Chung-Wen, as she toured Chinese communities along the American West Coast. These engagements would bring them to the Sun Sing Theater in San Francisco's Chinatown, the very same stage where Bruce's father had performed two decades earlier.

Originally known as the Mandarin Theater (before being renamed in 1949), the Sun Sing had long been one of the premiere venues in Chinatown. Situated on one of the busiest stretches of Grant Street, the theater was a key location in Chinatown's opera (and then cinema) culture for many decades throughout the twentieth century.

Built in 1924, the Mandarin quickly eclipsed the aging Liberty Theater on Broadway to become the epicenter of Chinatown's well-established opera culture. Residents of Chinatown weren't welcomed in venues anywhere else around town, and most couldn't understand the language being used on stage anyhow. As a result business within Chinatown's opera houses thrived. In the same period the newly constructed Great China Theater opened just one block east, down Jackson Street, to become the Mandarin's prime competition for many years to come. The two venues were constantly trying to out-bill each other with top-notch opera talent imported from China. In 1931 the Mandarin even brought over Ma Sze-tsang—likely the most famous actress in southern China at the time—for an eighteen-month run.

It was within this context, that the Mandarin Theater booked Bruce's father, Hoi Cheun, with other members of the Cantonese Opera in late 1939. The theater had deep enough pockets to post bonds with the Immigration Department for each individual it imported and paid the talent handsomely during their stay. However, by the time of Hoi Chuen's arrival to San Francisco, opera's heyday in Chinatown was on the descent. In the week before Bruce's birth at the Chinese Hospital in November 1940, the Grandview Theater opened just a block down the hill on Jackson Street as a state-of-the-art modern movie theater. It also served as the American headquarters of the Grandview production company, which produced films (of respectable quality considering the low budgets) for export back to Hong Kong. It was under Grandview that Esther Heng made *Golden Gate Girl* and bestowed a young Bruce with his first role. In time the Mandarin Theater would shift its own format to host opera performances during the day and then screen films in the evening. Later Orson Welles shot scenes in and around the theater for the film *The Lady from Shanghai*—with his estranged wife at the time, Rita Hayworth—in 1946, shortly before it was rechristened as the Sun Sing.

Just as the theater had done three decades earlier in securing one of China's premiere actresses with Ma Sze-tsang, it was now hosting the leading starlet of Hong Kong cinema—"The Most Beautiful Creature of Free China"—Diana Chang Chung-Wen. As Paul Fonoroff, longtime Hong Kong Cinema critic for the *South China Morning Daily*, explains it, "Diana Chang's voluptuous figure and sexy demeanor helped make her a Mandarin Marilyn Monroe of the late 1950s and early 1960s."

Born in Hebei Province in northern China, Diana eloped at the age of fifteen during the height of the war in 1941 and fled to Taiwan. Divorced two years later, she entered the film industry in her late teens under Taiwan's fledgling Central Motion Picture Corporation (where she had another short-lived marriage, to a studio executive).

As Fonoroff describes it, her rise to cinematic fame was a colorful one:

> Diana made her Hong Kong debut in *Three Sisters* (1957), notable for Chang's rendition of "Chop Suey Roll," sung to the tune of "Mambo Italiano" but with Chinese lyrics in which the amply endowed starlet invited listeners to partake of her cha shao bao ("roast pork buns"). Her passionate kiss in the Hong Kong–Thai co-production *Flame in Ash* (1958) caused a sensation, and she proved even more photogenic when filmed in Eastmancolor for *Calendar Girl* (1959).
>
> Diana was one of the busiest actresses in Mandarin pictures in the late 1950s, her credits including such escapist fare as *Wild Fantasies* (1958), *Loves of a Model* (1959), and *Fire-Breathing Lass* (1959) (which was also one of her nicknames).

In the fall of 1964 Diana embarked on a tour of the U.S. West Coast to promote her new film, *The Amorous Lotus Pan*. She was scheduled to appear at Chinatown theaters from Seattle to Los Angeles. Through his father's connections back home, Bruce was hired to accompany her along the tour, as well as dance the Hong Kong cha-cha on stage with her each night (and by some accounts, serve as a low-key bodyguard in the process).

During the final days of August, the tour was scheduled for a stop at the Sun Sing Theater, where Bruce and Diana were told to expect a packed house. As he had done to great effect for many years, Bruce was intent on seizing a down moment in the official program to take center stage for a martial arts performance. It would be, after all, a great opportunity to advertise his new Oakland school before all Chinatown. With Taky Kimura and James Lee unavailable, Bruce recruited his new friend Dan Inosanto to serve as a stage partner. The demonstration that ensued would become forever notorious among the Chinatown martial arts community.

Although Bruce carried a small degree of fame—derived from his Hong Kong films—his reputation within San Francisco's Chinatown by August 1964 was highly mixed. While neighborhood students of his dance instruction were very fond of him, members of the local martial arts scene considered him a troublemaker with little respect for his elders. To them he truly was the negative stereotype of a belligerent and egotistical Hong Kong Wing Chun practitioner, and his 1959 run-in with Lau Bun had only reinforced this type of impudent persona. So while his cha-cha performance that day may have been welcomed by some segments of the audience, his martial arts demonstration certainly was not by others.

Furthermore, in a wider context there is evidence of lingering tensions between James Lee and T. Y. Wong after their split, which pointed to antagonistic camps developing between Chinatown and Oakland. In this sense Bruce was regarded not as a lone practitioner but as a representative of a rival faction. Indeed, it was T.Y. who had labeled Bruce "a dissident with bad manners."

Not long after James left Kin Mon, T.Y. had published his own new book on his Sil Lum system of Kung Fu. Toward the end of the book he included a section titled "Soft Hand Stunts," in which T.Y. dismisses James Lee's type of Iron Hand techniques as mere gimmickry, concluding "Do not waste your time practicing this art." To drive the point home, in a not-so-subtle insult, the final page ran with an image of T.Y.'s small eight-year-old son mimicking the exact manner in which James had been portrayed breaking bricks in the previous book, under the headline: "See, I Can Break 'Em Too!"

Soon afterward, while compiling Bruce's book, James donned his old Kin Mon uniform for a section of photographs that was meant to illustrate "examples of a slower system against the more effective Gung Fu techniques." In those pages James is dismantled by Bruce in a photo-by-photo dismissal of specific techniques featured in T.Y.'s previous book. Both titles were readily for sale in Chinatown, and the slights could hardly have gone unnoticed among local martial artists.

(In fact, years later, in the introduction of James Lee's 1972 book *Wing Chun Kung-Fu*, his language became far more blunt: "Wing Chun has made a big difference in my life. Before taking it up, I studied the sil lum style, which featured such forms as 'A Dragon and Tiger in Conference' and 'Nine Dragons at Sea.' Not once during those years did I see students spar. We were told that this type of training would eventually lead to deadly 'internal strength.' I realized later that the whole repertoire was just a time-killing tactic to collect a monthly fee. In disgust, I quit practicing this particular sil lum style.")

James and Al Novak had also developed poor reputations among certain quarters in Chinatown. They had made a habit of hitting all the neighborhood bars and nightclubs after class at Kin Mon, which likely did not sit well with T. Y. Wong's "sturdy citizen" mentality. When one of these outings devolved into a vicious bar fight, James opened up a local resident's jaw with a powerful left cross before coming back with a savage backhand that only further dismantled his opponent's face (according to Al Tracy, this incident was so bad that the Hop Sing Tong demanded James pay for the victim's facial surgery). In this context the recent collaborations and business ventures of James, Bruce, and Novak were seen by some as a collusion of troublemakers.

Yet however much these issues and incidents may have added to the tensions between the Chinatown and Oakland martial arts camps, none were as incendiary as Bruce's contentious demonstrations throughout 1964, from Wally Jay's luau to his more recent showing in Long Beach. Stories of what had been said began to trickle around the neighborhood: of Bruce dismissing other styles, criticizing what the masters were teaching as impractical, and asserting the superiority of his own system. Now, in late August 1964, the question was whether Bruce would have the nerve to say those same things from the stage of the Sun Sing Theater in the heart of Chinatown?

*

Bruce started with a joke.

Mentioning that his new book would be for sale in the lobby afterward, he conveyed a coy observation. "Unlike the Chinese," he said, "I've noticed that Westerners don't appreciate what they read." Referencing the vertical nature of Chinese text, versus the horizontal rendering of English sentences, he said, "When they read in the East, you can see that they like it," he explained, moving his head up and down as if saying *yes*, "but when a Westerner reads, they go like this," now turning his head side to side, as if disagreeing, "because they don't really enjoy it."

Getting a brief laugh from the crowd, Bruce motioned for Inosanto and prepared to begin. Diana Chang had sung a few of the better-known numbers from her films and then, as planned, danced the cha-cha with Bruce. Now, in between performances, Bruce announced that he wanted to demonstrate the type of kung fu that he would be teaching at his new school over in Oakland.

Bruce worked through some basic Wing Chun concepts with Inosanto as his target, emphasizing the practicality and efficiency of the system. He made a point of saying that it was free of so many of the unnecessary wasted motions found in the Chinese martial arts today. Whereas in Long Beach Bruce had spanned cultures and styles, here he was talking solely about kung fu, and if he had started nice with some humor, it wasn't long before he was already using the term "classical mess" to disparage other styles. As he had done at the luau, he dipped into a bit of Northern Shaolin, before quickly dismissing the wide kicks as impractical. "Why would you kick high and leave yourself open," he said, pausing to allow Inosanto to counter. "Instead you can kick low and punch high," he explained while demonstrating each blow.

Letting forth a blast of chain punches, Bruce remarked how he had brought his skills from Hong Kong, and even there in China "80 percent of what they are teaching is nonsense. Here, in America, it is 90 percent." This comment drew an uneasy murmur from sections of the crowd. And then Bruce really drove it home. "These old tigers," he said, presumably referring to Chinatown's old masters, "they have no teeth."

A cigarette butt was tossed toward the stage in disgust. More followed. Savvy to the etiquette of stage culture, Bruce knew this to be no small insult.

"Bruce was saying these things that were offensive to the Chinese martial arts," explains Inosanto, "and they didn't like that sort of attitude coming from a young *sifu*."

Toward the far back of theater, a male audience member, seemingly making his way to the exit, turned to shout, "That's not kung fu!"

Bruce smiled, "Sir, would you care to come up on stage so I can demonstrate?"

The departing spectator shot back as he continued toward the exit. "You don't know kung fu!"

Bruce tried now to salvage his demonstration, asking, "Would anyone else care to volunteer?"

In the lower-left seats facing the stage, a hand shot up. Bruce, anxious to gain control over the situation, quickly called the volunteer up.

Sixteen-year old Adeline Fong sat with some of her friends, close to the stage. Born and raised in Chinatown, Fong came from a family that was deeply involved in the neighborhood's opera culture (in fact, her "great uncle" operated the Great China Theater on Jackson Street). At the age of eight, a good friend of her older sister—"Auntie" Gwynn—caught her jaywalking and pulled her into Chan Heung's Hung Gar school on Ross Alley to keep her out of trouble. Gwynn was a very early and enthusiastic fixture of the neighborhood martial arts scene who in her efforts to keep Fong safe inadvertently started her kung fu training at a young age. Later Fong would enroll with Bing Chan and become one of the first females in Chinatown to perform with a Lion Dance team. When her stepfather heard how serious she was about her studies, he arranged for her to also train with Lau Bun, essentially exposing her to a uniquely wide cross section of what the neighborhood martial arts culture had to offer.

Fong attended the Sun Sing that night with a sizable group of students from Bing Chan's school. When Bruce asked for a volunteer, her classmate Kenneth Wong didn't hesitate to raise his hand, much to the mischievous delight of his peers.

"When Bruce called Kenneth up, we began cheering and hollering," she explains, "egging him on."

Like Bruce, Kenneth was known as a bit of a hotshot.

Kenneth Wong ignored the stairs and just leapt onto center stage. This elicited some howls from his friends in the nearby row, and laughter from other sections of audience.

Bruce thanked him for volunteering and explained the demonstration he wanted to conduct. Instead of the one-inch punch, Bruce set the stage for his typical routine of closing the gap and tagging his opponent on the forehead, emphasizing speed and streamlined footwork. It was the same bit that he had already performed numerous times, including at Wally Jay's luau and the impromptu gathering the night before the Long Beach tournament. As always he explained that he would close from a wide distance of a few feet to deliver a light blow to the volunteer's forehead. He asked Kenneth to attempt to block him.

The two practitioners were ready, even as the crowd remained noisy. Bruce moved in fast. Kenneth blocked the blow clean. The crowd now roared. Bruce stepped back and motioned to go again. The volume in the theater stayed high. Bruce bolted in and delivered his blow. Blocked. And again. Blocked.

And as the crowd was near frenzy now with cheers and heckles, Kenneth stepped back and shifted to an offensive pose: fists up and outward toward the opponent. And for a brief moment, an explosive tension held heavy over the theater, as if right there on stage Chinatown's martial arts culture was finally going to square off against its detractor.

Realizing that the entire demonstration was completely off the rails and that the crowd was quickly going from surly to riotous, Bruce stepped back and smiled. He then offered an obligatory word, "Thank you for participating." The crowd erupted, reveling in his loss. A fresh round of cigarettes rained forth.

And then, stepping to the edge of center stage, Bruce signed off with a comment that is still hotly debated to this day in Chinatown martial arts circles: "I would like to let everybody know that any time my Chinatown brothers want to try out my Wing Chun, they are welcomed to come find me at my school in Oakland."

And with that Bruce left the stage, leaving many in the crowd to wonder—did he just put out an open challenge to all of Chinatown?

The neighborhood was abuzz.

"Bruce talked about how there were no good martial artists in America," explained James Wing Woo, a longtime local kung fu practitioner, "and word of that went quickly around Chinatown."

Descriptions of the errant demonstration were enthusiastically retold down in Hung Sing. At the Jackson Street Café, word reached Wong Jack Man that Bruce had performed and dismissed Northern Shaolin on stage. Word trickled into Kin Mon during the evening's class. Bing Chan heard about the incident and scolded Kenneth Wong for not retaliating against Bruce. Down Old Chinatown Lane members of the Gee Yau Seah discussed what had occurred.

If Bruce's final statement was being interpreted as a challenge, the question now was if anyone would step forward to meet it.

In the coming weeks a letter was drafted.

Wong Jack Man sat down at the Jackson Street Café after finishing his shift waiting tables, joining David Chin and Bing Chan. Chin was a regular at the Gee Yau Seah, a young practitioner in his midtwenties who studied Fut Gar under Mah Sek, the aging Qi Gong master who was widely known for his fantastical demonstrations.

They were also joined by Ronald "Ya Ya" Wu, a close friend of Chin. Wu had little connection to the Gee Yau Seah or martial arts in Chinatown. His nickname, Ya Ya, was a reference to his constantly yammering mouth. One longtime Chinatown resident remembers Wu as "the sort of guy that always had to insert himself into things."

The group concerned itself with penning a formal note to Bruce Lee in response to his words at the Sun Sing. Although the contents of the actual letter have likely long been lost to a wastebasket, the general consensus is that it sought to take Bruce up on his offer to "try out" his Wing Chun.

By the time the note was drafted and the small meeting at the Jackson Street Café concluded, it was Wong Jack Man who had signed his name to the letter.

Why Wong Jack Man, of all the people in the Chinatown martial arts community, had stepped forward remains a matter of much debate. Chin asserts that Wong had stated right there in the Jackson Café that he was set to open a Northern Shaolin kung fu school in Chinatown, and that beating Bruce Lee would give him immediate prestige. Others saw it as merely a macho gesture, spurred on by so much of the praise that Wong had received after recent demonstrations. Perhaps he was genuinely incensed by Bruce's insulting dismissal of the Northern Shaolin arts and intended to set the record straight by way of his fists. Among the more prevalent perspectives is the idea that Wong had been manipulated into the entire affair, the new kid in town naively lured into a fight without realizing the stakes.

Whatever the case, Chin soon made the trip across the Bay to hand-deliver the letter in Oakland. "I brought the note to Bruce Lee," Chin says, "and he looked at it and laughed, and said, 'Okay, set the date.'"

This started a back-and-forth over San Francisco Bay that went on for weeks. Bruce seemed unwilling to back down from the fight, but neither did he pursue it. He refused to fight in Chinatown and maintained that they would have to come to him instead.

As word of an impending showdown spread, anticipation began to build. Leo Fong heard a story that Wong Jack Man possessed a technique called "the vibrating fist," in which he could strike an opponent Taser-like, rendering him stunned from the blow. Meanwhile, as Chin traveled between the two potential participants, many began to consider him more an instigator than a messenger.

Regardless of the rumor mill, Bruce held firm to his position: if they wanted a fight, they'd have to come over to Oakland to get it.

The matter was settled on a weekday in November. The weather was sunny and pleasant. A frantic excitement spread around sections of Chinatown.

Bruce's childhood friend Ben Der, now living again in San Francisco, caught wind of the impending showdown. "The day of the fight," he explains, "everybody was talking about it. And everybody in the neighborhood seemed to favor Wong Jack Man."

Now assigned to a parish in Stockton, Leo Fong got a call from James Lee in the late afternoon: "It's all going down, man. Come on over." Caught on short notice, Fong couldn't make the drive in time. He anxiously told Jimmy to call him back right after the fight and let him know what happened.

Sam Louie recalls word coming down into Hung Sing, urging the senior students to go over to Oakland with Wong Jack Man. As disliked as Bruce was within Lau Bun's school, the affair was beyond the bounds of conduct that their teacher permitted. For years Lau Bun had prevented the local martial arts culture from devolving into a Hong Kong–style challenger culture. "We said, 'It has nothing to do with Hung Sing,'" Louie recalls. "And we explained to them, 'You go into someone's studio . . . it's no good. Whether you win or lose . . . it's no good.'"

By then the anticipation and adrenaline were too far along to be curbed. As the sun dipped low to the Pacific, Wong Jack Man got into a car and headed east, toward the city of Oakland.

14 EXCHANGING HANDS

James Lee bolted the door from the inside, the snap of the lock sending a charge through the already amplified atmosphere.

Wong Jack Man had arrived at Bruce Lee's school at 4157 Broadway in north Oakland with five other people in tow. The many weeks of back-and-forth had finally culminated in a showdown.

Bruce Lee stood facing them at the center of the room, blaring hostility. Behind him James returned to the rear of the studio to stand beside Linda. Outnumbered and unsure of just how many people were bound to show up, James kept a concealed handgun in case things spiraled out of control.

David Chin had driven the Chinatown group over the Bay Bridge in his beige Pontiac Tempest ("three sitting up front and three in the back") as autumn twilight fell on San Francisco Bay. The martial artists had sat clustered in the front seat: Chin, Wong Jack Man, and Chan "Bald Head" Keung. A well-respected tai chi practitioner, Keung was a longtime fixture of the Gee Yau Seah and was the oldest member of the group, in his midforties.

In the backseat Ronald "Ya Ya" Wu sat with Martin Wong and Raymond Fong. They were all at least a decade older than both Wong Jack Man and David Chin and carried the feel of mischievous hanger-on types, people who wanted to feel close to the action ("only there to see the hubbub," as Wong Jack Man would later explain). Yet for all the bluster in Chinatown that day, the ride over was unusually quiet.

They arrived at the Jun Fan Institute on Broadway Avenue in the early evening, and approached the two-story brick building. Formerly an upholstery business, the location's front door was recessed between glass showcase windows, and right inside the entrance a single step led down to the interior floor. The space was narrow: ten to fifteen feet across and about thirty feet deep, before another short step that led up to a partition separating off the back room. Lee had kept the studio simple and uncluttered. A student of his at the time remembers the school as "very unremarkable."

The Chinatown group stood near the front door, opposite the three Lees further inside, the space between them dense with tension. "It was serious business," Linda Lee recalls.

In time Wong Jack Man would try to spin the scenario into a more harmless context, asserting that he merely wanted to engage in a friendly sparring match. Chin, like Linda Lee, dismisses this notion as pure revisionism. "It was *not* a friendly atmosphere," he asserts. "The challenge was real."

David Chin stepped forward to introduce Wong Jack Man and articulate their intent. Bruce was having none of it: "Shut your mouth . . . you've already gotten your friend killed." The back-and-forth started in English, then hastily shifted in and out of Cantonese. Bruce pressed Wong on whether he had actually been at the Sun Sing, which he admitted he had not. When Chin tried to interject some ground rules, Bruce kept the tone harsh: "You came to my school to challenge me and now you want to set the rules?"

The Chinatown crowd briefly turned inward to confer. Perhaps they had finally begun to realize that Bruce's often-cited cockiness didn't stem from shallow egotism but from a genuine confidence: he really did believe he could beat any and all challengers. In this regard it was difficult to determine which fighter was underestimating his opponent.

Bruce barked toward their huddle, letting them know that high noon was the wrong hour for second guesses. "As far as I'm concerned," Bruce shouted, "there are no rules. It's all out!"

However contested the actual reasons for the fight were, the match-up itself had a singularly spectacular symmetry: two highly promising twenty-three-year-old kung fu practitioners wielding inverse styles of Shaolin and representing opposite shores of the bay.

Their appearances alone spoke to the yin-yang-like dynamic that existed between them. At five feet seven and a mere 140 pounds, Bruce stood in a tank top and jeans. Like the fight with Yoiche in Seattle, his opponent had arrived formally dressed. At five feet ten and about the same weight as Bruce, Wong Jack Man wore a traditional black *jing mo*, making him look far more handsome and naive than formidable or menacing.

Although fairly new to the area, Wong had an unassuming and low-key personality that quickly endeared him to many in Chinatown. Bruce, on the other hand, was entirely polarizing. He was known by many to be cocky, hyperactive, and outspoken. His close friends, by contrast, regarded him as charismatic, highly motivated, and fiercely loyal.

If the old boxing adage, "Styles make fights," was true, then the impending bout would be stellar. As a practitioner of the Northern Shaolin arts, Wong Jack Man's abilities were expansive, acrobatic, and oriented around long-range attacks. He was known for his kicking abilities, which—according to one student—could be delivered with "blinding speed and crushing power." Conversely, Bruce practiced a Southern Shaolin style—Wing Chun—which was short, linear, and economical. His abilities were anchored around an uncanny agility of the hands and otherworldly displays of speed, manifested in barrages of direct punches. Whereas Bruce had refuted the practicing of forms as "dry-land swimming," Wong was said to have mastered "close to a hundred of them at the time."

Both men had spent their early years growing up in Hong Kong, learning kung fu from established Chinese masters, before transplanting to the Bay Area. Whether intentional or otherwise, Wong Jack Man was representing the long-established and more traditional martial arts culture of Chinatown, while Bruce was a member of a very new and modern camp in Oakland.

Up until that very moment, the two men had actually never met.

"Step forward," Bruce demanded in Cantonese.

As Wong Jack Man emerged forth, Bruce was intent on replicating his eleven-second victory in Seattle from a few years earlier. Like so many other of their viewpoints, Bruce shared a similar philosophy with James, who was known to often articulate these situations in stark terms: "If you get in a fight, you've got to take the guy out in the first ten seconds. You can't give him a chance. Just destroy him." So whether it was this Oakland street-fighter code of quickly putting an opponent down or the old notion of a true master defeating an opponent in three moves or less, Bruce sought to end the conflict quickly.

Now in the late stages of pregnancy, Linda Lee watched with detached cool. "I suppose I ought to have been nervous," she recounted later in a memoir, "Yet, the truth is that I felt quite calm and composed under the circumstances.... I had no doubt that he [Bruce] could take care of himself."

Wong stepped into range, and Bruce took the initiative. As in the demonstration he so often exhibited, Bruce saw his chance to quickly close the gap and land a blow. Even in light of his recent failure with the technique at the Sun Sing Theater, Bruce didn't hesitate to seize on the opening and execute it, but instead of a mere tap to the head, he darted in and delivered a sharp punch to Wong's temple, just narrowly missing his eye. The tone of the fight was set. As Wong would convey to one of his students years later, "He really wanted to kill me."

Bruce pressed in, anxious for a fast resolution. Wong resorted to defensive maneuvers, sidestepping to avoid Bruce's straight assaults and using his forearms to deflect the blasts. By Chin's account Bruce employed low kicks to close in and then advanced with a flurry of punches. The melee soon moved through the building as Wong sought to evade his enraged attacker.

Shifting to offense, Wong delivered a wide diagonal blow—"like an ax punch coming down"—that narrowly missed Bruce's chin and instead caught him across his lower neck. For Bruce, who had been so untouchable in recent years during both *chi sao* and sparring, the blow stoked his fury even further. Now approaching a frenzy, he pressed in on Wong with blasts of "chain punches": a rhythmic succession of rapid blows that keeps the hands high in defense even as they are used offensively.

Despite the seemingly high-quality match-up, opposing a practitioner who had taken to calling his martial arts approach "scientific street fighting" with a Northern expert known for his elegance, the fight was quickly devolving into a wild and sloppy brawl that spilled across the entire room.

Wong sidestepped again as he deflected with his arms. In then backpedaling away from Bruce, he stumbled over one of the small riser steps that came up from the studio floor. Bruce was over him now, relentless with his punches, shouting in Cantonese: "Do you yield? Do you yield?" Having lost his feet, Wong had little choice.

"From there," explains Chin, "he said he gives up and we stopped the fight. The whole thing lasted . . . not more than seven minutes."

Wong Jack Man and his mismatched entourage got back into Chin's car and returned to San Francisco. In Chinatown they went upstairs to the Chin Family Association on Washington Street and applied a hardboiled egg to Wong's eye as a way to reduce the bruising. The mood was sullen.

Back in Oakland the atmosphere was far from triumphant. "After the fight, Bruce sat down on the stairs in the back of the studio," explains Linda Lee, "and he told me that he was so disappointed in himself, because the fight lasted way too long, that he couldn't get him [Wong] down right away, and that he was winded from running around."

Even as Linda would maintain that Wong was "soundly defeated," the fight was a far cry from Bruce's dominant victory over Yoechi years earlier in Seattle. After expounding all year in front of so many other martial artists about the ineffectiveness of so many practitioners and their techniques, Bruce now sat quietly in his school, wrestling with his own shortcomings.

The following afternoon Bruce's childhood friend Ben Der returned to Chinatown anxious to catch word of what had transpired.

"The day before, everybody was talking about it," he recalls, "saying how exciting it was gonna be. So I purposefully went down to Chinatown the next afternoon to see what everyone was saying. And it was dead quiet. Nobody was saying anything. And that's how I knew Bruce Lee won that fight."

15 AFTERMATH

There had actually been an agreement between the two camps to keep the incident quiet. However, that pledge of silence quickly unraveled on November 26, when a local Chinese newspaper reprinted an absurd account of the fight that had recently run in the celebrity gossip column of the *Hong Kong Ming Bao Daily*, alleging that the two combatants had actually been battling over the affections of Diana Chang Chung-Wen.

This then opened the floodgates, sparking a huge wave of gossip around Chinatown about what had actually occurred, and like any good schoolyard brawl the postfight chatter was heavy on hyperbole. Three weeks after the initial article, Bruce gave an interview to the local *Chinese Pacific Weekly*, in an attempt to clear up some of the assertions in the original article, particularly its connection to Diana Chang. This then sparked its own flurry of published responses, including anonymous letters to the editor and classified ads that were run like op-eds. Collectively, these missives debated numerous aspects of the incident, from the tangible (how many people were present, how long the fight lasted) to the outlandish (the manner in which Bruce Lee had fainted).

This all played out in a very public way, making the fight a hot topic in Chinatown and among the Bay Area martial arts scene not just in the immediate aftermath of the incident but for many years (and really decades) to come. Before long it began to sound like dozens of people were actually witnesses to the fight.

"Lots of people claim that they were there," states Chin. "I've heard all kinds of things: people say they broke up the fight, that they were the judge, that they knocked on the door and slipped in to watch. It's amazing how many people love to make these claims, but it's not true. They weren't there."

Indeed, stories from secondhand sources would attach all sorts of exaggerated detail to the match, at times straying wildly from the simple narrative of those in attendance; some insisted that the actual fight went for over twenty minutes, that Bruce slammed Wong's head through a wall, or that Wong had Bruce in a headlock and was poised to knock him out right when the police showed up. In Hong Kong, Bruce's mother heard that he had been killed in the fight.

There was a quality to all this that harkened to the classic Akira Kurosawa film *Rashomon*, which explores issues of truth, memory, and self-interest, amid contradictory accounts given by different characters who are recounting the very same incident. In this manner the Bruce Lee–Wong Jack Man fight can read like a case study in the fickle nature of human memory. For example, Ming Lum, a well-liked veteran member of the Chinatown martial arts scene, would recall that he saw Wong Jack Man working at the Jackson Street Café the very next morning after the fight, with a small scratch above his eye. Ben Der, on the other hand, asserts that Wong Jack Man missed two days at the café before returning to work, and when he finally did he was sporting a massive black eye ("like a panda.").

As with Rashomon the various accounts can seem to directly contradictory one another, though more likely, they are just intentionally selective. David Chin, very frank about the matter decades later, concedes, "I've always felt bad for Wong Jack Man, so I would tell people it was a draw."

Just as with Wally Jay's early shortcomings in judo competitions or Leo Fong's initial defeat at the smoker fights, so too would the stilted outcome of the Wong Jack Man fight have a tremendous influence on Bruce's evolution as a martial artist. The impact was as tangible as it was immediate.

Fong showed up for class in Oakland later that week to find Bruce punching at a boxing glove he had hung on a chain from the ceiling and "bouncing around like Muhammad Ali."

After the fight had occurred, James Lee had given Leo Fong a call to report back on what had transpired. Eventually the phone was passed to Bruce, who explained to Fong that his opponent's evasiveness posed a real challenge for him. Fong responded by suggesting that Bruce integrate more boxing technique into his repertoire: "Bruce, you gotta get some angles, man, straight blasts alone don't do it. You need to develop some uppercuts, some hooks."

The timing was right. Bruce had already been in the process of synthesizing so many of the influences that he had been exposed to in recent years, from James Lee's street-fighter sensibility, to Leo Fong's boxing aptitude, to Wally Jay's sense for innovation, among many others. He began formally developing a new integrated fighting approach that would bring together the best aspects of what he considered the most effective styles and nuanced techniques, yet all integrated around his emphasis of personalizing the system to the individual. In this regard the disappointing results in the Wong Jack Man fight had provided a catalyst to finally enact something new.

To begin with, Bruce was resolved to take his physical conditioning to the next level. After becoming so quickly winded during his fight in Oakland, Bruce resolved that fitness could no longer be a second priority. And with Allen Joe and James Lee as mentors, he soon took to serious bodybuilding with his typical zeal.

On a conceptual level the fight had made an even bigger impact. As Linda Lee would later write:

> The fact that the fight did not go the way Bruce wanted it to go initiated the idea that he should not be stuck on the system that he had learned in wing chun. . . . He realized that he had become stuck to those techniques and that he needed to broaden his array of skills to deal with a situation as it is unfolding. You cannot predict what is going to happen in a fight. . . . You just have to react to what is presented to you. And that was part of Bruce's broadening, both philosophically and technically.

Writing to Taky Kimura shortly after the fight, Bruce informed him: "My mind is made up to start a system of my own." A few months later he would describe it to James Lee, by writing, "This system is a combination of chiefly wing chun, fencing and boxing." In time Bruce would give it the name Jeet Kune Do, which translated as "the way of the intercepting fist." Being fond of the stop-hit technique in fencing (essentially employing an attack as a way of countering an opponent's attack), Bruce applied a term that emphasized this type of method. Yet Jeet Kune Do would be notable as much for its philosophical underpinnings as for its diverse and nuanced sense of technique. With JKD Bruce sought to design an approach that would transcend stylistic parameters and the dogmatic conditioning that he felt they entailed.

And much as he had done in Long Beach, Bruce placed the emphasis on the individual: "True observation begins when one sheds set patterns, and true freedom of expression occurs when one is beyond systems. . . . The core of understanding lies in the individual mind. . . . Truth cannot be perceived until we come to fully understand ourselves and our potentials. After all, *knowledge in the martial arts ultimately means self-knowledge.*"

This notion, of Bruce Lee's advocacy for an individual's self-awareness, lifelong evolution, and sense of boundless potential, would be at the core of his legacy and in time would inspire people well beyond the field of martial arts.

Standing there watching him dart and move around the suspended boxing glove, Fong suspected that Bruce was now poised for a bold step in his own personal evolution: "He was popping right jabs and following with the left, one-two. It was beautiful. He knew how to interpret stuff and integrate it into what he was doing. And I thought to myself, 'Man, nobody is gonna touch him now.'"

For all the outlandish gossip that would surround the big Oakland showdown, there were a few key points that would remain particularly controversial over the years. To begin with, there is debate that the opening blow that Bruce landed—the most successful of the entire fight—was delivered while Wong Jack Man was actually trying to shake hands. There has also been considerable speculation about whether Wong Jack Man was evading Bruce in a defensive posture or simply fleeing from him in a panic (the Oakland camp would long refer to Wong Jack Man as "the runner"). The fight also provided critics within the martial arts community with perceived evidence of each practitioner's shortcomings, to the effect that Wong Jack Man could only do forms and couldn't really fight, while Bruce lacked "knock-out" power and was far more talk than substance.

Clearly though, the hottest issue surrounding the fight was not the outcome but the cause. In time the prevailing sentiment that emerged was the idea that the bout had been fought over Chinatown's opposition to Bruce and James Lee teaching kung fu to non-Chinese students.

This narrative suggests that the original note sent to Oakland via David Chin was a sort of cease-and-desist letter handed down from the top brass in the tongs reprimanding Bruce for allowing non-Chinese students to study with him. In this context Wong Jack Man was sent over in the role of enforcer to drive the message home with fists, and that the true stakes of the fight were whether Bruce could continue to operate his school.

This idea would come to dominate the fight narrative over time (culminating in a bizarre Hollywood rendering of the affair decades later) and effectively nestle itself into the iconic and glossy mythos that would shroud Bruce in the years to come. Yet as tangible as the exclusion code was, martial artists from the Bay Area widely express skepticism at the idea of it being the core reason for that particular fight.

"It was never about that," says Leo Fong. "It really had to do with Bruce's personality." Al Tracy, who asserts that Bruce dropped by his kenpo school on Ocean Avenue the following Monday to lay out the whole story for posterity's sake, agrees with Fong: "It's very simple: the fight was a result of Lee's big mouth. The Chinese want respect, and when Bruce said, 'These tigers have no teeth,' that fight was inevitable." Al Novak couldn't explain the theory either, saying, "I think that's mostly made up." Clarence Lee dismisses the idea as well and instead explains the fight between the two twenty-three-year-olds in his typical terse, no-nonsense fashion: "Have you ever heard of macho bullshit?"

Indeed, a survey of the martial arts landscape in Chinatown up to late 1964 renders notable examples of non-Chinese students studying with local masters, including Noel O'Brien in Kin Mon and Clifford Kamaga in

Hung Sing. T. Y. Wong had not only performed on television but had also produced two English-language books and trained Al Novak as early as 1960. Ed Parker would often visit the old Chinatown masters whenever he was in town and would buy jars of herbal ointment from Lau Bun. The newest school in the neighborhood, Bing Chan's Lup Mo, had offered open enrollment from the get-go. Altogether then there is substantial evidence that the old tong code was well into its final throes by the time of the Bruce Lee–Wong Jack Man showdown.

However, that's not to say that the idea should be dismissed altogether. After all, the exclusion code was very prevalent during Lau Bun's generation in Chinatown, and Bruce himself dealt with it in tangible ways throughout his life, with Ip Man (both as his student and then later during his 1963 trip home), with Ruby Chow, and at times with spectators at his demonstrations.

The racial line didn't have an official clear-cut end date in the Chinese martial arts, as say, in Major League Baseball when it allowed Jackie Robinson into the league as the first African American. And even still, as in the case of Robinson, integration didn't mean the complete evaporation of racism and exclusion.

In this sense a little-known incident in Chinatown at the end of the decade provides an interesting and nuanced postscript to the debate surrounding the Oakland fight.

By the end of the 1960s, tai chi master Choy Kam Man gained a curious following. Just as his father, Choy Hak Pang, had attracted Gerda Geddes as a student in 1950s Hong Kong, Choy Kam Man soon found himself with a sizable following of young San Franciscans ("hippies," by most accounts) learning tai chi with him in Chinatown.

Michael Gilman, who would become one of his senior students, vividly remembers how he first encountered Master Choy: "There was a meeting out at Winterland in 1968 with a lot of spiritual teachers of the era, Timothy Leary, Alan Watts, and figures like that. Over in a corner away from the stage, I encountered Master Choy with some of his students performing tai chi. I had never seen it or heard of it before, but I was intrigued. Something struck me about the movements. The fliers for the classes called it 'mediation in motion.' So I signed up and was with him for years." Soon enough, Master Choy began to draw a huge following to the Chinatown YMCA for his Saturday tai chi salon. His young following even got him slots performing on stage at the Fillmore Auditorium before Grateful Dead concerts. It was a curious relationship spanning both generations and cultures, though strangely fitting for the times and indicative of the booming popularity of the martial arts that was manifesting itself by the end of the 1960s.

Around 1972 Choy began to receive threatening phone calls in the middle of the night, warning him to stop teaching non-Chinese students. This went on for months, harassing Choy and his family with very grave threats. Choy refused to cave in. Finally, he challenged his anonymous aggressors to meet him to settle the matter.

Choy and Gilman (who, years later, still confesses that he was "scared shitless") ventured to the predetermined site in the neighborhood only to find Choy's opponents to be a no-show. The calls stopped coming. Gilman asserts that Choy was positive that the harassment had come from other martial arts masters within the neighborhood.

The incident raises an important point for consideration. If the code could still apply to a well-respected insider like Choy as late as 1972, then surely it could have applied to Bruce—an outsider and perceived troublemaker—years earlier.

There is, however, another theory about the origin of the Oakland fight, which still quietly persists around Chinatown. In this scenario Bruce's demonstration at Sun Sing was not the last straw for the Chinatown martial arts community. Yes, it riled everybody, but there is evidence of an additional incident that was more formally responsible for provoking the confrontation.

Some time in early autumn of 1964, Bruce Lee apparently questioned the abilities of the aging Qi Gong master Mah Sek. A long-standing member of the Gee Yau Seah and a close friend of Lau Bun, Mah Sek was a highly respected master (who was in his late eighties at the time) and was widely known within California martial arts culture for his unique feats of the body. Purportedly, Bruce Lee not only expressed skepticism about Mah

Sek's skills but also boasted that he was going to personally "try him out." This was perceived as a sign of immense disrespect, and allegedly when word of this got around, Chinatown had finally had enough.

This theory is interesting because it not only explains why the fight took about ten weeks to happen after the contentious demonstration at the Sun Sing Theater but would also account for why members of the Gee Yau Seah (David Chin, Wong Jack Man, Chan "Bald Head" Keung) were so closely involved. Most notable perhaps is that this perspective implies that Wong Jack Man did in fact go over to Oakland with a purpose as handed down from top brass within the community.

There is an interesting point of reference to this as well. Later in his career Bruce had an incident where he essentially did "try out" the internal methods of another master. As Bruce's former student Doug Palmer recounted it:

> Several masters from other schools were with Bruce on a television show, a benefit for charity, as I recall. At any rate, one of the other masters was bragging about his "internal *Chi*," his inner power, goading Bruce and challenging him to strike his stomach. The master stood in a ready stance, one arm at his side the other pointing at his stomach, insisting that Bruce hit him there. Because of his internal *Chi*, he said it was impossible to hurt him. Bruce approached. The master insisted again. Bruce struck him a blow right on the nose, not that hard but enough to shock him. The master jumped back, startled and incensed, demanding to know what Bruce was doing. "Any one can learn to resist a blow he is prepared for," Bruce said. "A *Gung Fu* man must be prepared for the unexpected."

This is a good example of the kind of behavior that was so upsetting to the Chinatown martial artists and suggests what Bruce might have meant when he said he would "try out" Mah Sek. Whatever the case, it still speaks to the idea that Bruce's conduct and personality were ultimately at the root of the fight.

Regardless of the actual cause for the Oakland showdown in 1964, the idea that it was over the right for Bruce to teach non-Chinese students would plague Wong Jack Man for years to come, despite the great variety of pupils he would teach over the course of his career.

By late January 1965 the neighborhood gossip about the fight had gotten so outlandish that Wong Jack Man finally gave an account to the *Chinese Pacific Weekly*, in his own attempt to set the record straight. The article ran large on the front page alongside a dramatic picture of him performing a full split atop two chairs while holding a sword steadily aloft over his head. Like the interview Bruce had given one month earlier, Wong denied starting or losing the fight.

Surprisingly though, Wong went so far as to assert that his trip to Oakland was originally meant to be amicable, or rather "to have a friendly visit." The article concluded with an interesting sentiment: "[Wong] says that in the future he will not argue his case again in the newspaper, and if he is made to fight again, he will instead hold a public exhibition so that everyone can see with their own eyes." Although not an exact quotation from Wong, the wording is interesting—"made to fight"—and hints at the popular theory that he had been manipulated into the affair. Ever inclined to interpret things on the side of a challenge, Chinatown's martial arts culture widely regarded Wong's final sentiments as a call for a rematch.

Yet by the time this article ran on January 28, Bruce had numerous big things happening in his personal life. A second fight with Wong Jack Man was likely the last thing on his mind.

With the Chinese New Year, on February 1, 1965, Linda Lee gave birth to a baby boy. Their first child, Brandon Lee, arrived at Oakland Hospital, as the Year of the Green Dragon had finally come to an end.

Three days later Bruce caught a plane down to Los Angeles, for an opportunity in Hollywood.

EPILOGUE
Screen Test

As Bruce arrived in Los Angeles, the current issue of *Black Belt Magazine* found on newsstands featured local kung fu master Ark Wong on the cover, beneath the headline "Special: Ancient Fighting Arts of China."

Wong was the first Chinese martial artist ever to appear on the magazine's cover, and for many of the publication's readers, it would be their first real exposure to the art of kung fu. Most important was Wong's overt acknowledgment within the magazine that his door was open to every type of student. As a member of the Los Angeles chapter of the Hop Sing Tong, his published assertion was the closest thing to an official ending of the old tong segregation code surrounding the Chinese martial arts.

In this sense the Chinese code had run parallel to the American policy of exclusion. The two had mirrored each other for a long time and then wound down in unison. A new era was beginning. As historian Ben Judkins puts it: "1965 was a pivotal year for the traditional Chinese martial arts in North America. Simply put, it was the moment when everything changed."

Lau Bun passed in 1967, truly marking the end of an era. His career was a bridge to the modern age of the Chinese martial arts in America. As a pioneer who predated much of the martial arts media that surfaced in later years, he is scarcely acknowledged for his foundational contributions. Fifty years after his death, Hung Sing still operates in San Francisco. It is one of the oldest martial arts schools in the nation.

T. Y. Wong relocated Kin Mon up to Sacramento Street, where he taught into the midseventies. Amid the many martial arts masters who claim to be the first to accept non-Chinese students, T.Y.'s trailblazing contributions often go unacknowledged.

Master Choy taught a diverse array of students for years to come throughout Northern California. His family played a key role in the proliferation of tai chi all over the world.

Mah Sek practiced kung fu into his late nineties, until one afternoon he told his students that his friends and family were all gone and that he was tired of living. He passed just days later.

David Chin now teaches Tibetan Hop Gar in North Carolina. His views on the martial arts today echo many of the things Bruce Lee expressed during his demonstrations fifty years earlier: "The things Bruce was saying back then were true. I disagreed with him at the time, but he was right. And now even today, people still want to bury their heads in the sand."

After his fight with Bruce Lee, Wong Jack Man distanced himself from many of the martial artists in Chinatown but continued to teach until his retirement in 2005. The fight would—quite unfairly—attach itself to his reputation for the rest of his life.

In May 1965 Muhammad Ali fought Sonny Liston in a rematch, and the results would be forever shrouded in controversy. Ali knocked out Liston in the first with a quick right—the "phantom punch" as it would be known—that had many immediately alleging a fix, inferring that Liston simply took a clumsy dive. Their rematch had played out in front of 2,500 spectators and was broadcast on national television, while some of the world's best sportswriters were sitting ringside. Even still, the results of just what happened remain hotly contested by historians and biographers some fifty years later. By contrast Bruce Lee's fight with Wong Jack Man happened behind closed doors, with seven witnesses. In this sense it is unsurprising that their fight in Oakland remains subject to all manner of speculation and hyperbole.

With the change in immigration laws, Chinatown saw a fresh crop of martial artists arrive throughout the decade and establish their own long-term schools within the neighborhood: YC Wong, Brandon Lai, and Kuo Lien Ying were among the new masters who taught for many years and carved out legacies of their own.

In Chinatown gangs began to form among the neighborhood youth, and by the early seventies the ensuing violence around Chinatown was severe. The wealthier residents took advantage of new housing opportunities and moved to outlying areas. Many of the theaters, nightclubs, and opera houses fell into decline. In a sort of grand social irony, the heyday of Chinatown ended just as true equality for its residents had barely begun.

James Lee passed in 1972. Like Lau Bun and many of the other old masters of Chinatown, his role in martial arts history is often unsung. Kenpo master Al Tracy calls James "one of the great missing pieces of the martial arts in America."

Many of Bruce Lee's other colleagues around the Bay Area—Wally Jay, Ralph Castro, Al Novak, Leo Fong—taught for decades, their students over time collectively numbering in the many thousands. When asked how many students Wally Jay had taught in his lifetime, his widow, Bernice, takes on a look of wonder, as if asked to unravel a complex algorithm.

Ed Parker's model for kenpo karate schools eventually spread to locations all over the United States. One longtime kenpo practitioner surmises that the influence and infrastructure that Parker first began to lay out in the 1950s would over the years be responsible for millions of people practicing the martial arts in America.

There's a hint of nervousness to Bruce Lee as he sits and waits for his screen test to begin. Dressed sharp in a black suit with a black tie and sporting an immaculate haircut, it is little wonder that Allen Joe took him for a male model that night at Ruby Chow's years earlier.

His very presence in Hollywood was no small irony. Despite his time as a child actor in Hong Kong, Bruce never pursued show business upon his return to the United States. He never sought an agent, or went to casting calls, or sent around head shots. Instead, he immersed himself in the martial arts along the West Coast and in doing so caught Hollywood's attention.

Sitting there with his hands folded, waiting to begin, Bruce was on the cusp of beginning to accomplish what he told his godfather about over dinner on his first day back in the United States six years earlier: "I would like to let the world know about the greatness of the Chinese martial arts." It is hard to not consider it in fateful terms.

As the film rolls, a clear male voice speaks out from off-camera: "Now Bruce, just look right into the camera lens right here and tell us your name, your age and where you were born."

Bruce takes a breath and shifts in his seat.

"My last name is Lee. Bruce Lee. I am twenty-four-years-old. I was born in San Francisco."

ACKNOWLEDGMENTS

This book and the history it contains are based on a multitude of interviews with key sources from the era. The help and participation of many people made this possible.

Hung Sing's Dino Salvatera always left his door open for me and pointed me in the right direction whenever it was needed. He introduced me to Adeline Fong, who constantly resurfaced for additional interviews on her day off. I greatly appreciate all their help. If any readers are interested in Lau Bun's style of Choy Li Fut, they should know that Hung Sing is alive and well in San Francisco.

For Kin Mon, Warren Chan was instrumental in helping me convey the legacy of T. Y. Wong, putting me in touch with numerous people and opening all his files to me as well. Thank you, Warren! Also, my gratitude to Gilman Wong for his support in this project.

Bruce Lee's good friend Allen Joe was one of the very first people I interviewed for this project. He is a living legend of cool East Bay history and a dedicated friend in keeping the memory of Bruce Lee alive. I greatly appreciate his help at every turn.

I would like to thank Bernice Jay and her family for always welcoming me over to Eagle Avenue whenever I had questions. As Linda Lee said to me, "The Jay family is a Bay Area institution." Small Circle is still being taught there in the studio at the back of the house. Also, my appreciation to Wally's student Rick Wong for his steady interest and insight into this project.

A very big thank-you to the family of Ed Parker for their help and support. They not only provided me with great information but really hustled to get me everything I needed before deadline.

Leo Fong gave me full access from the first day I cold-called him a few years back. His personal history is one of the uniquely American tales that I encountered, and I can't think him enough for all his time and insight. Mr. Fong is still teaching in Southern California.

I also appreciate how helpful James Lee's son Greglon was over the last few years, embodying all the down-to-earth sensibility you would have expected from his father. Readers interested in the Oakland school should know that Greglon teaches martial arts classes in Berkeley, California.

Thank you to Jeff Chinn for answering my questions on all things Bruce Lee. I hope this book adds a thing or two to his collection.

Martial arts historian Ben Judkins was tremendously helpful in enabling me to grasp the trajectory of Chinese martial arts history. Ben is doing amazing work on his blog, Kung Fu Tea (chinesemartialstudies.com), and I highly recommend it to anyone holding this book.

Historian Philip Choy welcomed me into his house to answer questions. He is a pioneering Chinese American historian, and I greatly recommend his books for anyone wishing to further pursue the social history contained here.

I need to thank Rick Wing and David Tadman for their help with my initial article. If you are interested in Wong Jack Man's Northern Shaolin system, Rick has assumed leadership of the school and teaches regular classes. Also if you would like to read more about the Wong Jack Man–Bruce Lee fight, check out his book *Showdown in Oakland*. I also suggest Tadman's books on Bruce Lee, most notably, *Lee Siu Loong: Memories of the Dragon*.

Barney Scollan emailed me out of the blue one day and has since provided me with a wealth of material. I greatly appreciate all his support.

I would like to specifically thank Ben Der, Dan Inosanto, Al Tracy, Gary Cagaanan, Sam Louie, and Doc-Fai Wong for amazingly insightful interviews.

I would also like to express my gratitude to Linda Lee Cadwell, who took the time to send me a note of encouragement.

My reverence and admiration endure for those who passed in the time since I interviewed them: George Lee, Al Novak, Paul Eng, and James Wing Woo.

I need to thank friends and colleagues for their feedback on this project: Lily Bixler Clausen, Mark Jordan, Jay Seals, Domini Dragoone, Andrew Strawder, and Adam Korn. In particular I would like to express my great appreciation for Sara Hayden, who contributed major editing help on the original draft as well as all-around insight for the book.

I would like to thank my journalism professors and mentors over the years: Ken Kobre, Yumi Wilson, Jon Rochmis, and Clay Lambert.

Special thanks to Frank Parisi, who bumped into me one day at a coffee shop when I was starting my original article and has fielded an endless stream of questions and anxieties ever since. His insight had a profound influence on what's in these pages, and I appreciate every instance of advice and patience.

My agent, Danielle Svetcov, was on board with this project from day one and stuck with it ever since. Having her in my corner has made all the difference. Thank you.

Thanks to my parents and my sisters, who have always supported everything and anything I was ever inclined to do.

To my kids, Angelo, Marcello, and Cora, for being super dupe.

And finally . . . it would really take an entire book, rather than just these few sentences, to properly express my love and gratitude to my wife, Léla. Quite simply, this book doesn't exist without her support. Thank you. I love you.

AUTHOR'S NOTE

I should be the first to say that the information provided here is in no way a complete history of this early era of martial arts and martial artists in America. Really it is a testament to just how robust the Bay Area martial arts culture was during the early 1960s that so many other figures are deserving of more space and mention. Ming Lum, Clarence Lee, Chris Chan, Willie Cahill, Paul Pung, Mitz Kimura, Yosh Uchida, Raymond "Duke" Moore, E. Y. Lee, Ben Largusa, James Wing Woo, and Jew Leong are just some of the region's early practitioners who should have chapters (and entire books) all their own.

Furthermore, there were many pioneering American martial artists outside the Bay Area during this early era who deserve similar attention: Ark Wong, Gin Foon Mark, Wong Moon Toy, Adriano Emperado, Jhoon Rhee, Robert Trias, George Mattson, and Don Draeger, to name just a few. The list is long and noteworthy.

This book was never meant to be an encyclopedia but rather was organized as a history of a time and a place that is anchored around a particular narrative. To all those practitioners worthy of greater space . . . my humble apologies.

NOTES

PROLOGUE

1 **Wally Jay spent**: Jay family (Bernice, Alan, Alberta, and Antoinette), personal interview by the author, March 24, 2012. Also Bernice Jay, personal interviews by the author, September 18, 2012, and October 13, 2014; Alan Jay, phone interview by the author, January 3, 2015.

Alan Jay explained how the luau event was originally conceived one night in the Eagle Avenue kitchen (circa 1952) by Wally, Mark Egan (who was the founder of the Hawaii Visitor's Bureau), and Walter Napoleon, as part of an effort to start a Bay Area Hawaiian club. The luaus were originally a way to raise money for the club, and in time the parties grew into a very large community event. The martial arts connection to the luaus grew over time, starting in the late fifties.

1 **"All right, Wally"**: Bernice Jay interview, September 18, 2012.

2 **In the frenzy**: Bernice Jay interview, September 18, 2012.

2 **Even in the bustle**: Jay family interview; Bernice Jay interview, September 18, 2012, and October 13, 2014; Alan Jay interview.

2 **After her celebrated**: http://digicoll.manoa.hawaii.edu/music/Pages/syllabus.php?route=courses.php&course=5, accessed January 23, 2013. Lena Machado was the Ella Fitzgerald of the Hawaiian music scene. Wally Jay would regularly book top-notch island talent for his luau events. The anecdote about her performance at the World's Fair is typically included as part of her biographical information, such as the one linked here.

2 **Better yet for Wally**: Bernice Jay interview, September 18, 2012; Leo Fong, personal interview by the author, October 24, 2011.

2 **Leo Fong drove:** Fong interviews, October 24, 2011, and June 3, 2014. Also Fong interview, February 3, 2011, and December 17, 2014. The luau event stands out in Fong's mind as the first time he ever encountered Bruce Lee. Fong, a Methodist minister, cites Jesus Christ and Bruce Lee as the two big influences on his life.

4 **James Lee held a beer:** Al Novak, personal interview by the author, March 3, 2011.

4 **A favorite among:** Ralph Castro, personal interview by the author, February 10, 2011; Bernice Jay interview, September 18, 2012. James Lee's breaking demonstrations at Wally's luaus were legendary among Bay Area martial artists. Ralph Castro was among the many partygoers who vividly recalls how James would set up a stack of bricks and ask someone in the crowd to pick the one he should pinpoint with his strike. Then he would strike the stack, and upon destroying them all, James would step back, scratch his head, and say humorously, "Whoops, I made a mistake." He would then set up a new stack and strike again, but this time only destroying the specific brick in the column.

4 **The gathering in Colombo Hall:** Accounts of Wally Jay's luau come from personal interviews with the Jay family, March 24, 2012; Bernice Jay, September 18, 2012; Leo Fong, February 3, 2011 (phone), and October 24, 2011; Novak interview, March; Ralph Castro, February 10, 2011; George Lee, January 8, 2011; Allen Joe, June 18, 2014; Willy Cahill, August 20, 2014; Alan Jay, January 3, 2015.

4 **He spoke for some:** Castro interview.

4 **"The kid is tough":** Novak interview; James Wing Woo, personal interview by the author, February 26, 2014.

4 **Parker explained:** Novak interview; Dave Hebler, phone interview by the author, December 12, 2014.

5 **Leo Fong arrived:** Fong interviews, February 3, 2011, October 24, 2011, and June 3, 2014.

5 **A 260-pound:** Novak interview; also Ching, "Great American Great Grandmaster."

5 **As the island revelry:** Fong interview, October 24, 2011; Bernice Jay interview, September 18, 2012.

5 **Bruce Lee ignored:** Fong interviews, February 3, 2011, October 24, 2011, June 3, 2014, and December 17, 2014; Novak interview; George Lee interview.

5 **Leo Fong, on the**: Fong interview, October 24, 2011.

6 **"How could you"**: Fong interview, October 24, 2011.

6 **By the time**: George Lee interview.

6 **But by 1964**: Fong interviews, February 3, 2011, and October 24, 2011.

6 **As a result**: Novak interview; George Lee interview; Allen Joe, personal interview by the author, June 18, 2014; Castro interview; Fong interview, October 24, 2011; Linda Lee Cadwell, phone interview by the author, April 20, 2011; Al Tracy, phone interview by the author, August 26, 2014. Leo Fong likes to point out that prior to Bruce Lee being cast on *The Green Hornet*, his circle of friends in Oakland was actually rather small.

6 **"a dissident with"**: Joe Cervara, phone interview by author, February 14, 2014. Cervara attributed this quote to T. Y. Wong. The sentiment is a very succinct bit of insight into how Bruce was regarded with the established martial arts community in San Francisco's Chinatown.

6 **"The real significant"**: Al Tracy, phone interview by author, August 26, 2014.

6 **By the spring of 1964**: Campbell and Lee, *Dragon and the Tiger*, vols. 1 and 2.

7 **He would drop out**: Thomas, *Bruce Lee*, 57.

7 **He would marry**: Linda Lee, *Bruce Lee Story*, 18–19.

7 **He would travel**: Thomas, *Bruce Lee*, 57.

7 **And before the year's**: Linda Lee, *Bruce Lee Story*, 52–53.

7 **Standing on that stage**: Linda Lee, *Bruce Lee Story*, 70–71.

7 **Furthermore, his big challenge**: Linda Lee, *Bruce Lee Story*, 53–54.

7 **Bruce Lee's demonstration**: Fong interviews, February 3, 2011, and October 24, 2011; George Lee, personal interview by author, January 8, 2011; Novak interview.

7 **"There is no way"**: Fong interview, October 24, 2011; George Lee interview. See also Tommy Gong, "Jeet Kune Do," in Green and Svinth, *Martial Arts of the World*, 479.

7 **"Classical methods"**: Fong interview. See also Linda Lee, *Bruce Lee Story*, 43, 479

8 **A disjointed atmosphere**: Fong interviews, February 3, 2011, and October 24, 2011; Novak interview.

8 **"The techniques are smooth"**: Fong interview, October 24, 2011. See also Linda Lee, *Bruce Lee Story*, 49.

8 **"scientific street fighting"**: Cadwell interview.

8 **Finally he gave:** Fong interviews, February 3, 2011, and October 24, 2011; Novak interview; George Lee interview.

8 **"a big football":** Fong interview, October 24, 2011.

9 **"Now let's do it":** Fong interview, October 24, 2011; Novak interview.

9 **Fong took stock:** Fong interviews, February 3, 2011, and October 24, 2011; Novak interview.

1. THE PATRIARCH

13 **Lau Bun quietly:** James Wing Woo, personal interview by the author, February 26, 2014; Doc-Fai Wong, personal interview by the author, February 2, 2012; Dino Salvatera, personal interviews by the author, June 20, 2011, and November 7, 2011.

13 **At sixty-eight Lau Bun:** Kem K. Lee Photograph Collection, 1927–1986, Ethnic Studies Library, University of California, Berkeley, copy in possession of Dino Salvatera. Descriptions of Lau Bun's appearance at the time as well as subsequent descriptions of Portsmouth Square are drawn from the extensive visual record left by longtime Chinatown photographer Kem K. Lee, as found in his archives at the University of California, Berkeley. Lee actually photographed Hung Sing in early 1959, showing a formidable looking Lau Bun with his equally tough-looking senior students in the Brenham Place studio. Dino Salvatera, the current Sifu of Hung Sing in San Francisco, also has an extensive collection of photographs of Lau Bun and his students that dates back to the 1940s.

13 **"the Heart of Chinatown":** Philip P. Choy, personal interviews by the author, December 20, 2011, and March 30, 2013.

14 **Through the many:** Dino Salvatera, personal interviews by the author, June 20, 2011, November 7, 2011, and December 19, 2012; Wong interview; Sam Louie, personal interview by the author, February 1, 2012; Adeline Fong, personal interviews by the author, June 28, 2011, December 12, 2012, and December 3, 2014; Leo Fong, personal interview by the author, October 24, 2011; James Wing Woo, personal interview by the author, February 26, 2014; Al Tracy, phone interview by the author, August 26, 2014.

14 **The wisdom of his:** Garvey, *San Francisco Police Department*, 74. Herbert P. Lee had been sworn in just two years earlier (1957) as the first regular Asian member of the SFPD. There are, however, accounts of Chinese Americans serving in the force's auxiliary ranks back in the 1940s (Garvey, *San Francisco*

Police Department, 74) See Dillon, *Hatchet Men*, 2–3, for consideration of the original policing dynamic of Chinatown.

14 **In a wider sense:** Choy interviews, December 20, 2011, and March 30, 2013; Salvatera interviews, June 20, 2011, and November 7, 2011.

14 **If a curious social:** Choy interviews, December 20, 2011, and March 30, 2013.

15 **With more than twenty-five:** Wing Woo interview; February 26, 2014; Tracy interview.

15 **They murmured stories:** Wong interview; Adeline Fong interviews, June 28, 2011, and December 12, 2012; Salvatera interviews, June 20, 2011, and June 28, 2011; Leo Fong, personal interview by the author, October 24, 2011; Wing Woo interview. Lau Bun's proficiency with the straight sword was well known and factors into many recollections of his abilities. As a young teenager Doc-Fai Wong was drawn to studying with Lau Bun on the prospect of straight-sword training. The killing of the rat in the dark comes specifically from Adeline Fong, who conveys the story not only with great detail but almost as the by-product of an entirely different anecdote. The incident occurred while she was alone with Lau Bun in the Hung Sing studio. So as a young teenage girl, his request for her to turn off all the lights greatly alarmed her. She was then relieved to realize he was only hunting the rat.

15 **Not that Lau Bun's:** Wong interview; Sam Louie, personal interview by the author, February 1, 2012; Leo Fong interview; Wing Woo interview.

16 **Young arrivals to Chinatown:** Wong interview; Salvatera interview, June 28, 2011. Doc-Fai Wong, for example, experienced this dynamic of how native-born Chinese children would discriminate within the neighborhood against newcomers. He arrived in Chinatown from China in 1960 as a young adolescent and quickly had local kids ganging up on him after school: "They scared the hell out of me all the time . . . so I knew that I had to learn to protect myself."

16 **In that underground space:** Adeline Fong interviews, June 28, 2011, and December 12, 2012; Leo Fong interview; Wong interview; Louie interview; Salvatera interviews, June 20, 2011, June 28, 2011, and December 19, 2012.

16 **This softer side:** Louie interview; Wong interview; Adeline Fong interview, June 28, 2011; Salvatera interview, June 28, 2011.

16 **Standing beside them:** Salvatera interviews, June 20, 2011, June 28, 2011, November 7, 2011, and December 19, 2012; Wong interview; Louie interview; Adeline Fong interviews, June 28, 2011, and December 12, 2012; Leo Fong interview. Like his straight sword mastery, Lau Bun's insistence on rigorous

horse-stance training was well known and factors into numerous recollections by his past students. (Dino Salvatera compares Lau Bun to Pai Mei, the legendary master of many kung fu tales and movies, who trains Uma Thurman's character in the second *Kill Bill* film.)

17 **Lau Bun continued**: Wing Woo interview.

17 **The area's native people**: "First Peoples of California." See also "Muwekma Ohlone Tribe of the San Francisco Bay Area."

17 **The Spanish arrived**: Choy, *San Francisco Chinatown*, 23.

18 **Shortly after Mexico declared**: "The families of Richardson and Leese were the only households between the Mission and Presidio" (Choy, *San Francisco Chinatown*, 24). Dillon, *Hatchet Men*, 4.

18 **Even as Montgomery**: Choy, *San Francisco Chinatown*, 25–28.

18 **Events in the spring**: Choy, *San Francisco Chinatown*, 27–28.

18 **By the mid-nineteenth**: Takaki, *Strangers from a Different Shore*, 31–33; Chang, *Chinese in America*, 12–17.

18 **From Havana to Johannesburg**: Takaki, *Strangers from a Different Shore*, 31–33; Chang, *Chinese in America*, 12–17. "But the greatest outflow of the Chinese occurred in the nineteenth century: between 1840 and 1900, an estimated two and a half million people left China. They went to Hawaii and the United States as well as to Canada, Australia, New Zealand, Southeast Asia, the West Indies, South America, and Africa" (Takaki, *Strangers from a Different Shore*, 32).

19 **The region, through its**: Choy, *San Francisco Chinatown*, 15–20. Also *The Scramble for China* by Robert Bickers is an excellent source with extensive detail on Canton's history as China's international trading point.

19 **and by 1850 was suffering**: Lai, Chinn, and Choy, "History of the Chinese in California," 11–14. The first chapter of Iris Chang's book *The Chinese in America* provides a thorough, vivid, and accessible account of the turmoil within nineteenth-century China.

19 **With stories trickling back**: Lai, Chinn, and Choy, "History of the Chinese in California," 9.

19 **"golden romance"**: Takaki, *Strangers from a Different Shore*, 80, quoting an 1852 article in the *Daily Alta California*.

19 **By 1852 over twenty thousand**: Takaki, *Strangers from a Different Shore*, 79. Also Chang notes, "Although the Chinese came from the most populous

nation on earth, at the time of the gold rush perhaps fewer than fifty of them lived in the continental United States" (*Chinese in America*, 26).

19 **The Chinese who arrived**: "During the 1850s, some 85 percent of the Chinese in California were engaged in placer mining" (Chang, *Chinese in America*, 38). See Chang (46) on the topic of the Sacramento Street enclave; also Lai, Chinn, and Choy, "History of the Chinese in California," 10. In *Hatchet Men*, Dillon points out in his first chapter that other Chinese enclaves existed in San Francisco, most notably a fishing village along the Bay near the mouth of Mission Creek (where AT&T Park is located today).

19 **particularly after massive fires**: Dillon, *Hatchet Men*, 4. See also Bagwell, *Oakland*, 19.

19 **In light of the widespread**: See Takaki, *Strangers from a Different Shore*, chap. 3 ("Initially, the Chinese were welcomed in California") as well as Choy in the early sections of *San Francisco Chinatown*. In *Hatchet Men*, Dillon's first chapter, "The Era of Good Feeling," also provides articulate detail. All three offer numerous anecdotes and local newspaper quotes. The Mark Twain quote is also cited by Chang, *Chinese in America*, 39.

19 **At the federal level**: Takaki, *Strangers from a Different Shore*, 22.

19 **In 1852 Governor John**: Dillon, *Hatchet Men*, 6.

20 **"Born and reared under"**: Nathaniel Bennett, quoted in Takaki, *Strangers from a Different Shore*, 80.

20 **"yet vote at the same polls"**: The quote appeared in the *Alta California* of May 13, 1851, featured in Choy, *San Francisco Chinatown*, 33.

20 **"A disorderly Chinaman"**: Chang, *Chinese in America*, 39.

20 **This honeymoon proved**: Choy, *San Francisco Chinatown*, 35–37; Dillon, *Hatchet Men*, chap. 1, "Little Chinatown."

20 **"In 1852 the Chinamen"**: Testimony from San Francisco resident John F. Swift, November 10, 1876, from the Report of the Joint Special Committee to Investigate Chinese Immigration, published in 1877. Dillon uses this quote in *Hatchet Men*, 54.

20 **By 1882 Congress had passed**: Choy, *San Francisco Chinatown*, 34–40; Chang, *Chinese in America*, chap. 8; Dillon, *Hatchet Men*, chap. 2.

21 **Just a few years later**: For a summary, see Choy, *San Francisco Chinatown*, 34–40. For greater detail, see Chang, *Chinese in America*, chap. 9.

21 **Among the ranks**: Lau Bun's early history—as well as the preceding material on Yuen Hai—is based on Wong interview; and Salvatera interview, June 20,

2011, November 7, 2011, and December 19, 2012. See also Judkins, "Lives of Chinese Martial Artists (5)"; Doc-Fai Wong, "Great Grandmaster Lau Bun" and "Remembering Lau Bun."

22 **He set up a legal:** "The fire destroyed much of the city, but most important for the Chinese, it destroyed city birth and citizenship records. The loss of these municipal files allowed many immigrants to claim that they were born in San Francisco, not China, thereby enabling them to establish U.S. citizenship. . . . A Chinese immigrant who managed to convince the American government that he was a citizen could then return to his homeland and claim citizenship for children born in China. Or he could tell American authorities that his wife in China had given birth to a son, when in reality no child had been born, and then sell the legal paperwork of the fictitious son to a younger man eager to migrate to the United States" (Chang, *Chinese in America*, 146–47).

22 **In an incident:** Salvatera interviews, June 20, 2011, June 28, 2011, and December 19, 2012; Leo Fong interview; Louie interview; Wong interview; Adeline Fong interviews, June 28, 2011, December 12, 2012, and December 3, 2014; Tracy interview; Wing Woo interview. There are many versions of the Lau Bun immigration agents story. While it typically varies in detail, the general tale is consistently the same. The only dissenting version I have heard came from James Wing Woo, who asserted that Lau Bun had killed a Japanese man who had stolen his wallet in Los Angeles, and he was subsequently wanted by the local authorities.

23 **The event made:** Judkins, "Lives of Chinese Martial Artists (5)."

23 **It also caught:** Salvatera interviews, June 20, 2011, and November 27, 2012; Wing Woo interview.

24 **The tongs were modeled:** Chang, *Chinese in America*, 80–85; Takaki, *Strangers from a Different Shore*, 118–19; Dillon, *Hatchet Men*, 23.

24 **In its early years:** While there are many accounts of the nineteenth-century Tong Wars in Chinatown, Dillon's *Hatchet Men* remains one of the most comprehensive.

24 **Yet as anti-Chinese:** Dillon, *Hatchet Men*, xii–xvii.

24 **On the morning of April 18:** See Choy, *San Francisco Chinatown*, 40–42; Chang, *Chinese in America*, 145; Chen, *Chinese San Francisco*, 163–66; see also Davies, *Saving San Francisco*.

24 **City leaders perceived:** Chen, *Chinese San Francisco*, 165.

24 **The leaders of Chinatown:** see Choy, *San Francisco Chinatown*, 43–46.

25 **as one sociologist pointed out:** This is from Rose Hum Lee in 1942: "Wherever the Chinese are it has been possible to count the variations in the ways they can earn their living on the fingers of the hand—chop suey and chow mein restaurants, Chinese art and gift shops, native grocery stores that sell foodstuffs imported from China to the local Chinese community and Chinese laundries" (quoted in Takaki, *Strangers from a Different Shore*, 251).

25 **However, in a mind-set:** Salvatera interviews, June 20, 2011, June 28, 2011, November 27, 2012, and December 19, 2012; Adeline Fong interviews, June 28, 2011, December 12, 2012, and December 3, 2014; Leo Fong interview; Tracy interview; Wing Woo interview.

26 **He had sent them southeast:** Wing Woo interview.

27 **"Boys," he said:** Wing Woo interview.

2. NATIVE SON

28 **It had been almost three:** Thomas, *Bruce Lee*, 30. See also Linda Lee, *Bruce Lee Story*, 35.

28 **"become famous in America":** Vincent Lacey, phone interview by the author, February 10, 2011.

28 **The voyage across the Pacific:** Thomas, *Bruce Lee*, 30; Gong, *Bruce Lee*, 15; Linda Lee, *Bruce Lee Story*, 35; Campbell and Lee, *Dragon and the Tiger*, 1:14–16.

28 **his fellow travelers took turns:** Photograph from Tadman and Kerridge, *Bruce Lee*, unpaginated.

28 **he had been deeply introspective:** Linda Lee, *Bruce Lee Story*, 35. See also Campbell and Lee, *Dragon and the Tiger*, 1:14–16.

29 **The years that transpired:** Thomas, *Bruce Lee*, 27–30. Gong, *Bruce Lee*, 15–17; Ben Der, personal interview by the author, February 12, 2014.

29 **His present trip to America:** Linda Lee, *Bruce Lee Story*, 31–35. Campbell and Lee, *Dragon and the Tiger*, 1:3–4.

30 **His apartment, on the lower:** Gong, *Bruce Lee*, 249–50; Der interview, February 12, 2014. See also Tadman and Kerridge, *Bruce Lee*, "Walking Tour Map."

30 **"The Largest Chinatown":** Morin. "31 Beautiful Photos."

30 **Bruce knew before Mr. Quan:** Linda Lee, *Bruce Lee Story*, 21; Der interview, February 12, 2014. See also Lee Family Immigration Files, interviews with Lee Hoi Chuen and Grace Lee.

30 **In the autumn of 1939:** Thomas, *Bruce Lee*, 3–4; Gong, *Bruce Lee*, 7; Campbell and Lee, *Dragon and the Tiger*, 1:1; Lee Family Immigration Files.

30 **Mr. Quan explained how the**: Choy, *San Francisco Chinatown*, 150–51. Also Kar and Bren, *Hong Kong Cinema*, 76-77; Der interview, February 12, 2014.

31 **Yet his own relationship:** Thomas, *Bruce Lee*, 7, 30.

31 **rich tradition of the Cantonese**: Choy, *San Francisco Chinatown*, 150–51; Chen, *Chinese San Francisco*, 90-95.

31 **The article displayed the face**: "Four Words Win a Trip"; Chinese Historical Society, *Glamour and Grace*. See also Chen, *Chinese San Francisco*, 192-96.

31 **A published poet himself**: Ben Der, personal interview by the author, April 2, 2012. Der expressed frustration in losing a copy of Mr. Quan's book, which had been personally inscribed to him.

31 **Mr. Quan was referring to**: Choy, *San Francisco Chinatown*, 152. For a longer history, see Morgan and Peters, *Howl on Trial*.

32 **The Lion's Den, one of**: Dong, *Forbidden City, USA*; Robbins, *Forbidden City*.

32 **The neighborhood may have been**: Lai, "Short History of the Chinese Media."

32 **One of the city's two**: "Giants Win—in 2nd Place."

32 **The Giants had arrived**: Pace, "George Christopher, 92, Dies." While researching photos in the Kem K. Lee archive at UC Berkeley, I came across images of a massive parade that the city had staged for the Giants to officially welcome them to San Francisco.

33 **Ironically, Mays had gone**: Rosenbaum, "S.F. Fans Can Boo with Best of 'Em."

33 **"And this," he explained**: Lee Family Immigration Files; Der interview, February 12, 2014; Tadman and Kerridge, *Bruce Lee*, "Walking Tour Map."

33 **It was a handsome building**: Lai, "Chinese Hospital"; Choy, *San Francisco Chinatown*, 158-60. See also "Chinese Hospital." Sadly, the city of San Francisco failed to preserve this building during recent renovations. As the Associated Press reported, the hospital was one of ten historic sites lost in 2013 as cited by the National Trust for Historic Preservation. The new building is rather lackluster in comparison.

33 **"Your parents lived here"**: Lee Family Immigration Files; Tadman and Kerridge, *Bruce Lee*; "Walking Tour"; Der interview, February 12, 2014.

33 **Hoi Cheun was performing**: Lee Family Immigration Files; Campbell and Lee, *Dragon and the Tiger*, 1:1; Thomas, *Bruce Lee*, 4.

33 **"The true meaning of Bruce's name"**: "Biography." However, a more personal reason exists for the name Jun Fan. When Bruce was born in San

Francisco, his mother was by herself in the Chinese Hospital since her husband, Lee Hoi Chuen, was in New York with the Chinese Opera group. She chose the name Jun Fan since baby Bruce would be her protector while in San Francisco. So Jun Fan means "Protector of San Francisco"; see Gong, *Bruce Lee*, 4.

33 **At the Chinese hospital**: Thomas, *Bruce Lee*, 4.

34 **The American name would later**: Interview with Lee Hoi Chuen, from Lee Family Immigration Files.

34 **Bruce would be entirely unaware**: Gong, *Bruce Lee*, 8.

34 **Before departing the United States**: Thomas, *Bruce Lee*, 9. For more on the life and career of Esther Eng, see *Golden Gate Girls*. On the history of the Grandview Film Company, see Kar and Bren, *Hong Kong Cinema*.

34 **Most surprising to Mr. Quan**: Der interview, February 12, 2014. See also interview with William Cheung, in Rafiq, *Bruce Lee Conversations*, 91: "On the first day, after he did the lesson he said to me he's going to make Wing Chun or Chinese Kung Fu a common name on households. I said to him, 'What? And how are you going to do that?' Because he had a vision and also he was experienced in movies and so on. When you have something good you can make it worldwide."

34 **The "Father of Modern China"**: "Father of Modern China."

34 **"China's George Washington"**: Sharman, *Sun Yat-sen*.

34 **While in exile during**: Choy, *San Francisco Chinatown*, 46–50; "The future of China was plotted right here in Chinatown" (204–5). For a fuller account, see Lai, "Memorable Day 70 Years Ago."

35 **Bruce was familiar with**: Ho, *Tracing My Children's Lineage*, 139–40.

35 **For many other residents of**: Philip P. Choy, personal interview by the author, March 30, 2013. See also Anspacher, "Madame Chiang."

35 **After many decades of**: Choy interview.

35 **Madame Chiang had traveled**: Li, *Madame Chiang*, 193–237. You can listen to her 1943 address to the U.S. Congress at http://www.history.com/speeches /madame-chiang-kai-shek-addresses-congress#madame-chiang-kai-shek -addresses-congress.

35 **In San Francisco her tour**: Anspacher, "Madame Chiang," 1. See also Li, *Madame Chiang*, 223: "As she headed west her receptions became grander and grander, as each city tried to outdo the last. In San Francisco she was escorted into the city on a navy ship with Coast Guard cutters flanking it and

a fire ship throwing out water displays. Tens of thousands of residents lined the streets. . . . The local Chinese community put up 'a hell of a fight' to get her to go to Chinatown, and in the end she went."

35 **Although she never spoke about:** Li, *Madame Chiang*, 244.

35 **From a more behind-the-scenes:** Li, *Madame Chiang*, 217–21.

36 **However, this change in perceptions:** "Unnoticed Struggle."

36 **In San Francisco the Chinese:** Choy interview.

36 **Recently, the city of San Francisco:** Garvey, *San Francisco Police Department*, 74.

36 **Nationally, Hiram Fong would soon:** "Hiram Leong Fong."

36 **just as Daniel Inouye:** McFadden. "Daniel Inouye."

36 **As they walked back:** Der interview, February 12, 2014. Tadman and Kerridge, *Bruce Lee*, "Walking Tour Map."

3. THE GOOD LONG FIST

37 **the altar within the Kin Mon:** From the personal files of Warren Chan.

37 **Wong Tim Yuen sat in:** Leo Fong, personal interview by the author, October 24, 2011; Al Novak, personal interview by the author, March 3, 2011; Warren Chan, personal interview by the author, November 12, 2013; Dean Kimball, phone interview by the author, February 22, 2013.

37 **The name of his school:** Kimball interview; Warren Chan, personal interview by the author, November 12, 2013; Campbell and Lee, *Dragon and the Tiger*, 1:88–89.

37 **Although he was almost:** James Wing Woo, personal interview by the author, February 26, 2014. Woo points out that T.Y. was also highly proficient in the obscure Bear Style of kung fu.

38 **On the wall behind him:** Kem K. Lee, Kem Lee Photograph Collection; Chan interview, November 12, 2013; Joe Cervara, phone interview by the author, February 14, 2014.

38 **Leong Tin Chee spent many:** T. Y. Wong, *Chinese Kung Fu*, 1–2; Dean Kimball, phone interview by the author, February 22, 2013; Cervara interview; personal files of Warren Chan.

38 **He studied under Leong:** T. Y. Wong, *Chinese Kung Fu*, 1–2; Kimball interview; Cervara interview; personal files of Warren Chan.

38 **Later, during the Japanese invasion:** Gilman Wong, personal interview by the author, May 15, 2015.

38 **Upon arriving in San Francisco's:** Wing Woo interview.

39 **students of Kin Mon smiling:** Personal files of Gilman Wong. See also Wong and Lee, *Chinese Karate Kung-Fu*, i. Students of Kin Mon appeared on the *Home* show on January 15, 1955. Still images from the broadcast show four of the students performing in the school's distinctive black *jing-mo* uniforms on what looks to be a "Chinese opera-themed" episode. A large Buddha statue is used as a decoration in the background, and an elegantly dressed woman plays a Chinese yangqin (traditional dulcimer). T.Y. doesn't perform but is seen in a suit and tie while his students are being given exaggerated makeup for the performance. Later Arlene Francis presented them with a plaque to commemorate the performance. I have searched far and wide for a copy of this episode (having contacted NBC, Arlene Francis's son, and many others) with no success.

39 **More recently, he began collaborating:** T. Y. Wong, *Chinese Kung Fu*; Campbell and Lee, *Dragon and the Tiger*, 1:11–12; Warren Chan, personal interview by the author, November 11, 2013; Greglon Lee, personal interview by the author, June 18, 2014.

39 **The hulking Novak was:** Novak interview. See also Gene Ching, "Great American Great Grandmaster."

39 **"All martial arts under heaven":** "History of Shaolin Kung Fu."

39 **Located along the Songshan:** Shahar, *Shaolin Monastery*, 9–12. Shahar's work is widely regarded by academics as the key scholarly work on the history of the Shaolin Monastery.

40 **Tang Hao was a Chinese historian:** Kennedy and Guo, *Chinese Martial Arts Training Manuals*, 38–60. See also Judkins, "Lives of Chinese Martial Artists (12)."

40 **The early folklore attributed:** Shahar, *Shaolin Monastery*, 11–17.

40 **"the symbolic crossing point":** Shahar, *Shaolin Monastery*, 13.

40 **The martial arts, as the story:** Kennedy and Kuo, *Chinese Martial Arts Training Manuals*, 69.

41 **Tang Hao dismissed much:** Kennedy and Kuo, *Chinese Martial Arts Training Manuals*, 42–48.

41 **Shaolin military activity:** Shahar, *Shaolin Monastery*, 21–22; phone interview with Ben Judkins, August 23, 2014.

41 **ritualistic black magic:** Shahar, *Shaolin*, 37–42; Ben Judkins, phone interview by the author August 23, 2014. As Shahar writes in the conclusion to chap. 2,

"the connection between monastic martial practice and the veneration of Buddhist military deities can be traced back to medieval times. It is likely that as early as the Tang Period Shaolin Monks beseeched the divine warrior Vajrapani to supply them with physical strength. More pertinently, the Buddhist guardian provided the monks with religious sanction for violence."

41 **Later, when Shaolin did earn**: Shahar, *Shaolin Monastery*, 55-67; Judkins interview.

42 **Qi Jiguang was a celebrated**: Gyves, "English Translation," 9-15; Shahar, *Shaolin Monastery*, 128-30. See also Matuszak, "'Practical Isn't Pretty.'"

42 **Beginning in 1560**: Gyves, "English Translation," 9-12.

42 **Over the course of his**: Shahar, *Shaolin Monastery*, 128-30; Gyves, "English Translation," 9-15.

42 **These skills would be**: Gyves, "English Translation," 9-11. "Hand combat, Qi Jiguang argued, could be used for troops' training. The experienced general was well aware that bare-handed methods were useless in the battlefield. He suggested, however, that they were not without merit in instilling courage. Moreover, bare-handed practice was a good starting point for armed training" (Shahar, *Shaolin Monastery*, 130).

42 **"The popularity of the unarmed"**: Judkins, "Book Club."

42 **Historians refer to it**: Shahar, *Shaolin Monastery*, 173-75. In the conclusion of chapter 6, Shahar writes: "Shaolin monks were probably fascinated by the medical, religious, and philosophical opportunities that were opened by the new empty-handed techniques. The synthesis of martial, therapeutic, and religious goals has been a primary reason for the popularity of hand combat both in its native land and in the modern West. If modern hand combat is not only a fighting method but also a system of thought, then it is not surprising that its evolution was partially spurred by intellectual developments. Late Ming syncretism provided a philosophical foundation for the integration of bare-handed fighting and *daoyin* calisthenics, permitting Daoist mystics to explore Buddhist-related martial arts and allowing Shaolin monks to study Daoist gymnastics."

43 **Yet away from the elite**: Judkins interview. See also Robinson, *Bandits, Eunuchs*, 2-11: "Coercive force by the government and illicit violence in society were a very real part of everyday life in Ming China."

43 **Throughout history the Chinese martial**: Kennedy and Kuo, *Chinese Martial Arts Training Manuals*, 7.

44 **During the early 19th century**: Judkins, "'Fighting Styles' or 'Martial Brands'?" Abbreviated for clarity with permission by the author. The original text runs as follows: "During the early 19th century (before the market reforms of the Republican era) China had a huge number of local fighting styles. Most of them were very small village or family affairs. A lot of what they did actually focused on militia training, opera or banditry. Many of these styles did not actually have names, though there were some notable exceptions. Why did so many of these pedagogical systems lack names? They were not studied so much as a particular 'style' of fighting (or in the case of opera, acting). They simply were fighting (and acting). Later in the 19th century as the demand for martial instruction increased, and the number of reasons it was pursued diversified, it became necessary to market these skills on a broader scale than had been undertaken in the past. Names and shiny new creation myths began to appear as the fighting techniques of the previous generation were increasingly repackaged as a 'martial commodity.'"

45 **Just as the Bodidharma**: Shahar, *Shaolin Monastery*, 181.

45 **"The goal of most martial arts"**: Kennedy and Kuo, *Chinese Martial Arts Training Manuals*, 34.

45 **"invented tradition"**: Judkins interview.

45 **For Wing Chun**: Wing Woo interview.

45 **It was in an era**: Kennedy and Kuo, *Chinese Martial Arts Training Manuals*, 38–60. See also Judkins, "Tang Hao."

46 **"as many sacred cows"**: Judkins, "Lives of Chinese Martial Artists (12)."

46 **"some ruthless and self-proclaimed"**: Kennedy and Kuo, *Chinese Martial Arts Training Manuals*, 49.

46 **and the fact that people**: Judkins interview.

4. THE LITTLE DRAGON

47 **A few audience members**: George Lee, personal interview by the author, January 8, 2011.

47 **"The showmanship, not the killer"**: Cheung, "Bruce Lee's Hong Kong Years."

47 **In the summer of 1959**: Campbell and Lee, *Dragon and the Tiger*, 1:17; Ben Der, personal interview by the author, February 12, 2014; "Harriet Lee's Reflections on the Dragon," from Tadman and Kerridge, *Bruce Lee*, unpaginated.

48 **Not far from the stage**: George Lee interview.

48 **"Any chance you'll come back"**: George Lee interview.

48 **"What style were you doing"**: George Lee interview.

48 **Located along China's southern**: Lai, "Guangzhou to Hong Kong."

48 **"barren island"**: British Foreign Secretary Lord Palmerston, quoted in Carroll, *Concise History of Hong Kong*, 15: "Although he would go down in history for later dismissing Hong Kong as little more than 'a barren island with hardly a house upon it,' Foreign Secretary Lord Palmerston declared his intention to seize Hong Kong."

48 **would experience a huge influx**: "In 1849 after gold was discovered in California, the first shipload of Chinese laborers came through Hong Kong, en route to the United States. By December 1850, two thousand Chinese had left China for California. Between January and June 1850, some ten thousand tons of shipping were loaded or partly loaded in Hong Kong and shipped to the western coast of the United States. With this growth of overseas trade also came new Chinese labor and talent. . . . From 1853 to 1859 the Chinese population of Hong Kong rose from approximately forty thousand to around eighty-five thousand, even with mass departures during the Second Opium War" (Carroll, *Concise History of Hong Kong*, 29–30).

49 **The place that developed**: "Mega Cities Hong Kong."

49 **Hoi Cheun and Grace**: Lee Family Immigration Files; Thomas, *Bruce Lee*, 3–4; Gong, *Bruce Lee*, 9.

49 **They had arrived home**: Carroll, *Concise History of Hong Kong*, 115–19.

49 **The occupation that followed**: Carroll, *Concise History of Hong Kong*, 121–26.

49 **The Le family weathered**: Gong, *Bruce Lee*, 11.

49 **With the passing of his brother**: Linda Lee, *Bruce Lee Story*, 20–21; Thomas, *Bruce Lee*, 6–7.

50 **After becoming smitten with him**: Thomas, *Bruce Lee*, 3; Ho, *Tracing My Children's Lineage*, 140.

50 **Although raised in Shanghai**: Ho, *Tracing My Children's Lineage*, 136–45.

50 **"final piece in the jigsaw"**: Ho, *Tracing My Children's Lineage*, 140.

50 **Grace's exact racial makeup**: Lee Family Immigration Files. See Ho, *Tracing My Children's Lineage*, 140, for specifics on Grace, though the entire chapter on Ho Kom-tong (136–45) is worth consideration.

50 **Grace and Hoi Chuen's first son**: William Cheung, interviewed in Rafiq, *Bruce Lee Conversations*, 88; Linda Lee, *Bruce Lee Story*, 20; Thomas, *Bruce Lee*, 4. "Bruce had many nicknames, but his family called him Sai Fong or

'Little Peacock' a girl's name. This was to fool the Chinese gods into thinking Bruce was a girl because they might be jealous that the family had a second boy and take him away" (Gong, *Bruce Lee*, 9).

51 **With the 1949 victory**: Carroll, *Concise History of Hong Kong*, 135–43. "From 1946 to the mid-1950s, approximately 1 million people came to Hong Kong from China—an average of almost three hundred people per day" (140).

51 **"a wasteland of an island"**: Carroll, *Concise History of Hong Kong*, 135.

51 **As Bruce's childhood friend Hawkins**: Cheung, "Bruce Lee's Hong Kong Years."

51 **This environment contrasted starkly**: Thomas, *Bruce Lee*, 6; Der interview, February 12, 2014.

51 *mo si tung,* **meaning**: Gong, *Bruce Lee*, 9.

51 **Later, the sum total**: Linda Lee, *Bruce Lee Story*, 22–31; Thomas, *Bruce Lee*, 11–12.

51 **In the Kowloon section**: Der interview, February 12, 2014; Thomas, *Bruce Lee*, 13–14; Linda Lee, *Bruce Lee Story*, 26; Cheung interview in Rafiq, *Bruce Lee Conversations*, 89.

52 **Bruce exhibited a tough**: Cheung interview in Rafiq, *Bruce Lee Conversations*, 89 In Linda Lee, *Bruce Lee Story*, 26–31, she quotes Bruce's brother, Robert: "You didn't have to ask Bruce twice to fight."

52 **Many of Bruce's classmates**: Thomas, *Bruce Lee*, 13–14; Cheung interview in Rafiq, *Bruce Lee Conversations*, 89.

52 **The combined impact of Japan's**: James Wing Woo, personal interview by the author, February 26, 2014; Stanley Henning, "The Martial Arts in Chinese Physical Culture, 1865–1965," in Green and Svinth, *Martial Arts*, 29–30.

52 **Ip Man arrived**: Ching and Heimberger, *Ip-Man*, 25, 33–34. See also "Yip Man."

53 **Economical, swift, and direct**: Cheung, "Bruce Lee's Mother Art"; Taky Kimura, personal interview by the author, March 19, 2014; Al Novak, personal interview by the author, March 3, 2011; Linda Lee, *Bruce Lee Story*, 49; Gong, *Bruce Lee*, 9–10.

53 **The folk history attached**: Thomas, *Bruce Lee*, 17.

53 **Ip Man's approach**: "Yip Man"; Gong, *Bruce Lee*, 10.

53 **Bruce had taken up**: Cheung interview, in Rafiq, *Bruce Lee Conversations*, 89–91; Gong, *Bruce Lee*, 10–11; Thomas, *Bruce Lee*, 14, 20–21; Linda Lee, *Bruce Lee Story*, 27.

54 **"Upstart"**: "Yip Man."

54 **"fighting crazy"**: Thomas, *Bruce Lee*, 14.

54 **"Everyone wanted to be"**: Cheung, "Bruce Lee's Hong Kong Years."

54 **A core practice**: Cheung, "Bruce Lee's Mother Art"; Thomas, *Bruce Lee*, 18–19; Kimura interview.

54 **They responded by pointing**: Cheung interview, in Rafiq, *Bruce Lee Conversations*, 90; Thomas, *Bruce Lee*, 26–27. See also *I Am Bruce Lee*.

54 **In training now with**: Cheung interview, in Rafiq, *Bruce Lee Conversations*, 89–91; Linda Lee, *Bruce Lee Story*, 30–31; Gong, *Bruce Lee*, 10–11.

55 **With the colony housing**: Ben Judkins, phone interview by the author, February 17, 2014; Linda Lee, *Bruce Lee Story*, 22–26.

55 **"As he taught us"**: Cheung, "Bruce's Classical Mess."

55 **This facet of Bruce's**: Cheung, "Bruce's Classical Mess." Beginning in November 1991, Hawkins Cheung produced a series of essays for *Inside Kung Fu* magazine on the topic of growing up in Hong Kong, and his time learning Wing Chun under Ip Man with Bruce Lee. I highly recommend these essays for their detail and insight into Bruce's formative teenage years as well as the atmosphere of Ip Man's school. For example, as Cheung explained on the topic of real fighting experience: "Back in the 1950s, Yip Man trained us to fight, not be technicians. Because we were so young, we didn't understand the concepts or theories. As he taught us, Yip Man said, 'Don't believe me, as I may be tricking you. Go out and have a fight. Test it out.' In other words, Yip Man taught us the distance applications of wing chun. First he told us to go out and find practitioners of other styles and test our wing chun on them. If we lost, we knew on what we should work. We would go out and test our techniques again. We thought to ourselves, 'Got to make that technique work! No excuses!' We learned by getting hit. When you are in a real fight, you find out what techniques are good for you. Just because your technique may work for one person doesn't guarantee it will work for you. When you test your techniques on someone you don't know, you experience a different feeling than when training with your friends. If you discover through your own experience, it's much better than relying on another's experience."

55 **His sister Agnes notes**: Thomas, *Bruce Lee*, 25: "Bruce's sister Agnes says, 'He began to get into more and more fights for no reason at all. And if he didn't win, he was furious. Losing, even once in awhile, was unbearable for him.'"

55 **This deep-seated drive:** Linda Lee, *Bruce Lee Story*, 30–31; Ben Der, personal interview by the author, March 19, 2014; Cheung interview, in Rafiq, *Bruce Lee Conversations*, 90; Gong, *Bruce Lee*, 13–15.

56 **Bruce also thrived:** Thomas, *Bruce Lee*, 9; Gong, *Bruce Lee*, 7–8.

56 **He could be gregarious:** Der interview, February 12, 2014; George Lee interview; Vincent Lacey, phone interview by the author, February 10, 2011; Linda Lee, *Bruce Lee Story*, 27.

56 **"He was a little hyper":** Der interview, February 12, 2014.

56 **Fellow students assert:** Thomas, *Bruce Lee*, 27–28; Linda Lee, *Bruce Lee Story*, 31.

56 **Popular urban mythology:** "Interview with Robert Lee"; Greglon Lee, phone interview by the author, February 15, 2011.

56 **Whatever the specifics:** Cheung interview, in Rafiq, *Bruce Lee Conversations*, 97. Cheung asserts that it was Ip Man who finally got their names cleared from the list.

57 **With high school graduation:** Linda Lee, *Bruce Lee Story*, 31, 35.

57 **Bruce walked along:** Sam Louie, personal interview by the author, February 2, 2012; Der interview, February 12, 2014. While many members of the Chinatown martial arts community relate this story, this anecdote comes from the eyewitness account of Sam Louie, one of Lau Bun's senior students of the time, and—after James Wing Woo—the most veteran primary source on Chinatown's martial art history. Louie, a well-respected member of the San Francisco community who went on to become a very successful chef, relayed this story in an almost offhand manner without any passion or sense of embellishment. The entire incident jibes well with Ben Der's accounts from this period: Der asserts that Bruce had first heard of Lau Bun from a patron in a bar on Jackson Street. Furthermore, it's worth considering Louie's take on Bruce Lee so many years later: "I really respect Bruce Lee. We worked hard. He worked harder."

57 **"When Bruce came to":** Louie interview.

57 **"Don't worry; if you lose":** Dino Salvatera, personal interview by the author, March 2, 2013.

57 **Ip Man's teenage students:** Der interview, February 12, 2014; James Wing Woo, personal interview by the author, February 26, 2014.

58 **The room went quiet:** Louie interview.

58 **"Don't bother"**: Louie interview.

58 **"Did your teacher"**: Louie interview.

5. THE SOFT ARTS

59 **At the start**: Dan Inosanto, personal interview by the author, June 2, 2014; Leo Fong, personal interviews by the author, October 24, 2011, and June 3, 2014; James Wing Woo, personal interview by the author, February 26, 2014; "Violent Repose." See also Green and Svinth, *Martial Arts in the Modern World*; Smith, *Martial Musings*.

59 **Their presence within**: Doc-Fai Wong, personal interview by the author, February 2, 2012.

59 **"the spirit of the lion"**: Adeline Fong, personal interview by the author, December 3, 2014.

60 **"Horse Stable Alley"**: Wing Woo interview.

60 **Far less a formal**: Ben Der, personal interview by the author, April 2, 2014; David Chin, personal interview by the author, March 31, 2011; Wing Woo interview.

60 **In 1939 the Chinese Consolidated**: Hagood, "Choy Kam Man"; Wing Woo interview.

60 **his arrival in San Francisco**: Wing Woo interview; "Master Choy Hak Pang." See also Hagood, "Choy Kam Man," 35: "Though Choy Hok Pang taught no Americans himself, he carried on an extensive training program among the Chinese in this country, many who later became teachers. Because he nurtured the seed that spread it, it is Choy Hok Pang who must be remembered as the father of Tai Chi in America."

60 **While in Chinatown**: Hagood, "Choy Kam Man"; Wing Woo interview. See also "Master Choy Hak Pang."

60 **Gerda Geddes was born**: Ronnie Robinson, "Tai Chi Interview-Gerda Geddes." For a complete bio, see Woods, *Dancer in the Light*, 2008.

61 **"As I watched I had"**: Woods, *Dancer in the Light*, 2.

61 **"They did not seem"**: Woods, *Dancer in the Light*, 143.

61 **In the same culture**: In a personal letter to Gerda Geddes at the time (March 4, 1957), now in Geddes family personal archives. Choy Kam Man not only acknowledged the insular nature of the Chinese martial arts but went as far as to urge her to teach tai chi back in Europe: "I indeed consoled for that you will consummation of my wishes for that you could to promote and to

teaching of Chinese Shadow Boxing to your own people when and if you go back to England. As I have told you that there are still have many narrow mind Chinese Shadow Boxers and Chinese people as they're never be teaching to foreigners, and when there are if have someone will does, then they may say his is a rebellious!"

61 **Classes were in private**: Woods, *Dancer in the Light*, 144–47.

61 **The younger Choy's martial**: Jack Wada, personal interview by the author, March 26, 2015; Michael Gilman, personal interview by the author, December 8, 2012.

62 **"disappeared"**: Wada interview.

62 **brief segment performing**: Woods, *Dancer in the Light*, 158.

62 **Geddes was routinely met**: Geddes is quoted in Ronnie Robinson, "Tai Chi Interview-Gerda Geddes": "Nobody had the faintest idea what I was taking about, when I mentioned Tai Chi." See also Woods, *Dancer in the Light*, 158–59.

62 **Interestingly enough, this**: See Dunning, "Sophia Delza Glassgold." See also Woods, *Dancer in the Light*, 192.

62 **Meanwhile, the younger Choy**: Hagood, "Choy Kam Man." See also letter from Choy Kam Man to Gerda Geddes, dated January 18, 1959, Geddes family letters. Choy would have been about forty years old at the time of his return to the United States.

62 **"Master Choy could fold"**: Wada, "Master Choy." Also Bob Cook, phone interview by the author, March 28, 2013. Cook is an interesting figure in this early culture, who, like Leo Fong, had trained with many different teachers at the time. After speaking with him for a while about a variety of different practitioners from the era, I finally asked him about Master Choy, to which he responded, "That guy was amazing! I had never seen anyone kick like that before. He was unbelievably good."

63 **Choy lived in a tiny**: Gilman interview; Mark Small, phone interview by the author, March 26, 2013.

63 **Within the neighborhood**: Gilman interview; Robyn Silverstein, phone interview by the author, December 10, 2012.

63 **A genuine glimpse**: David Cox. "Mah Sek: The Odyssey of a Kung Fu Master," *Official Karate*, Fall 1973. Also Leo Fong, personal interview by the author, October 24, 2011; David Chin, personal interview by the author, March 31, 2011; Wing Woo interview. Chin's website also has a bio; see Lamia, "Grandmaster Mar Sik."

64 **"like a hard rubber ball"**: Leo Fong interview. This quote comes from a fascinating story that Leo Fong related about Mah Sek. In 1973 Fong worked closely with Mah Sek for the profile article that ran in *Official Karate*. During the time they spent together, Mah Sek insisted that no one talk while they were driving in a car together because he had been in two horrible rollover crashes in his life. As Fong related: "Everyone else in the car had gotten hurt but him, because he would feel where the car was rolling and he would give into that and roll like a rubber ball. He was in two serious accidents but never got hurt. He came from the old . . . way old old school."

64 **His Iron Shirt**: Chin interview; Leo Fong interview; Wong interview; Wing Woo interview.

64 **Historically, martial arts**: Judkins, "Through a Lens Darkly (17)": "These individuals are maligned in almost all of the same accounts that record their existence. The idea of 'selling one's art for money' is universally reviled in period accounts. Performers . . . usually get the brunt of this aggression."

6. THREE MOVES OR LESS

65 **Bruce let Jesse Glover**: Jesse Glover, quoted in Bax, *Disciples of the Dragon*, 21.

65 **Glover was Bruce's**: Thomas, *Bruce Lee*, 35. Interview with Jesse Glover, in Rafiq, *Bruce Lee Conversations*, 20. See also Glover's obituary in the Seattle Times, June 29, 2012: Vaughn, "Jesse Glover."

65 **Not long afterward**: Interview with James Demile, in Rafiq, *Bruce Lee Conversations*, 27–29.

66 **"deadly" Asian fighting techniques**: Demile, "Evolving from the Darkside."

66 **"Bruce looked about as dangerous"**: James Demile, quoted in Brewster and Buerge, *Washingtonians*, 421.

66 **"You look like you"**: James Demile, quoted in Green and Svinth, *Martial Arts*, 115–16.

66 **"I felt myself being jolted"**: Demile, "Evolving from the Darkside."

66 **"Hello? Is there anybody home?"**: Demile interview, in Rafiq, *Bruce Lee Conversations*, 28.

67 **More students soon followed**: Taky Kimura, personal interview by the author, March 19, 2015. See also Thomas, *Bruce Lee*, 36–37; Halpin, "The Little Dragon," in Brewster and Buerge, *Washingtonians*, 419–39. For Skip Ellsworth, see "Biography of Skip Ellsworth."

66 **At nineteen Bruce would:** James Wing Woo, personal interview by the author, February 26, 2014; Al Tracy, phone interview by the author, August 26, 2014.

67 **The result was the most:** This point seems to either get completely overstated or just entirely lost in the shuffle. Within the nuance of it, however, there are some really fascinating conclusions to draw. In looking at other Chinese martial arts schools in America circa 1960, you would be hard-pressed to find a class as racially diverse as Bruce's in Seattle. For this reason many of the Seattle students like to joke that the class looked "like the United Nations." In this regard Bruce Lee genuinely was a pioneering force of the Chinese martial arts in America years before he was famous via Hollywood (especially when considering that he was among the first—if not the very first—to teach Wing Chun in the United States). Furthermore, and perhaps more notably, as Bruce's teaching in Seattle become more formal, he had a significant number of female students, which was also very rare at the time.

67 **When Ruby Chow, the stern:** Jesse Glover, in Bax, *Disciples of the Dragon*, 24.

67 **Bruce was settling nicely:** Thomas, *Bruce Lee*, 35–42; interview with Ed Hart, in Bax, *Disciples of the Dragon*, 23–24; Gong, *Bruce Lee*, 17–19.

67 **"We were all dummies":** Bax, *Disciples of the Dragon*, 49.

67 **Open to drawing on more:** Interviews with Taky Kimura (10–11), Jesse Glover (26), and James Demile (28–29), all in Bax, *Disciples of the Dragon*. In the interview Demile states: "There were two reasons Bruce modified his Wing Chun. First, was to beat his seniors in Wing Chun. . . . The second reason for modifying his Wing Chun was the Westerners were bigger and stronger than him and once they learned the basics of Wing Chun they could become a real threat to him. Bruce became very selfish in his personal training. He would explore efficient fighting concepts with different students, never really teaching everyone the same thing."

67 **At the moment, however:** Thomas, *Bruce Lee*, 44–45; Gong, *Bruce Lee*, 18.

68 **Glover knew of Yoiche's:** Interview with Jesse Glover, in Bax, *Disciples of the Dragon*, 21.

68 **The origin of their conflict:** Interview with Jesse Glover, in Bax, *Disciples of the Dragon*, 21

68 **Standing in the yard:** Interview with Jesse Glover, in Rafiq, *Bruce Lee Conversations*, 24.

68 **"Let's get this straight"**: Campbell and Lee, *Dragon and the Tiger*, 1:210-11. See also Kimura interview, in Bax, *Disciples of the Dragon*, 12.

69 **"Are you the teacher?"**: Warren Chan, personal interview by the author, November 12, 2013; Joe Cervara, phone interview by the author, February 14, 2014; also a written account from the personal files of Warren Chan. This incident is well known among students of Kin Mon. Warren Chan was an eyewitness standing just a few feet away when it happened.

69 **There is a notion**: Gong, *Bruce Lee*, 60; Tracy interview. From the personal files of Warren Chan: writings on T. Y. Wong's teacher Leong Tin Chee assert this notion as well.

69 **In the courtyard**: Interviews with Jesse Glover (21) and Ed Hart (27), in Bax, *Disciples of the Dragon*; Thomas, *Bruce Lee*, 44-45; Linda Lee, *Bruce Lee Story*, 45. See also Campbell and Lee, *Dragon and the Tiger*, 1:210-13.

70 **"drove his opponent"**: Glover interview, in Bax, *Disciples of the Dragon*, 21; interview with James Demile, in Rafiq, *Bruce Lee Conversations*, 31.

70 **"The man took a long time"**: Glover interview, in Bax, *Disciples of the Dragon*, 21.

70 **"eleven-second fight"**: Kimura personal interview.

70 **Bruce landed a multitude**: Interviews with Jesse Glover (21) and Ed Hart (27), in Bax, *Disciples of the Dragon*; Thomas, *Bruce Lee*, 44-45.

7. THE INNOVATOR

73 **The brick breaking**: Greglon Lee, personal interview by the author, June 18, 2014; Al Novak, personal interview by the author, March 3, 2011; Al Tracy, personal interview by the author, August 26, 2014; Campbell and Lee, *Dragon and the Tiger*, 1:78-80, 97-99. I should point out that I could not nail down where James Lee first learned his breaking technique. I asked numerous sources about this point, but nobody could say for certain. The general consensus, including the opinion of his son, was that he learned during his time in Hawaii.

73 **His upper body was rugged**: Photos from the personal files of Greglon Lee. Tracy interview; Allen Joe, personal interview by the author, June 18, 2014.

73 **testimony to the achievements**: Campbell and Lee, *Dragon and the Tiger*, 1:12. Greglon Lee, phone interview by the author, February 15, 2011.

73 **A welder by trade**: Campbell and Lee, *Dragon and the Tiger*, 1:86, 109, and captions to the photographs; Thomas, *Bruce Lee*, 65; interview with Greglon

Lee, in Rafiq, *Bruce Lee Conversations*, 100; George Lee, personal interview by the author, January 8, 2011. George Lee worked as a machinist at the Mare Island Naval Shipyard for thirty-six years. Along with James Lee and Allen Joe, he developed a close personal relationship with Bruce. When Bruce relocated to Southern California, George Lee would build many of the devices and contraptions that Bruce conceived.

74 **After dinners with**: Campbell and Lee, *Dragon and the Tiger*, 1:78; Greglon Lee interview, June 18, 2014.

74 **Though an unlikely candidate**: Greglon Lee interview, June 18, 2014; Campbell and Lee, *Dragon and the Tiger*, 1:86, 91–92; Gong, *Bruce Lee*, 48. See also Zimmer's articles: "Take Note, Grasshopper, of Kung Fu" and "How 'Kung Fu' Entered the Popular Lexicon."

74 **In short order, packages**: Campbell and Lee, *Dragon and the Tiger*, 1:91–92.

74 **While considering a title**: Zimmer, "Take Note, Grasshopper, of Kung Fu"; Zimmer, "How 'Kung Fu' Entered the Popular Lexicon."

74 **Born and raised in**: Campbell and Lee, *Dragon and the Tiger*, 1:7; Allen Joe, personal interviews by the author, June 18, 2014, and August 26, 2014; Greglon Lee interview, February 15, 2011.

74 **Most notable**: Joe interview, June 18, 2014; Tracy interview; Greglon Lee interview, February 15, 2011.

75 **After school he took**: Campbell and Lee, *Dragon and the Tiger*, 1:7–9.

75 **After returning to Oakland**: Campbell and Lee, *Dragon and the Tiger*, 1:7–9.

75 **James eventually proposed**: Campbell and Lee, *Dragon and the Tiger*, 1:104–5. Personal interviews with Greglon Lee, June 18, 2014 and Gilman Wong, May 15, 2015.

75 **The project proved**: Leo Fong, personal interview by the author, October 24, 2011; Novak interview; Greglon Lee interview, June 18, 2014; Campbell and Lee, *Dragon and the Tiger*, 1:111. Leo Fong asserts that he was present when James stormed out of Kin Mon and has always said that the fallout was over just a few dollars. There are theories, however, that after witnessing T. Y. Wong's children practice, James realized that he was being taught a watered-down version of the techniques.

75 **Talking with his close**: Novak interview; Campbell and Lee, *Dragon and the Tiger*, 1:111–20.

75 **As James would explain**: J. Yimm Lee. *Wing Chun Kung-Fu*, introduction.

76 **The two of them**: Joe interviews, March 3, 2011, and June 18, 2014.

76 **First, his brother, Robert:** "Harriet Lee's Reflections on the Dragon," in Tadman and Kerridge, *Bruce Lee*, unpaginated.

76 **Just recently, his friend:** Bernice Jay, personal interview by the author, October 13, 2014.

76 **If a more modern:** Novak interview; Fong interview.

76 **Allen Joe ordered:** Joe interviews, March 3, 2011, and June 18, 2014. See also Gong, *Bruce Lee*, 47–48.

76 **Allen had grown up:** Joe interviews, March 3, 2011, and June 18, 2014. See also Gong, *Bruce Lee*, 47–48.

77 **James and Allen had:** Goldstein, "Jack Lalanne"; Finacom, "Jack La Lanne"; Allen Joe interviews, March 3, 2011, and June 18, 2014; phone interview with Elaine Lalanne, October 21, 2015; Gong, *Bruce Lee*, 50–52.

77 **But for the East Bay:** Franklin, "Ed Yarick Gym"; Yarick, "Steve Reeves I Know"; Joe interviews, March 3, 2011, and June 18, 2014; LaLanne interview; Gong, *Bruce Lee*, 50–52.

78 **Later, after his service:** Joe interviews, March 3, 2011, and June 18, 2014; Gong, *Bruce Lee*, 50–52.

78 **Working on a second Scotch:** Joe interviews, March 3, 2011, and June 18, 2014. See also Gong, *Bruce Lee*, 47–48.

78 **"I was told about you":** Joe interview, June 18, 2014.

78 **Bruce's face lit up:** Joe interview, June 18, 2014.

78 **"You practice Gung Fu?":** Joe interview, June 18, 2014.

78 **"Yes, with Robert's brother":** Joe interview, June 18, 2014.

78 **"Come on, let's":** Joe interview, June 18, 2014.

78 **The two of them made:** Joe interview, June 18, 2014; Gong, *Bruce Lee*, 47–48.

79 **"Before we go in":** Joe interview, June 18, 2014; Gong, *Bruce Lee*, 47–48. "He then asked Allen to throw a punch at him, and when he did, he found Bruce lo sao-ing him (grabbing his arm) all over the place: 'When he lop sao-ed me, he jerked my shoulder so hard that might be why my socket is still sore today!' It was the beginning of a great friendship!" (Gong, *Bruce Lee*, 47).

79 **Driving his black Ford:** Campbell and Lee, *Dragon and the Tiger*, 1:244, 251–53.

79 **Allen Joe had returned:** Joe interview, June 18, 2014.

79 **"James, the kid is amazing":** Joe interview, June 18, 2014.

79 **Bruce and Allen had stayed**: Joe interview, June 18, 2014; Gong, *Bruce Lee*, 47-48.

79 **Two hundred years**: Bagwell, *Oakland*, 15-20.

80 **As San Francisco blossomed**: Bagwell, *Oakland*, 15-20. "The price of redwood lumber skyrocketed. In 1847, it was $30 per one thousand board feet. In 1849, it $350 to $600 per thousand board feet. Fortunes were to be made in the redwoods, and miners came quickly back" (18).

80 **Bruce continued south, anxious**: Campbell and Lee, *Dragon and the Tiger*, 1:251-53.

80 **In 1868 Oakland**: Bagwell, *Oakland*, 50-53.

80 **At the time there was**: Bagwell, *Oakland*, 60.

80 **With the turn**: Bagwell, *Oakland*, 178-79.

80 **"There were those who thought"**: Bagwell, *Oakland*, 178-79.

81 **With the opening**: Bagwell, *Oakland*, 189.

81 **Aeronautics soon followed**: Bagwell, *Oakland*, 197-200.

81 **Amelia Earhart operated**: "Leamington Hotel."

81 **By the 1920s the city**: Bagwell, *Oakland*, 196.

81 **The industry and job**: Bagwell, *Oakland*, 232-42.

81 **For Bruce the view**: George Lee interview.

81 **If James Lee was searching**: Campbell and Lee, *Dragon and the Tiger*, 1:251.

81 **Juggling a variety**: Gong, *Bruce Lee*, 17-19; Campbell and Lee, *Dragon and the Tiger*, 2:102.

81 **He was planning a trip**: Phoebe Lee et al., *Lee Siu Loong*. This book, by Bruce's siblings, is entirely focused on his 1963 trip home.

82 **All that aside, Bruce**: Campbell and Lee, *Dragon and the Tiger*, 1:251; Joe interview, June 18, 2014.

82 **On Monticello Avenue**: Campbell and Lee, *Dragon and the Tiger*, 1:254.

82 **"how does this thing work?"**: Campbell and Lee, *Dragon and the Tiger*, 1:256; George Lee interview; Joe interview, June 18, 2014; Novak interview.

82 **As the entire house**: Campbell and Lee, *Dragon and the Tiger*, 1:254.

82 **James Lee and his colleagues**: Bernice Jay, personal interviews by the author, September 18, 2012, and October 13, 2014; Linda Lee Cadwell, phone interview by the author, April 20, 2011; Greglon Lee interview, February 15, 2011.

82 **"Bruce was smart"**: Greglon Lee interview, February 15, 2011.

83 **"Allen, the kid is amazing"**: Joe interview, June 18, 2014.

84 **It was getting late:** Al Novak, personal interview by the author, March 3, 2011; Bernice Jay, personal interview by the author, October 11, 2014.

84 **Bruce Lee jumped:** Novak interview.

84 **Bruce was down from Seattle:** Novak interview; Bernice Jay interview, October 11, 2014; Greglon Lee, phone interview by the author, February 15, 2011.

84 **The talk came packaged:** Novak interview; Bernice Jay interview, October 11, 2014. "I can't tell you the number of late nights that were spent with Ralph Castro, and Wally Jay, James Lee, Allen Joe, all those guys. Many late nights where they would go around the living room demonstrating things . . . 'Hey get up, let me show you this one move'" (Linda Lee Cadwell, phone interview by the author, April 20, 2011).

84 **"all just go out back":** Bernice Jay interview, October 11, 2014.

84 **On the topic of kung fu:** Novak interview.

85 **On his feet now:** Novak interview.

85 **Bruce's buddy Hawkins:** Cheung, "Bruce Lee's Hong Kong Years."

85 **Bruce explained how:** Novak interview.

85 **In time Bruce would exhibit:** Leo Fong, personal interview by the author, October 24, 2011.

85 **The conversations continued on:** Novak interview.

85 **On the subject of American:** Novak interview. Numerous sources testified to Bruce's great interest in American boxing and his admiration for these particular fighters (Robinson, Dempsey, and Ali). There is a great segment from the *I Am Bruce Lee* documentary that is worth watching on this topic; in it Dan Inosanto and Linda Lee relate that Bruce watched an 8 mm boxing film of Muhammad Ali backward to see how he could apply the moves from Ali's left-foot-forward stance to his own right-foot-forward stance. "He studied these films meticulously," explains Linda Lee.

85 **"Dempsey was out for the kill":** Al Tracy, phone interview by the author, August 26, 2014.

85 **spurred Wally forward:** Novak interview.

85 **Prior to his jujitsu training:** Alan Jay, phone interview by the author, January 3, 2015.

85 **topic steered to the kid:** Novak interview. Again, Bruce's admiration for Ali surfaces in many interviews with people who knew him. Leo Fong, for example, can talk about this at great length.

86 **Bruce held the present company**: Cadwell interview.

86 **Novak would have fit**: Novak interview; also Gene Ching, "Great American Great Grandmaster."

86 **Bruce was also becoming**: Bernice Jay interview, October 11, 2014.

86 **In fact, when Wally's**: Alan Jay interview.

86 **As Bruce was becoming**: Cadwell interview.

86 **Often over the course**: Novak interview.

87 **In 1922 British heavyweight**: Edwards and Edwards, "Historical Perspectives."

87 **Starting in the mid-nineteenth**: "Japanese Laborers Arrive"; Takaki, *Strangers from a Different Shore*, chap. 4.

87 **In the social turbulence**: Takaki, *Strangers from a Different Shore*, 42-46.

87 **the Japanese would compose**: Takaki, *Strangers from a Different Shore*, 132.

87 **just before a new federal**: "Immigration Act of 1924."

87 **"preserve the ideal"**: "Immigration Act of 1924."

88 **Filipinos, who were exempt from**: "Immigration Act of 1924"; "Filipino Laborers Arrive."

88 **All these migrant groups**: Takaki, *Strangers from a Different Shore*, 164-66.

88 **"Hawaii was the first great"**: Dan Inosanto, personal interview by the author, June 2, 2014.

88 **By the time that Morris**: Edwards and Edwards, "Historical Perspectives."

88 **In seeking out a practitioner**: Edwards and Edwards, "Historical Perspectives."

88 **During the late nineteenth century**: Takaki, *Strangers from a Different Shore*, 43. Edwards and Edwards, "Historical Perspectives."

88 **During family financial turmoil**: Edwards and Edwards, "Historical Perspectives."

88 **Living in the Hilo**: Bernice Jay, personal interview by the author, October 13, 2014; Edwards and Edwards, "Historical Perspectives."

89 **If there was a fighter**: Edwards and Edwards, "Historical Perspectives."

89 **The fighting method**: Skoss, "Jujutsu and Taijutsu."

89 **"the art of gaining victory"**: Joseph R. Svinth, "Professor Yamashita Goes to Washington," in Green and Svinth, *Martial Arts*, 50.

89 **eventually employed to describe**: Svinth, "Professor Yamashita."

89 **These methods—with their**: Skoss, "Jujutsu and Taijutsu."

89 **Later, in an effort**: William J. Long, "Judo," in Green and Svinth, *Martial Arts of the World*, 127-32.

89 **"all the nasty bits out"**: Personal interview with the Jay family (Bernice, Alan, Alberta, and Antoinette), personal interview by the author, March 24, 2012.

89 **Whereas the Chinese martial**: Judkins, "Lives of Chinese Martial Artists (14)."

89 **so much so that President**: Svinth, "Professor Yamashita."

90 **In preparing for the Morris**: Edwards and Edwards, "Historical Perspectives."

90 **On May 19, 1922**: Edwards and Edwards, "Historical Perspectives."

90 **In 1926 Okazaki returned**: Edwards and Edwards, "Historical Perspectives."

90 **Photos of his students**: From the personal files of Bernice Jay.

90 **Although the local**: Edwards and Edwards, "Historical Perspectives."

91 **Okazaki always maintained**: Bernice Jay interview, October 13, 2014.

91 **With the Japanese attack**: Edwards and Edwards, "Historical Perspectives."

91 **Born to Chinese immigrants**: Jay family interview; Rick H. Wong, personal interviews by the author, September 25, 2014, July 8, 2012 and December 4, 2014; Inosanto interview; Bernice Jay interviews, September 18, 2012, and October 13, 2014; Alan Jay interview. See also "History of Small Circle Jujitsu."

91 **In 1950 Wally**: Bernice Jay interview, September 18, 2012.

91 **However, Wally's evolution**: Bernice Jay interviews, September 18, 2012, and October 13, 2014; Alan Jay interview; Wong interviews, July 8, 2012, and December 4, 2014; "History of Small Circle Jujitsu."

92 **"When we first came"**: Alan Jay interview.

92 **Wally became a popular**: Wong interview, July 8, 2012; Alan Jay interview; Bernice Jay interviews, September 18, 2012, and October 13, 2014; Inosanto interview. From interview with Dan Inosanto: "Well . . . Wally Jay is kinda like my own personal hero."

92 **Wally would field criticism**: Bernice Jay interview, October 13, 2014; Alan Jay interview, January 3, 2015; Wong interview, December 4, 2014; "History of Small Circle Jujitsu."

92 **"There was a kind of"**: Inosanto interview.

9. THE HAWAIIAN CONNECTION (PART TWO)

93 **"Are you ready?"**: Campbell and Lee, *Dragon and the Tiger*, 2:88; Ralph Castro, personal interview by the author, February 10, 2011.

93 **Ralph Castro steadied himself**: Castro interview.

93 **Parker and Castro had:** Campbell and Lee, *Dragon and the Tiger*, 2:58-95; Castro interview.

93 **the group all put on:** From the personal files of Greglon Lee; Campbell and Lee, *Dragon and the Tiger*, 2:81-82.

93 **Parker began to warm:** Campbell and Lee, *Dragon and the Tiger*, 2:72-78.

94 **Parker and Castro were both:** Castro interview.

94 **Castro had a tough:** Willy Cahill, personal interview by the author, August 20, 2014.

94 **In California his students:** Barney Scollan, personal interview by the author, January 11, 2014; James Wing Woo, personal interview by the author, February 26, 2014.

94 **As a Bay Area:** Linda Lee Cadwell, phone interview by the author, April 20, 2011.

94 **Bruce was ready now:** Campbell and Lee, *Dragon and the Tiger*, 2:88; Ralph Castro interview.

94 **"fist law":** Lee Wedlake, "Kenpo Karate," in Green and Svinth, *Martial Arts of the World*, 49-55.

94 **It is a broad:** "Currently, kenpo is a dynamic martial art. A careful reading of the history of this art indicates that innovation and change are its hallmarks . . . a martial system as flexible and adaptable as the people who have embraced it" (C. Jerome Barber, "Kenpo," in Green and Svinth, *Martial Arts of the World*, 259).

94 **Kenpo's origins in Hawaii:** Bruce Juchnik, phone interview by the author, December 17, 2014; Al Tracy, personal interview by the author, August 26, 2014; "Origin 'Ideas' of Kenpo." See also Barber, "Kenpo."

94 **Born in Hawaii, Mitose:** Juchnik interview; "James."

95 **Parker and Castro learned kenpo:** Castro interview.

95 **He was known to be:** Tracy, "Professor William K. S. Chow."

95 **"He was into full-on":** "In the martial arts . . . we teach people to respect themselves and others" (Samuel Alama Kuoha, quoted in Avent, "In the Martial Arts").

95 **Born into the Mormon:** "Ed Parker Biography"; Darlene Parker and Antwone Alferos, phone interview by the author, June 18, 2015.

95 **Parker arrived on the mainland:** Parker and Alferos interview.

95 **During the halftime:** Broad. "Tribute to Ed Parker."

95 **He corresponded with Professor:** Parker and Alferos interview.

95 **"High Priest of Hollywood's"**: "Violent Repose."

96 **Over time his celebrity**: Wedlake, "Kenpo Karate." See also "Ed Parker Biography."

96 **Without many years**: "Ed Parker Biography"; Leo Fong, personal interview by the author, October 24, 2011; Parker and Alferos interview; Dave Hebler, personal interview by the author, December 11, 2014.

96 **He already had a small**: Parker and Alferos interview; Tracy interview; Lee Wedlake, email correspondence with the author, June 27, 2015.

96 **event that Parker was planning**: Phone Interview with Dave Hebler, phone interview by the author, December 12, 2014; Parker and Alferos interview.

10. WAY OF THE INTEGRATED FIST

97 **"the ultimate"**: Leo Fong, phone interview by the author, February 3, 2011; Leo Fong, personal interview by the author, October 24, 2011.

97 **Fong had spent**: Fong interviews, February 3, 2011, and October 24, 2011.

97 **"radical overhaul"**: "Timing."

97 **Fong practiced his main**: Fong interview, October 24, 2011.

97 **"pah-pah . . . pah-pah"**: Fong interview, October 24, 2011. I've noticed that the many martial artists I interviewed all seem to have their own sounds that they attach to recollecting certain moves or techniques. For Fong, "pah-pah" is one of the sounds he ascribes to combinations of punches being thrown and landed.

97 **He had racked up**: Fong interviews, October 24, 2011, and June 3, 2014.

98 **These odd hours**: Fong interview, October 24, 2011.

98 **At the age of fifteen**: Leo Fong interview, October 24, 2011; Leo Fong, phone interview by the author, December 17, 2014.

98 **The match was held**: Fong interviews, October 24, 2011, and December 17, 2014.

98 **The residents of Widener**: Fong interviews, October 24, 2011, and June 3, 2014.

98 **"Population 92"**: Fong interviews, October 24, 2011, and June 3, 2014.

99 **"Ching Chong Chinaman–kinda chant"**: Fong interviews, October 24, 2011, and June 3, 2014.

99 **Later that day Fong**: Fong interviews, October 24, 2011, and June 3, 2014.

99 **"The racism was so deep"**: Fong interviews, October 24, 2011, and June 3, 2014.

99 **In addition to the regular**: Fong interviews, October 24, 2011, and December 17, 2014.

99 **the book** *Fundamentals of Boxing*: Fong interviews, October 24, 2011, and December 17, 2014.

99 **So walking home after**: Fong interviews, October 24, 2011, and June 3, 2014.

100 **"a sliding right"**: Fong interview, December 17, 2014.

100 **Yet even with a record**: Fong interview, October 24, 2011.

100 **While Fong sparred with his**: Fong interviews, October 24, 2011, and December 17, 2014.

101 **One would gain momentum**: Bruce Lee, *Chinese Gung Fu*.

101 **while the other would enjoy**: Thomas A. Green, phone interview by the author, January 27, 2015.

101 **After months of enthusiastic**: Bruce Lee, *Chinese Gung Fu*; Campbell and Lee, *Dragon and the Tiger*, vol. 2. Sid Campbell and Greglon Lee's second volume mainly concerns itself with James and Bruce collaborating to publish *Gung Fu: The Philosophical Art of Self-Defense*. Their book is likely the most thorough account of that particular history.

101 **Somewhat uncharacteristically**: Bruce Lee, *Gung Fu*. "Bruce intentionally wrote this introductory book about Chinese gung fu for those in America, which included very little of the wing chun gung fu that he had been practicing and teaching. The book illustrates a more basic, generalized approach and primer to the theories of gung fu, including much of the classical approach Bruce later criticized" (Gong, *Bruce Lee*, 48).

101 **The book opened with**: Bruce Lee, *Gung Fu*, 1–8.

101 **He not only showcased**: Bruce Lee, *Gung Fu*; Gong, *Bruce Lee*, 48.

101 **Conversely,** *Secret Fighting Arts*: Gilbey, *Secret Fighting Arts*.

101 **"a book crammed full"**: Gilbey, *Secret Fighting Arts*.

101 **Gilbey's book hopped**: Gilbey, *Secret Fighting Arts*.

102 **"an heir to a textile"**: Gilbey, *Secret Fighting Arts*.

102 **the book was a hoax**: Smith, *Martial Musings*, 113–18; Green interview.

102 **A World War II veteran**: Smith, *Martial Musings*.

102 **But the parody**: Smith, *Martial Musings*; Green interview.

102 **"What we were reading in"**: Green interview.

103 **the authors shared common**: I should note that Robert W. Smith would have been appalled to be lumped together with Bruce Lee on this point. In fact, the quote, "So much of what passes for the fighting arts in America and Asia is

bogus," is taken from a chapter in Smith's memoir in which he skewers Bruce Lee and his role in the prevailing perceptions of the martial arts. I could write a lengthy article on this topic, and ultimately I would conclude that Smith was unable to distinguish what Lee was doing on screen with what Lee was doing in the garage on Monticello Avenue in Oakland. By only considering the former and not the latter, I think Smith assessed Bruce incorrectly. After all, the quote cited above sounds remarkable similar to what Bruce was already saying in the early 1960s.

103 **"So much of what passes"**: Smith, *Martial Musings*, 342.

103 **At the end of the year**: Allen Joe, personal interview by the author, June 18, 2014; Linda Lee interview. See also Gong, *Bruce Lee*, 49.

103 **James presented Bruce**: Campbell and Lee, *Dragon and the Tiger*, 2:230–31.

103 **He had found a location**: Thomas, *Bruce Lee*, 55; Gong, *Bruce Lee*, 22, 31–33.

103 **Over the summer Bruce**: Gong, *Bruce Lee*, 22. See also Phoebe Lee et al., *Lee Siu Loong*. This book chronicles Bruce's trip back to Hong Kong in the summer of 1963. It is a thorough account of his time there.

104 **With James Lee, Allen Joe**: Joe interview.

11. YEAR OF THE GREEN DRAGON

107 **City coordinators and police**: "Chinatown's Biggest Night"; "King-Sized Traffic Snarl." See also Ludlow, "300,000 . . . and a Dragon."

107 **"monumental"**: From *San Francisco Examiner* headline, February 23, 1964, A-1.

107 **Both the Golden Gate**: "King-Sized Traffic Snarl."

107 **In Chinatown police barricades**: "Chinatown's Biggest Night." See also Ludlow, "300,000 . . . and a Dragon."

107 **SFPD patrolman William Goodwin**: "Chinatown's Biggest Night."

107 **The parade itself was**: Kem K. Lee, Photograph Collection, 1927–1986; "Chinatown's Biggest Night." See also Ludlow, "300,000 . . . and a Dragon."

108 **"a combination of marvelous"**: Ludlow, "300,000 . . . and a Dragon."

108 **Lau Bun's Lion Dance**: Kem K. Lee, Photograph Collection, 1927–1986.

108 **T. Y. Wong and his squad**: Kem K. Lee, Photograph Collection, 1927–1986.

108 **careful to conduct their lions**: Adeline Fong, personal interview by the author, December 12, 2012.

108 **As expected, the Forbidden City**: "Chinatown Parade Tomorrow." For Coby Yee history, see Dong, *Forbidden City, USA*.

108 **"A flower boat with"**: "Chinatown Parade Tomorrow."

108 **However, the float briefly**: Ludlow, "300,000 ... and a Dragon."

108 **"ten saddened beauties"**: "Chinatown's Biggest Night."

108 **tempered by the steady stream**: Kem K. Lee, Photograph Collection, 1927–1986.

108 **star of the festivities finally**: "Chinatown's Biggest Night." See also Ludlow, "300,000 ... and a Dragon"; Kem K. Lee, Photograph Collection, 1927–1986.

109 **"Parade officials didn't know"**: Ludlow, "300,000 ... and a Dragon."

109 **"Chinatown's Greatest Night"**: Ludlow, "300,000 ... and a Dragon."

109 **"In Chinatown, it's the Year"**: Caen, "Phenomenal Week."

109 **On February 9 the Beatles**: Margolis, *Last Innocent Year*, 139–42.

109 **Bob Dylan had already**: Marqusee, "Fifty Years."

109 **"the year that everything"**: Margolis, *Last Innocent Year*, 266.

109 **On February 25 Cassius Clay**: Gallender, *Sonny Liston*, 104–76; Tosches, *Devil and Sonny Liston*, 185–203; Margolis, *Last Innocent Year*, 148–49.

110 **defeating Floyd Patterson**: Tosches, *Devil and Sonny Liston*, 157–67; Gallender, *Sonny Liston*, 63–97.

110 **"the big Negro in every"**: As quoted in Gallender, *Sonny Liston*, 89.

110 **Somehow, Cassius Clay**: Gallender, *Sonny Liston*, 104–76; Tosches, *Devil and Sonny Liston*, 185–203.

110 **"I don't have to be who"**: Margolis, *Last Innocent Year*, 149.

111 **"It is unthinkable that anyone would"**: Caen, "Phenomenal Week."

111 **Within a year the federal**: "Unnoticed Struggle."

111 **The rise of Chinatown youth**: Bill Lee, *Chinese Playground*.

111 **Furthermore, a series of new**: Choy, *San Francisco Chinatown*, 57; "History of Fair Housing."

111 **As spirited as Coby Yee's**: Dong, *Forbidden City, USA*, 34–36.

111 **local dancer Carol Doda made**: Dong, *Forbidden City, USA*, 34–36.

112 **Bing Chan opened his own**: Dino Salvatera, personal interviews by the author, June 20, 2011, November 7, 2011, and December 19, 2012; Doc-Fai Wong, personal interview by the author, February 2, 2012; Sam Louie, personal interview by the author, February 1, 2012; Adeline Fong, personal interviews by the author, June 28, 2011, December 12, 2012, and December 3, 2014.

112 **T.Y. had taken on Irish**: Warren Chan, personal interview by the author, November 12, 2013.

112 **Lau Bun was teaching Hawaiian**: Louie interview; James Wing Woo, personal interview by the author, February 26, 2014.

112 **There was also a notable**: Wing Woo interview, February 26, 2014; Ben Der, personal interview by the author, February 2, 2014; Paul Eng, personal interview by the author, May 16, 2014; David Chin, phone interview by the author, March 31, 2011; Dorgan, "Bruce Lee's Toughest Fight."

112 **"elegantly athletic"**: Dorgan, "Bruce Lee's Toughest Fight."

112 **He frequented the Ghee**: Chin interview.

112 **"the one-inch punch"**: Leo Fong, personal interviews by the author, October 24, 2011, and June 3, 2014; phone interview by the author, February 3, 2011.

112 **James Lee had put**: Al Novak, personal interview by the author, March 31, 2011; Leo Fong interview, October 24, 2011; George Lee, personal interviews by the author, January 8, 2011.

112 **Fong was still uncertain**: Leo Fong interviews, February 3, 2011, and October 24, 2011.

113 **George Lee, who had been**: George Lee interview, January 8, 2011.

113 **First, James announced**: Leo Fong interview, October 24, 2011.

113 **In deciding to move**: Thomas, *Bruce Lee*, 57.

113 **Initially James considered**: Greglon Lee, personal interview by the author, June 18, 2014; Al Tracy, phone interview by the author, August 26, 2014. See also Gong, *Bruce Lee*, 46.

113 **Taking a cue**: Thomas, *Bruce Lee*, 57; Gong, *Bruce Lee*, 46; Linda Lee, personal interview by the author, April 20, 2011. At the end of 1963, Bruce and Linda traveled to Pasadena, presumably to see the Washington Huskies in the Rose Bowl. Bruce really wanted to visit Ed Parker. The young couple picked up James Lee, and while down there, Parker took them over to the Long Beach Auditorium and explained the current state of his plans for the tournament that coming summer. A photo from this visit shows Linda, Bruce, James, Ed Parker, and Ed Parker Jr. The back of the photo is dated December 30, 1963. I asked Linda Lee about this directly because it seemed like a mismatch from the date of the 1964 tournament.

113 **Bruce talked for a bit**: Leo Fong interview, October 24, 2011.

113 **"classical mess"**: Leo Fong interview, October 24, 2011.

113 **"explosive power"**: Leo Fong interview, October 24, 2011.

113 **Bruce moved the coffee table**: Leo Fong interview, October 24, 2011.

113 **"Bruce knocked him"**: Leo Fong interview, October 24, 2011; Barney Scollan, personal interview by the author, January 22, 2014. Leo Fong and Barney Scollan describe different demonstrations of Bruce performing the one-inch punch at James Lee's house in almost the exact same manner. Scollan signed up with Bruce and James later that year but seemed to attend a similar sort of orientation meeting in the living room at Monticello Avenue. Scollan was actually the volunteer during this particular meeting. While the account from this chapter is from Fong, here is Scollan's account. Notice the similarities: "I went through the air with the one-inch punch. In James Lee's living room. We were skeptical, like, 'C'mon, one inch?' And he said, 'Okay.' So he moved the coffee table out of the way, and he had me stand with a pillow from the couch. And I was holding it like this, like in a football stance. And he went— *whap*. And I flew, hit the couch, the couch tipped over, and I was almost about to go through the living room window when my roommates caught me. I outweighed Bruce by like thirty or forty pounds. I don't know how he did it. I talked to my old roommate recently, and I said, 'You were there, weren't you?' And he said, 'Yeah, I caught you as you were about to go through the window. Two of us did.'"

114 **As everyone settled down**: Leo Fong interview, October 24, 2011.

114 **"Until the new school is ready"**: Leo Fong interview, October 24, 2011.

114 **The few people in attendance**: Novak interview; Leo Fong interview, October 24, 2011; George Lee interview.

12. LONG BEACH

115 **At the 1964 Summer**: "Judo at the 1964 Tokyo Summer Games."

115 **Ed Parker sought to**: Chris Trevino, "Bruce Lee Put U.S. Martial Arts"; Darlene Parker and Antwone Alferos, phone interview by the author, June 18, 2015.

115 **There had been a few**: Trevino, "Bruce Lee Put U.S. Martial Arts"; Parker and Alferos interview.

115 **"Chicago was a real mess"**: Trevino, "Bruce Lee Put U.S. Martial Arts."

115 **Parker invited him down**: Linda Lee Cadwell, phone interview by the author, April 20, 2011; Thomas, *Bruce Lee*, 57.

115 **"He (Bruce) was very"**: Ed Parker, quoted in Thomas, *Bruce Lee*, 57.

115 **Bruce was entirely disdainful**: *I Am Bruce Lee*.

116 **"organized despair"**: George Lee, personal interview by the author, January 8, 2011. Bruce's former Seattle student Pat Strong had a different way of phrasing it: "To Bruce, this kind of sparring was more a form of constipation" (quoted in Bax, *Disciples of the Dragon*, 47).

116 **When Bruce arrived**: Dan Inosanto, personal interview by the author, June 2, 2014. As Inosanto recalls, "Ed Parker gave me seventy-five dollars and said, 'Make sure that he eats, and show him around the Long Beach area.'"

116 **Slomanski had brought**: Inosanto interview.

116 **Inosanto studied for a time**: Inosanto interview.

116 **"I was completely flabbergasted"**: Inosanto, quoted in Thomas, *Bruce Lee*, 58.

117 **The night before the tournament**: Inosanto interview; Barney Scollan, personal interview by the author, January 22, 2014.

117 **Dressed in a black leather**: Scollan interview; photographs from personal files of Barney Scollan.

117 **"That one . . . is the only"**: As related by Pat Strong, in Bax, *Disciples of the Dragon*, 44.

117 **many observers in the room**: Inosanto interview; Scollan interview. It's worth noting that Inosanto says he was as impressed with this performance by Bruce—"in front of the black belts"—as he was with the one at the tournament the following day.

117 **a seminal moment for**: Trevino, "Bruce Lee Put U.S. Martial Arts."

117 **The turnout at the**: Dave Hebler, phone interview by the author, December 11, 2014.

117 **"It truly was international"**: Hebler interview.

117 **Bruce's demonstration was slated**: Gong, *Bruce Lee*, 54–56; Thomas, *Bruce Lee*, 56; Hebler interview. It's worth noting that there is some discrepancy over Bruce's slot amid the demonstrations. Whereas Dave Hebler asserts that Bruce was a minor presenter, most Bruce Lee biographers slate him as the final presenter and, as a result, a sort of headliner. It seems that Bruce did perform toward the end of the day, but whether his billing had "headliner status" remains unclear.

118 **"My dad started the internationals"**: Parker and Alferos interview.

118 **There in Long Beach, Ed**: Trevino, "Bruce Lee Put U.S. Martial Arts"; Parker and Alferos interview; Hebler interview.

118 **Bruce took the floor**: Thomas, *Bruce Lee*, 56.

118 **Dressed in a black *jing-mo***: Thomas, *Bruce Lee*, 56.

118 **Unlike his succinct**: Scollan interview.

118 **"Bruce was absolutely electric"**: Cadwell interview.

118 **"I had seen it all"**: Richard Bustillo, quoted in Trevino, "Bruce Lee Put U.S. Martial Arts."

118 **Bruce performed the Wing Chun**: Scollan interview; Inosanto interview; Gong, *Bruce Lee*, 54–56; Thomas, *Bruce Lee*, 56; *I Am Bruce Lee*. See also Trevino, "Bruce Lee Put U.S. Martial Arts." There are some notable discrepancies in the accounts of what Bruce performed at Long Beach in 1964 versus later years.

119 **"Although they were impressive, Bruce"**: Thomas, *Bruce Lee*, 56–57.

119 **he took the floor to**: Scollan interview; Inosanto interview.

119 **Bruce insulted a lot**: Scollan interview; Inosanto interview; Clarence Lee, personal interview by the author, October 7, 2014.

119 **"The prevailing attitude"**: Hebler interview.

119 **"kicking a guy in the nuts"**: Scollan interview.

119 **"He got up there and"**: Scollan interview.

119 **The horse stance is**: Inosanto interview.

119 **"of the classical mess"**: Scollan interview.

120 **"There's stability, but"**: Inosanto interview.

120 **By contrast he then**: Scollan interview.

120 **"He said the individual"**: Richard Bustillo, in *I Am Bruce Lee*.

120 **"He was heavily into"**: Inosanto interview.

120 **This was a popular point**: Leo Fong, personal interview by the author, October 24, 2011; Inosanto interview; Al Novak, personal interview by the author, March 3, 2011.

120 **"Back then, it was"**: Leo Fong interview.

120 **"Teachers should never impose"**: Inosanto interview.

120 **"There was a high percentage"**: Inosanto interview.

121 **"Guys were practically lining"**: Clarence Lee interview.

121 **Months earlier Scollan**: Scollan interview.

121 **"Bruce made a number of**: Barney Scollan, email communication with the author, June 7, 2011.

121 **Jay Sebring was the hair**: "Jay Sebring." See also "Jay Sebring Trailer."

121 **At Long Beach, Sebring**: Thomas, *Bruce Lee*, 67; Linda Lee, *Bruce Lee Story*, 70. See also *I Am Bruce Lee*.

121 **Sebring's life was fated**: "Jay Sebring."

121 **Not long after Parker's**: Thomas, *Bruce Lee*, 67; Linda Lee, *Bruce Lee Story*, 70. See also *I Am Bruce Lee.*

122 **Not only was it Dozier's**: "The Man behind TV's Batman."

122 **During haircutting chitchat**: Thomas, *Bruce Lee*, 67; Linda Lee, *Bruce Lee Story*, 70. See also *I Am Bruce Lee.*

13. INCIDENT AT THE SUN SING THEATER

123 **Barney Scollan couldn't sign**: Barney Scollan, personal interview by the author, January 22, 2014; Dick Miller, phone interview by the author, December 4, 2014.

123 **"So, Bruce"**: Scollan interview.

123 **"That is why"**: Scollan interview.

123 **Scollan and his Berkeley**: Scollan interview; Thomas A. Green, phone interview by the author, January 27, 2015.

123 **"I would get into fights"**: Scollan interview.

124 **In this sense the growing**: Green interview.

124 **"There will always be"**: Green interview.

124 **"emphasizing practicality and renouncing"**: Kennedy and Kuo, *Chinese Martial Arts Training Manuals*, 45. Interestingly enough, the famous Chinese General Qi Jiguang had also chimed in on this issue of practicality in the martial arts, writing, "The pretty is not practical, and the practical is not pretty" (see Matuszak, "'Practical Isn't Pretty'").

124 **"untouchable"**: Scollan interview; George Lee, personal interview by the author, January 8, 2011.

124 **George Lee remembers how**: George Lee interview; Greglon Lee, personal interview by the author, February 15, 2011.

124 **Bob Cook, a well-traveled**: Bob Cook, phone interview by the author, March 28, 2013.

124 **"a hand-grenade"**: Bob Cook, phone interview by the author, March 28, 2013.

125 **"Leo, are you serious, man?**: Leo Fong, personal interview by the author, October 24, 2011.

125 **"Yeah, Bruce, I'm"**: Leo Fong interview, October 24, 2011.

125 **"No, Leo"**: Leo Fong interview, October 24, 2011.

125 **A lot had happened in**: Linda Lee, *Bruce Lee Story*, 16–19; Gong, *Bruce Lee*, 33.

126 **In the coming weeks**: Linda Lee, *Bruce Lee Story*, 51; Gong, *Bruce Lee*, 49.

126 **In the wake of his:** *I Am Bruce Lee.*

126 **"This guy":** Gong, *Bruce Lee*, 56.

126 **"We were both very excited":** Linda Lee, *Bruce Lee Story*, 71.

126 **Bruce went back out:** Dan Inosanto, personal interview by the author, June 2, 2014.

126 **Originally known as the Mandarin:** Kar and Bren, *Hong Kong Cinema*, 76. See also Choy, *San Francisco Chinatown*, 150–51.

127 **The two venues were constantly:** "The following theatrical decline reached bottom after the destruction of Chinatown in the great San Francisco Earthquake of 1906. But the theater scene gradually recovered in a rebuilt Chinatown and boomed during the 1920s and 1930s, thanks to intense competition between two theaters: the Mandarin at 1021 Grant Street and the Great China at 630 Jackson Street" (Kar and Bren, *Hong Kong Cinema*, 76).

127 **In 1931 the Mandarin:** Kar and Bren, *Hong Kong Cinema*, 76.

127 **Mandarin Theater booked Bruce's:** Lee Family Immigration Files. There tend to be discrepancies concerning exactly where Bruce's father performed while in San Francisco. Some sources cite the Great China (or, as it was later known, the Great Star), yet Lee Hoi Chuen's immigration documents clearly cite the Mandarin as his place of employment.

127 **The theater had deep:** Kar and Bren, *Hong Kong Cinema*, 77.

127 **opera's heyday in Chinatown:** Choy, *San Francisco Chinatown*, 150–51.

127 **In the week before:** Kar and Bren, *Hong Kong Cinema*, 82.

127 **It was under Grandview:** Kar and Bren, *Hong Kong Cinema*, 97–98. See also *Golden Gate Girls.*

127 **the Mandarin Theater would shift:** Choy, *San Francisco Chinatown*, 150–51.

127 **Later Orson Welles:** "The Lady from Shanghai."

128 **"The Most Beautiful Creature":** Paul Fonoroff, email correspondence with the author, October 22, 2014.

128 **"Diana Chang's voluptuous figure":** Paul Fonoroff, email correspondence.

128 **Born in Hebei Province:** Paul Fonoroff, email correspondence.

128 **Diana made her Hong Kong:** Paul Fonoroff, email correspondence.

128 **In the fall of 1964 Diana:** Paul Fonoroff, email correspondence; Inosanto interview.

128 **Bruce was intent on seizing:** Inosanto interview.

129 **While neighborhood students:** George Lee interview. "Harriet Lee's Reflections on the Dragon," in Tadman and Kerridge, *Bruce Lee*, unpaginated.

129 **negative stereotype:** Leo Fong, personal interviews by the author, October 24, 2011, and June 3, 2014; Al Novak, personal interviews by the author, March 3, 2011; Linda Lee Cadwell, phone interview by the author, February 14, 2014; Joe Cervara, phone interview by the author, February 14, 2014.

129 **evidence of lingering tensions:** Mancuso, "Kung Feud?"

129 **Indeed, it was T.Y.:** Cervara interview.

129 **T.Y. had published his:** T. Y. Wong, *Chinese Kung-Fu.*

129 **"Soft Hand Stunts":** T. Y. Wong, *Chinese Kung-Fu,* 103.

129 **"Do not waste your time":** T. Y. Wong, *Chinese Kung-Fu,* 103.

129 **"See, I Can Break":** T. Y. Wong, *Chinese Kung-Fu,* 106.

129 **Soon afterward, while compiling:** Bruce Lee, *Chinese Gung Fu,* 88–97.

129 **"examples of a slower system":** Bruce Lee, *Chinese Gung Fu,* 88–97.

129 **In those pages James:** Bruce Lee, *Chinese Gung Fu,* 88–97; T. Y. Wong, *Chinese Kung-Fu.* See also Mancuso, "Kung Feud?" For example, compare the rendering of the "pow chuie" punch in Bruce's book on pp. 88–89 with the one in T. Y. Wong's first book on pp. 100–101.

130 **introduction of James Lee's:** J. Yimm Lee, *Wing Chun Kung-Fu,* introduction.

130 **"Wing Chun has made":** J. Yimm Lee, *Wing Chun Kung-Fu,* introduction.

130 **They had made a habit:** Allen Joe, personal interview by the author, June 18, 2014.

130 **When one of these outings:** Al Tracy, phone interview by the author, August 26, 2014.

130 **none were as incendiary:** Leo Fong interviews, October 24, 2011, and June 3, 2014; James Wing Woo, personal interview by the author, February 26, 2014.

131 **Bruce started with a joke:** Jeff Chinn, personal interview by the author, February 4, 2014.

131 **"Unlike the Chinese":** Chinn interview; Ralph Castro, personal interview by the author, February 10, 2011.

131 **Bruce motioned for Inosanto:** Inosanto interview.

131 **Diana Chang had sung:** Adeline Fong, personal interview by the author, December 12, 2012; Inosanto interview.

131 **Bruce worked through:** Inosanto interview.

131 **"classical mess":** Wing Woo interview.

131 **"Why would you kick high":** Scollan interview.

131 **"80 percent of what they are":** Tracy interview; Wing Woo interview. Both of these men identify this particular quote (including the "tigers have no

teeth" sentiment below) as the deal-breaking line for much of the audience at Bruce's Sung Sing performance. Interestingly enough, this type of quote surfaces again and again on the topic of Bruce's public criticisms of the legitimacy of what was being practiced in martial arts schools at the time. For example, in Linda Lee's memoir she makes a similar reference to this kind of sentiment, presumably referring to his Long Beach demonstration: "How could this individual have stood in front of the entire martial arts community in the United States and said that over 95 percent of what he saw and heard was utter nonsense" (*Bruce Lee Story*, 41).

131 **"These old tigers"**: Tracy interview; Wing Woo interview.

132 **A cigarette butt was**: Adeline Fong, personal interviews by the author, December 12, 2012, and December 3, 2014.

132 **"Bruce was saying"**: Inosanto interview.

132 **"That's not kung fu"**: Inosanto interview.

132 **"Sir, would you care"**: Inosanto interview.

132 **"You don't know"**: Inosanto interview.

132 **"Would anyone else care"**: Adeline Fong interview, December 12, 2012.

132 **In the lower-left seats**: Adeline Fong interview, December 12, 2012.

132 **Sixteen-year old Adeline**: Adeline Fong interviews, June 28, 2011, December 12, 2012, and December 3, 2014.

133 **"When Bruce called Kenneth"**: Adeline Fong interview, December 3, 2014.

133 **Kenneth Wong ignored the stairs**: Adeline Fong interviews, June 28, 2011, December 12, 2012, and December 3, 2014; Doc-Fai Wong, personal interview by the author, February 16, 2012; Wing Woo interview.

133 **"Thank you for participating"**: Adeline Fong interview, June 28, 2011.

133 **Bruce signed off**: Doc-Fai Wong interview; Wing Woo interview; Adeline Fong interview, June 28, 2011; Ben Der, personal interview by the author, February 12, 2014; David Chin, phone interview by the author, March 31, 2011; Greglon Lee interview; Tracy interview.

133 **"I would like to let everybody"**: Wing Woo interview; Adeline Fong interview, June 28, 2011.

134 **In the coming weeks**: Chin interview, March 31, 2011; Doc-Fai Wong interview.

134 **Wong Jack Man sat down**: David Chin, phone interviews by the author, February 8, 2011, and March 31, 2011; Doc-Fai Wong interview. It's interesting to note that Doc-Fai was a busboy at the Jackson Street Café at the time, while Wong Jack Man was a waiter.

134 **They were also joined:** David Chin, phone interviews by the author, February 8, 2011, and March 31, 2011; Doc-Fai Wong interview.

134 **"the sort of guy":** Personal interview with Dino Salvatera, December 12, 2012.

134 **The group concerned itself:** Chin interviews, February 8, 2011, and March 31, 2011. There is a general consensus that the note was fairly short and to the point. Al Tracy's assessment of what the letter said is consistent with many other accounts: "Dear Mr. Lee, We understand you have a set of hands called Wing Chun Pai. We have a representative that would like to exchange hands with you."

134 **"try out":** Chin interview, March 31, 2011.

135 **Chin asserts that Wong:** Chin interview, March 31, 2011.

135 **Others saw it as merely:** Personal interview with Clarence Lee, March 3, 2011.

135 **Among the more prevalent:** Der interview; Leo Fong, phone interview by the author, February 3, 2011.

135 **"I brought the note":** Chin interview, March 31, 2011.

135 **This started a back-and-forth:** Chin interview, March 31, 2011; Leo Fong interview, February 3, 2011.

135 **"the vibrating fist":** Leo Fong interview, February 3, 2011.

135 **many began to consider him:** Leo Fong interview, February 3, 2011.

135 **The matter was settled:** Der interview; Leo Fong interview, February 3, 2011; Chin interview, February 17, 2011.

135 **"The day of the fight":** Der interview.

136 **"It's all going down":** Leo Fong interview, February 3, 2011.

136 **Sam Louie recalls word:** Sam Louie, personal interview by the author, February 1, 2012.

136 **"It has nothing to do":** Louie interview.

136 **By then the anticipation:** Der interview.

14. EXCHANGING HANDS

137 **James Lee bolted the door:** David Chin, personal interview by the author, March 31, 2011.

137 **Wong Jack Man had arrived:** Chin interview, March 31, 2011.

137 **Bruce Lee stood facing:** Gong, *Bruce Lee*, 58.

137 **David Chin had driven:** Chin interview, March 31, 2011; Ben Der, personal interview by the author, February 12, 2014.

137 **"three sitting up front"**: Chin interview, March 31, 2011.

137 **A well-respected tai chi**: Chin interview, March 31, 2011; Der interview.

137 **In the backseat**: Chin interview, March 31, 2011.

137 **"only there to see"**: Dorgan, "Bruce Lee's Toughest Fight."

138 **Formerly an upholstery**: Chin interview, March 31, 2011; Dick Miller, phone interview by the author, December 4, 2014.

138 **"very unremarkable"**: Miller interview.

138 **"It was serious business"**: Linda Lee Cadwell, phone interview by the author, April 20, 2011.

138 **In time Wong Jack Man**: Chin interview, March 31, 2011.

138 **"It was *not* a friendly"**: Chin interview, March 31, 2011.

138 **"Shut your mouth"**: Ralph Castro, personal interview by the author, February 10, 2011; James Wing Woo, personal interview by the author, February 26, 2014; Al Tracy, phone interview by the author, August 26, 2014; Dorgan, "Bruce Lee's Toughest Fight." This is the most notorious bit of dialogue that is typically ascribed to this incident, with some variation. The Wong Jack Man camp usually says that Bruce said it directly to him, along the lines of "You've been killed by your friend." Ralph Castro (who says he spent the next day with Bruce and had the fight thoroughly explained to him) suggests this line was more expletive laced. Al Tracy describes it this way as well, saying the line was directed to Chin (and yes, that it was laced with expletives).

138 **"As far as I'm concerned"**: Linda Lee, quoted in Gong, *Bruce Lee*, 57.

139 **At five feet seven and a mere**: Dorgan, "Bruce Lee's Toughest Fight."

139 **his opponent had arrived**: Der interview.

139 **At five feet ten and about**: Dorgan, "Bruce Lee's Toughest Fight."

139 **Wong had an unassuming and**: Ming Lum, quoted in Wing, *Showdown in Oakland*.

139 **Bruce, on the other hand**: Der interview.

139 **"Styles make fights"**: "Styles Make Fights."

139 **As a practitioner of**: Dorgan, "Bruce Lee's Toughest Fight."

139 **"blinding speed and crushing power"**: Dorgan, "Bruce Lee's Toughest Fight."

139 **Conversely, Bruce practiced**: Gong, *Bruce Lee*, 10–11; Thomas, *Bruce Lee*, 16–21; Linda Lee, *Bruce Lee Story*, 27.

139 **"dry-land swimming"**: Leo Fong, personal interview by the author, October 24, 2011.

139 **"close to a hundred of them"**: Chin interview, March 31, 2011.

139 **Both men had spent**: Der interview.

139 **Up until that very**: Chin, interview, March 31, 2011.

139 **"Step forward"**: Chin, interview, March 31, 2011.

139 **"If you get in"**: Tracy interview.

140 **Bruce sought to end**: Gong, *Bruce Lee*, 57. Paul Bax's interview with Jesse Glover is pretty telling on this theme: [Bax] "If you could pick the most important principle about fighting that Bruce taught you, what do you think it would be?" [Glover] "Close on the guy, and get it over with" (*Disciples of the Dragon*, 19).

140 **Now in the late stages**: Cadwell interview, April 20, 2011.

140 **"I suppose I ought"**: Linda Lee, *Bruce Lee Story*, 53.

140 **Wong stepped into range**: Chin interview, March 31, 2011; Linda Lee, quoted in Gong, *Bruce Lee*, 57; Dorgan, "Bruce Lee's Toughest Fight."

140 **he darted in and delivered**: David Chin, phone interviews by the author, February 8, 2011, and March 31, 2011; Linda Lee, quoted in Gong, *Bruce Lee*, 57.

140 **"He really wanted"**: Dorgan, "Bruce Lee's Toughest Fight."

140 **Bruce pressed in, anxious**: Chin interviews, February 8, 2011, and March 31, 2011.

140 **By Chin's account**: Chin interview, February 8, 2011.

140 **The melee soon**: Chin interviews, February 8, 2011, and March 31, 201; Linda Lee, quoted in Gong, *Bruce Lee*, 57.

140 **"like an ax punch"**: Chin interview, February 8, 2011.

140 **"chain punches"**: Chin interview, February 8, 2011.

140 **"scientific street fighting"**: Cadwell interview, April 20, 2011.

140 **Northern expert known for**: Dorgan, "Bruce Lee's Toughest Fight"; Der interview.

140 **In then backpedaling**: Chin interviews, February 8, 2011, and March 31, 2011.

141 **"Do you yield"**: Linda Lee, quoted in Gong, *Bruce Lee*, 57.

141 **"From there"**: Chin interview, February 8, 2011.

141 **Wong Jack Man and his**: Chin interview, February 17, 2011.

141 **"After the fight, Bruce"**: Cadwell interview.

141 **"soundly defeated"**: Cadwell interview.

141 **"The day before, everybody"**: Der interview.

142 **There had actually been:** Dorgan, "Bruce Lee's Toughest Fight"; Al Tracy, phone interview by the author, August 26, 2014.

142 **However, that pledge of silence:** Wing, *Showdown in Oakland*. When it comes to the issue of what played out in the Chinese press in the aftermath of the fight, Rick Wing's book contains a phenomenal account of what ran in the papers.

142 **This then opened:** Wing, *Showdown in Oakland*; Tracy interview.

142 **This then sparked:** From the personal files of Arthur Chin, as translated by Janet T. Shih.

142 **Before long it began:** Dorgan, "Bruce Lee's Toughest Fight." As Dorgan puts it, "Due to the human desire to be known as an eye witness to a famous event, it is easier to obtain firsthand accounts of the fight from persons who were not there than from those who were" ("Bruce Lee's Toughest Fight").

143 **"Lots of people claim":** David Chin, phone interview by the author, February 8, 2011.

143 **fight went for over twenty:** Tracy interview.

143 **Bruce slammed Wong's head:** Barney Scollan, personal interview by the author, January 22, 2014.

143 **Wong had Bruce in:** James Wing Woo, personal interview by the author, February 2, 2014.

143 **Bruce's mother heard:** Tracy interview.

143 **classic Akira Kurosawa film:** *Rashomon*.

143 **For example, Ming Lum:** Dorgan, "Bruce Lee's Toughest Fight."

143 **Ben Der, on the other:** Ben Der, personal interview by the author, February 12, 2014.

143 **"like a panda":** Der interview.

143 **"I've always felt bad":** David Chin, phone interview by the author, March 31, 2011. It's interesting to note here that Ben Der (a childhood friend of Bruce Lee who was living in San Francisco at the time of the fight, and presently a respected Wing Chun teacher in Northern California who has taught for years) has some very vivid accounts of two other eyewitnesses of the fight: Ronald "Ya Ya" Wu and Chan "Bald Head" Keung. Wu had practiced Wing Chun with Der for a time, and Keung gave Der an extensive account of the fight one afternoon down in Y. C. Wong's school during the late sixties. When

I conveyed this specific quote from Chin to Der, he replied, "Yep, even Chan Keung said that to me too."

143 **The impact was as tangible**: Linda Lee Cadwell, phone interview by the author, April 20, 2011. There is widespread agreement among biographers, close friends, and longtime enemies that the Wong Jack Man fight was a turning point in Bruce Lee's career.

143 **"bouncing around like"**: Leo Fong, personal interview by the author, October 24, 2011.

144 **James Lee had given Leo**: Leo Fong, phone interview by the author, February 3, 2011.

144 **"Bruce, you gotta get"**: Fong interview, February 3, 2011.

144 **He began formally developing**: Cadwell interview, April 20, 2011; Dan Inosanto, personal interview by the author, June 2, 2014.

144 **Bruce was resolved to**: Gong, *Bruce Lee*, 57; Allen Joe, personal interview by the author, June 18, 2014.

144 **The fact that the fight**: Linda Lee, quoted in Gong, *Bruce Lee*, 57–58.

144 **"My mind is made up to"**: Gong, *Bruce Lee*, 84.

145 **"this system is a combination"**: Gong, *Bruce Lee*, 87.

145 **"True observation begins"**: Bruce Lee, "Liberate Yourself from Classical Karate."

145 **"He was popping right jabs"**: Leo Fong interview, October 24, 2011.

145 **the opening blow that Bruce**: Dorgan, "Bruce Lee's Toughest Fight."

145 **simply fleeing from him**: Linda Lee, *Bruce Lee Story*, 53.

146 **"the runner"**: Bruce himself would use this term in letters to James and George Lee. Gong, *Bruce Lee*, 58; George Lee, *Regards from the Dragon: Oakland*. It should be noted that many people say that the term was not derived from the fight but rather originated when Bruce saw Wong Jack Man at the Jackson Street Café a few days after the fight. Purportedly, Wong Jack Man bolted upon seeing Bruce come through the front door. (Ralph Castro, for instance, recounts this with great enthusiasm.)

146 **Wong Jack Man could only**: James Wing Woo, personal interview by the author, February 26, 2014.

146 **while Bruce lacked**: Tracy interview, August 26, 2014.

146 **In time the prevailing**: Linda Lee, *Bruce Lee Story*, 52; Dorgan, "Bruce Lee's Toughest Fight."

146 **"It was never about that"**: Fong interview, February 3, 2011.

146 **"It's very simple: the fight"**: Tracy interview.

146 **"I think that's mostly"**: Al Novak, quoted in Gene Ching, "Great American Great Grandmaster."

146 **"Have you ever heard"**: Clarence Lee, personal interview by the author, March 3, 2011.

146 **including Noel O'Brien**: Warren Chan, personal interview by the author, November 12, 2013.

146 **Clifford Kamaga in**: Wing Woo interview, February 26, 2014.

147 **T. Y. Wong had not only**: Chan interview.

147 **Ed Parker would often**: Darlene Parker and Antwone Alferos, phone interview by the author, June 18, 2015.

147 **The newest school**: Wing Woo interview, February 26, 2014; Adeline Fong, personal interview by the author, December 19, 2012.

147 **exclusion code was very**: Dino Salvatera, personal interviews by the author, June 20, 2011, June 28, 2011, November 27, 2012, and December 19, 2012; Adeline Fong, personal interviews by the author, June 28, 2011, December 12, 2012, and December 3, 2014; Leo Fong interview, October 24, 2011; Tracy interview; Wing Woo interview, February 26, 2014.

147 **Bruce himself dealt with it**: Jesse Glover, in Rafiq, *Bruce Lee Conversations*, 24; Doug Palmer's essay, in Phoebe Lee, *Lee Siu Loong*, 70–82. Palmer explains how while visiting Bruce in Hong Kong during the summer of 1963, he had to be coy around Ip Man and not let on that he was learning from Bruce. Then, he tells another story about a demonstration during a stopover in Hawaii on the way home that sparked some tension when spectators realized that Bruce was training a Caucasian.

147 **By the end of the 1960s**: Michael Gilman, phone interview by the author, December 8, 2012; Mark Small, phone interview by the author, March 26, 2013; Robyn Silverstein, phone interview by the author, December 10, 2012.

147 **"There was a meeting out"**: Michael Gilman, phone interview by the author, December 19, 2014.

148 **Fillmore Auditorium before Grateful**: Small interview.

148 **"scared shitless"**: Gilman interview, December 8, 2012.

148 **only to find Choy's opponents**: Gilman interview, December 8, 2012.

148 **Gilman asserts that Choy**: Gilman interview, December 19, 2014.

148 **There is, however, another theory**: Sources confidential.

149 **Several masters from other schools:** Doug Palmer's essay, in Phoebe Lee, *Lee Siu Loong.*

150 **plague Wong Jack Man:** It is next to impossible to find an article on Wong Jack Man's martial arts career (apart from those penned by his students) that does not reference the Bruce Lee fight. Wong Jack Man attempted legal action against Linda Lee at some point in what seems to have been a defamation suit, but the suit was purportedly dismissed from court.

150 **Wong Jack Man finally gave:** Wing, *Showdown in Oakland.*

150 **"to have a friendly visit":** Wing, *Showdown in Oakland.*

150 **"[Wong] says that in":** Wing, *Showdown in Oakland.*

150 **"made to fight":** Wing, *Showdown in Oakland.*

150 **Wong's final sentiments:** "Wong wrote a detailed description of the fight which concluded with an open invitation to Lee to meet him for a public bout if Lee was not satisfied with Wong's account" (Dorgan, "Bruce Lee's Toughest Fight").

150 **Linda Lee gave birth:** Thomas, *Bruce Lee,* 56.

EPILOGUE

151 **the current issue:** Judkins, "Lives of Chinese Martial Artists (14)."

151 **"1965 was a pivotal year":** Judkins, "Lives of Chinese Martial Artists (14)."

151 **Lau Bun passed in 1967:** Doc-Fai Wong, "Great Grandmaster Lau Bun."

151 **Hung Sing still operates:** Sifu Dino Salvatera runs Hung Sing in San Francisco's Sunset District.

152 **T. Y. Wong relocated:** Warren Chan, personal interview by the author, November 12, 2014.

152 **Master Choy taught a diverse:** Michael Gilman, phone interview by the author, December 8, 2012; Robyn Silverstein, phone interview by the author, December 10, 2012.

152 **Mah Sek practiced:** Lamia, "Grandmaster Mar Sik."

152 **"The things Bruce was":** David Chin, phone interview by the author, February 8, 2011.

152 **Wong Jack Man distanced:** Ben Der, personal interview by the author, February 12, 2014.

152 **continued to teach until:** Paul Eng, personal interview by the author, May 16, 2014. See also "Grandmaster Wong Jack Man."

152 **In May 1965 Muhammad:** Gallender, *Sonny Liston,* 212–42.

152 **"phantom punch"**: Snowden, "Phantom Punch Hits 50."

152 **many immediately alleging**: Snowden, "Phantom Punch Hits 50";Gallender, *Sonny Liston*, 212–42. It's interesting to note one of Ali's explanations for the fight: "It's a chop, so fast you can't see it. . . . It's karate. It's got a twist to it. Just one does the job" (Gallender, *Sonny Liston*, 233).

152 **Chinatown saw a fresh**: Gene Ching, "Keeping Secrets."

153 **In Chinatown gangs began**: Bill Lee, *Chinese Playground*.

153 **James Lee passed in 1972**: Dill, "Meet James Yimm Lee."

153 **"one of the great missing"**: Tracy interview.

153 **When asked how many**: Bernice Jay, personal interview by the author, October 13, 2014.

153 **Ed Parker's model**: Darlene Parker and Antwone Alferos, phone interview by the author, June 25, 2015; Bruce Juchnik, phone interview by the author, December 17, 2014.

153 **There's a hint of nervousness**: *I Am Bruce Lee.*

154 **"I would like to let"**: Der interview, February 12, 2014. See also interview with William Cheung, in Rafiq, *Bruce Lee Conversations*, 91.

154 **"Now Bruce, just look"**: *I Am Bruce Lee.*

154 **"My last name is Lee"**: *I Am Bruce Lee.*

BIBLIOGRAPHY

Anspacher, Carolyn. "Madame Chiang: First Lady of the Orient Talks to City's Chinese, Urges Aid to War Effort." *San Francisco Chronicle*, March 29, 1943, A-1.

Avent, G Jeanette. "In the Martial Arts . . . We Teach People to Respect Themselves and Others." *Los Angeles Times*, March 11, 1990.

Bagwell, Beth. *Oakland: The Story of a City*. 1982. Oakland CA: Oakland Heritage Alliance, 2012.

Bax, Paul. *Disciples of the Dragon*. High Ridge MO: Baxtard Unlimited, 2006.

Bickers, Robert. *The Scramble for China: Foreign Devils in the Qing Empire, 1832–1914*. London: Penguin Books, 2011.

"Biography." http://www.BruceLeeFoundation.com. Accessed November 2014.

"Biography of Skip Ellsworth." http://www.Hollowtop.com. Accessed April 4, 2014.

Bowman, Paul. *Beyond Bruce Lee: Chasing the Dragon through Film, Philosophy and Popular Culture*. New York: Wallflower Press, 2013.

——. "When Bruce Lee Meets Alain Badiou." http://www.Academia.edu. Accessed November 2014.

Brewster, David, and David M. Buerge, eds. *Washingtonians: A Biographical Portrait of the State*. Seattle: Sasquatch Books, 1988.

Broad, Bill. "A Tribute to Ed Parker." Essay. Parker Family Archives, Pasadena CA.

Cabrera, Manny. "Complete Interview with Grandmaster Michael Pick." http://www.ChineseKarateFederation.com. September 21, 2010. Accessed August 3, 2014.

Caen, Herb. "A Phenomenal Week." *San Francisco Chronicle*, February 16, 1964, 23.

Campbell, Sid, and Greglon Yimm Lee. *The Dragon and the Tiger*. Vol. 1. Berkeley: Frog, 2005.

——. *The Dragon and the Tiger*. Vol. 2. Berkeley: Frog, 2005.

Carroll, John M. *A Concise History of Hong Kong*. Lanham MD: Rowman & Little-field, 2007.

Chang, Iris. *The Chinese in America*. New York: Penguin, 2003.

Chen, Yong. *Chinese San Francisco, 1850–1943: A Trans-Pacific Community*. Stanford CA: Stanford University Press, 2000.

Cheung, Hawkins. "Bruce Lee's Hong Kong Years." *Inside Kung-Fu*, November 1991. http://www.hawkinscheung.com/wp/about.

——. "Bruce Lee Discovers Jeet Kuen Do." *Inside Kung-Fu*, December 1991. http://www.hawkinscheung.com/wp/about/part2/.

——. "Bruce Lee's Mother Art: Wing Chun." *Inside Kung-Fu*, January 1992. http://www.hawkinscheung.com/wp/about/part2/part3.

——. "Bruce's Classical Mess: Cleaning up the Mess the 'Little Dragon' Left Behind," *Inside Kung-Fu*, February 1992. http://www.hawkinscheung.com/wp/about/part2/part3/part4.

"Chinatown Parade Tomorrow." *San Francisco Chronicle*, February 21, 1964, 9.

"Chinatown's Biggest Night." *San Francisco Chronicle*, February 23, 1964, 1.

Chinese Historical Society. *Glamour and Grace: The History and Culture of Miss Chinatown USA*. Chinese Historical Society of America Museum, 2007. Civil RightsSuite.org. Accessed October 15, 2014.

"Chinese Hospital." http://www.SanFranciscoChinatown.com. Accessed September 2, 2014.

Ching, Gene. "Great American Great Grandmaster." *Kung Fu Magazine*, January/February 2010. http://www.kungfumagazine.com/magazine/article.php?article=87.

——. "Keeping Secrets." *Kung Fu Magazine*, July/August 2006. http://www.kungfumagazine.com/magazine/article.php?article=661.

Ching, Ip, and Ron Heimberger. *Ip-Man: Portrait of a Kung Fu Master*. Translated by Eric Li. Springville UT: King Dragon Press, 2001.

Choy, Philip P. *San Francisco Chinatown: A Guide to Its History and Architecture*. San Francisco: City Lights, 2012.

Choy, Philip P., Lorraine Dong, and Marlon K. Hom, eds. *Coming Man: Nineteenth-Century American Perceptions of the Chinese*. Seattle: University of Washington Press, 1994.

Cox, David. "Mah Sek: The Odyssey of a Kung Fu Master." *Official Karate* (Fall 1973): 52–61.

Davies, Andrea Rees. *Saving San Francisco: Relief and Recovery after the 1906 Disaster.* Philadelphia: Temple University Press, 2012.

Demile, James. "Evolving from the Darkside." http://www.WingChunDo.com. Accessed September 12, 2014.

Dill, Gary, "Meet James Yimm Lee: 'The Man Who Helped Make Bruce Lee a Success." *Blackbelt Magazine*, April 21, 2014. http://www.blackbeltmag.com/daily /traditional-martial-arts-training/jeet-kune-do/meet-james-yimm-lee-the -man-who-helped-make-bruce-lee-a-success/.

Dillon, Richard H. *Hatchet Men: The Story of the Tong Wars in San Francisco's Chinatown.* Sanger CA: The Write Thought, 1962.

Dong, Arthur. *Forbidden City, USA: Chinese American Nightclubs, 1936–1970.* Los Angeles: Deep Focus Productions, 2014.

Dorgan, Michael. "Bruce Lee's Toughest Fight." *Official Karate*, July 1980. http:// www.kungfu.net/brucelee.html.

Duerr, Fred. "Madame Chiang: City Takes Lovely Visitor to Its Heart." *San Francisco Chronicle*, March 26, 1943, A-1

———. "Madame Chiang: City Honors Chinese Leader at the Most Magnificent Banquet of a Generation." *San Francisco Chronicle*, March 27, 1943, A-1.

Dunning, Jennifer. "Sophia Delza Glassgold, 92, Dancer and Teacher." *New York Times*, July 7, 1996.

"Ed Parker Biography." http://www.EdParkerSr.net. Accessed June 10, 2015.

Edwards, Gene, and Laura Edwards. "Historical Perspectives." http://www.ChristianJuJitsu.com. September 16, 2014.

Emch, Tom. "The Chinatown Murders." *San Francisco Sunday Examiner and Chronicle*, September 9, 1973.

"The Father of Modern China: Sun Yat-sen (1866–1925). http://www.CNN.com. Accessed December 14, 2014.

"Filipino Laborers Arrive." http://www.HawaiiHistory.org. Accessed September 1, 2014.

Finacom, Steven. "Jack La Lanne—A Berkeley (not Oakland) Original." *Berkeley Daily Planet*, January 25, 2011.

"The First Peoples of California." California History Collection. http://lcweb2.loc .gov/. Accessed October 29, 2014.

"Four Words Win a Trip for Lovely Leona." *Straits Times*, October 25, 1959.

Franklin, Logan. "Ed Yarick Gym, Home of Champions." http://www.Senior
-Exercise-Central.com. Accessed August 2014.

Gallender, Paul. *Sonny Liston: The Real Story behind the Ali-Liston Fights*. Pacific
Grove CA: Park Place, 2012.

Garvey, John. *San Francisco Police Department*. Charleston SC: Arcadia, 2004

Gewu, Kang. *Spring Autumn: The Spring and Autumn of Chinese Martial Arts—5000
Years*. Santa Cruz CA: Plum, 1995.

"Giants Win—in 2nd Place." *San Francisco Chronicle*, May 17, 1959.

Gilbey, John F. *Secret Fighting Arts of the World*. Tokyo: Charles E. Tuttle, 1963.

Golden Gate Girls. Documentary film. Directed by S. Louisa Wei. Produced by Law
Kar. Blue Queen Cultural Communication. 2012. DVD.

Goldstein, Richard. "Jack Lalanne, Founder of Modern Fitness Movement, Dies
at 96." *New York Times*, January 23, 2011.

Gong, Tommy. *Bruce Lee: The Evolution of a Martial Artist*. Los Angeles: Bruce Lee
Enterprises, 2013.

"Grandmaster Wong Jack Man." http://www.jingomo.com/wongjackman. Accessed
January 9, 2015.

Green, Thomas. *Martial Arts of the World: An Encyclopedia*. Vol. 1, A–Q. Santa Barbara CA: ABC-CLIO, 2001.

Green, Thomas A., and Joseph R. Svinth, eds. *Martial Arts in the Modern World*.
Westport CT: Praeger, 2003.

———. *Martial Arts of the World: An Encyclopedia of History and Innovation*. Santa
Barbara CA: ABC-CLIO, 2010.

Gyves, Clifford Michael. "An English Translation of General Qi Jiguang's 'Quanjing
Jieyao Pian' (Chapter on the Fist Canon and the Essentials of Nimbleness)
from the *Jixiao Xinshu* (New Treatise on Disciplined Service)." MA thesis,
University of Arizona, Department of East Asian Studies, 1993.

Hagood, Roger D. "Choy Kam Man: Tai Chi Pioneer." *Kungfu Magazine*, Summer
1992, 36–44.

Halpin, Jim. "Bruce Lee: The Seattle Years." In *Washingtonians: A Biographical
Portrait of the State*, edited by David Brewster and David M. Buerge, 419–39.
Seattle: Sasquatch Books, 1988.

"Hiram Leong Fong: 1906–2004." http://www.SenatorFong.com. Accessed June
14, 2015.

"History of Fair Housing." U.S. Department of Housing and Urban Development.
http://www.HUD.gov. Accessed June 3, 2015.

"History of Shaolin Kung Fu." http://www.ShaolinKungFuguan.com.au. Accessed July 7, 2014.

"The History of Small Circle Jujitsu." http://www.SmallCircleJujitsu.com. Accessed September 3, 2014.

Ho, Eric Peter. *Tracing My Children's Lineage*. Hong Kong: Hong Kong Institute for the Humanities and Social Sciences, University of Hong Kong, 2010.

Hsu, Adam. *The Sword Polisher's Record: The Way of Kung-Fu*. Boston: Charles E. Tuttle, 1997.

I Am Bruce Lee. Documentary film. Directed by Pete McCormack. Leeway Media, 2012. DVD.

"Immigration Act of 1924 (The Johnson-Reed Act)." U.S. Department of State, Office of the Historian, http://www.history.state.gov. Accessed September 1, 2014.

"Interview with Robert Lee." http://www.CityonFire.com. January 17, 2011. Accessed December 2, 2014.

"James." http://www.Jamesmitose.org. Accessed December 10, 2014.

"Japanese Laborers Arrive." http://www.HawaiiHistory.org. Web. Retrieved September 1, 2014.

"Jay Sebring." http://www.CieloDrive.com. Accessed November 3, 2014.

"Jay Sebring Trailer." (Unofficial trailer for the Jay Sebring documentary.) Directed by Anthony DiMaria. 1010 Films, LLC. YouTube. July 24, 2013. Accessed November 3, 2014.

Judkins, Ben. "The Book Club: The Shaolin Monastery by Meir Shahar, Chapters 5–Conclusion: Unarmed Combat in the Ming and Qing Dynasties." http://www.ChineseMartialStudies.com. December 7, 2012. Accessed August 5, 2014.

———. "'Fighting Styles' or 'Martial Brands'? An Economic Approach to Understanding 'Lost Lineages' in the Chinese Martial Arts." http://www.ChineseMartialStudies.com. June 12, 2014. Accessed August 5, 2014.

———. "Lives of Chinese Martial Artists (5): Lau Bun—A Kung Fu Pioneer in America." http://www.ChineseMartialStudies.com. February 20, 2013. Accessed March 31, 2013.

———. "Lives of Chinese Martial Artists (12): Tang Hao—The First Historian of the Chinese Martial Arts." http://www.ChineseMartialStudies.com. March 14, 2014. Accessed April 25, 2014.

———. "Lives of Chinese Martial Artists (14): Ark Yuey Wong—Envisioning the Future of the Chinese Martial Arts." http://www.ChineseMartialStudies.com. November 17, 2014, Accessed November 18, 2014.

———. "Through a Lens Darkly (17): 'Selling the Art': Martial Artists in the Marketplace, 1900–1930." http://www.ChineseMartialStudies.com. March 21, 2013. Accessed November 30, 2014.

"Judo at the 1964 Tokyo Summer Games." http//www.sports-reference.com/olympics/summer/1964/JUD/. Accessed May 2, 2015. Kar, Law, and Frank Bren. *Hong Kong Cinema: A Cross-Cultural View*. New York: Scarecrow Press, 2004.

Kennedy, Brian, and Elizabeth Kuo. *Chinese Martial Arts Training Manuals: A Historical Survey*. Berkeley CA: Blue Snake Books, 2005.

"King-Sized Traffic Snarl." *San Francisco Chronicle*, February 23, 1964, A-1.

"The Lady from Shanghai." http://www.FilmReference.com. Accessed, November 4, 2014.

Lai, Him Mark. *Becoming Chinese American: A History of Communities and Institutions*. Walnut Creek CA: Alta Mira Press, 2004.

———. "Chinese Hospital: An Institution of, for, and by the Chinese Community." Him Mark Lai Digital Archive. http://www.HimMarkLai.org. Accessed June 21, 2014.

———. "Guangzhou to Hong Kong, Geographical and Historical Notes." Him Mark Lai Digital Archive. http://www.HimMarkLai.org. Accessed March 28, 2014.

———. "A Memorable Day 70 Years Ago." Parts 1 and 2. Him Mark Lai Digital Archive. http://www.HimMarkLai.org. Accessed June 21, 2014.

———. "Short History of the Chinese Media in North America." Him Mark Lai Digital Archive. http://www.HimMarkLai.org. Accessed December 2, 2014.

Lai, Him Mark, with Thomas W. Chinn, and Philip P. Choy. "History of the Chinese in California: A Syllabus." Parts 1–9. San Francisco: Chinese Historical Society of America, 1969. Him Mark Lai Digital Archive. http://www.HimMarkLai.org. Accessed June 21, 2014.

Lamia, Nick. "Grandmaster Mar Sik." http://www.TibetanHopGar.com. Accessed March 3 2014.

Lee, Bill. *Chinese Playground: A Memoir*. Self-published, 2014.

Lee, Bruce. *Chinese Gung Fu: The Philosophical Art of Self-Defense*. 1963. Santa Clara CA: Ohara, 2008.

———. "Liberate Yourself from Classical Karate." *Black Belt Magazine*, September 1971. Republished for the Web, September 26, 2011. Accessed March 4, 2012. http://www.blackbeltmag.com/daily/traditional-martial-arts-training/jeet-kune-do/liberate-yourself-from-classical-karate/.

———. *The Tao of Jeet Kun Do*. Valencia CA: Black Belt Communications, 2011.

Lee, George. *Regards from the Dragon: Oakland*. Compiled by David Tadman. Los Angeles: Empire Books, 2008.

Lee, J. Yimm. *Wing Chun Kung-Fu*. Santa Clara CA: Ohara, 1972.

Lee, Kem K. Kem Lee Photograph Collection, 1927–1986. Ethnic Studies Library, University of California Berkeley.

Lee, Linda. *The Bruce Lee Story*. Santa Clara CA: Ohara, 1989.

Lee, Phoebe, et al. *Lee Siu Loong: Memories of the Dragon*. Hong Kong: Bruce Lee Club, 2004.

Lee Family Immigration Files. Scans from 12017/53752. Record Group 85, ARC 296477. National Archives and Records Administration, San Francisco.

"Leamington Hotel." http://www.LocalWiki.org/Oakland/. Accessed March 10, 2015.

Leslie, Scott. http://www.Kinmon.org. Accessed 2012.

Li, Laura Tyson. *Madame Chiang Kai-Shek: China's Eternal First Lady*. New York: Grove Press, 2006.

Ludlow, Lynn. "300,000 . . . and a Dragon." *San Francisco Examiner*, February 23, 1964, 1.

"Machado, Lena: Performer Biography." Hawaiian Music Collection, University of Hawaii at Manoa Library. http://www.digicoll.manoa.hawaii.edu/. 2013.

"The Man behind TV's Batman: CBC Archives." YouTube. October 24, 2012. Accessed November 2, 2014.

Mancuso, Ted. "Kung Feud?" *PLUM Publications*. http://www.PlumbPub.com. November 27, 2009. Accessed July 21, 2013.

Margolis, Jon. *The Last Innocent Year: America in 1964; The Beginning of the "Sixties."* New York: William Morrow, 1999.

Marqusee, Mike. "Fifty Years of Bob Dylan's Stark Challenge to Liberal Complacency." *Guardian*, February 21, 2014.

"Master Choy Hak Pang, 1885–1958." Choy family video. From the personal files of Jack Wada.

Matuszak, Sacha. "'The Practical Isn't Pretty': General Qi Jiguang on Martial Arts for Soldiers." http://www.Fightland.Vice.com. March 3, 2015. Accessed June 9, 2015.

McFadden, Robert D. "Daniel Inouye, Hawaii's Quiet Voice of Conscience in Senate, Dies at 88." *New York Times*, December 17, 2012.

"Mega Cities Hong Kong." National Geographic Documentary. Discovery HD Channel & National Geographic (via YouTube). Feb 12, 2015. Accessed June 20, 2015.

Morgan, Bill, and Nancy J. Peters, eds. *Howl on Trial: The Battle for Free Expression.* San Francisco: City Lights Books, 2006.

Morin, Natalie. "31 Beautiful Photos of Life in San Francisco's Chinatown in the '50s." http://www.Buzzfeed.com. July 23, 2103. Accessed, September 5, 2014.

Morinaga, Dayton. "Emperado Kick-Started Mixing of Martial Arts." *Honolulu Advertiser,* May 22, 2009.

"Muwekma Ohlone Tribe of the San Francisco Bay Area." http://www.Muwekma .org. Accessed October 29, 2014.

O'Brien, Jess, ed. *Nei Jia Quan: Internal Martial Arts, Teachers of Tai Ji Quan, Xing Yi Quan, Ba Gua Zhang.* Berkeley CA: Blue Snake Books, 2004.

"The Origin 'Ideas' of Kenpo." Jamesmitose.org. Accessed December 10, 2014.

Pace, Erik. "George Christopher, 92, Dies; Lured Giants to San Francisco." *New York Times,* September 16, 2000.

Parker, Ed. *Kenpo Karate: The Law of the Fist and the Empty Hand.* Alliance NE: Iron Man Industries, 1960.

Patterson, James T. *The Eve of Destruction: How 1965 Transformed America.* New York: Basic Books, 2012.

Rafiq, Fiaz, ed. *Bruce Lee Conversations: The Life and Legacy of a Legend.* Manchester, England: HNL, 2009.

Rashomon. Directed by Akira Kurosawa. Daiei Motion Picture Company, 1950. DVD.

Richter, Robert. "Fundamentals of Fut Gar Kung Fu." *Karate Kung-fu Illustrated,* December 1988, 48–51.

———. "Fut Gar Kung Fu." *Black Belt Magazine,* August 1989, 62–65.

Robbins, Trina. *Forbidden City: The Golden Age of Chinese Nightclubs.* New York: Hampton Press, 2009.

Robinson, David. *Bandits, Eunuchs, and the Son of Heaven: Rebellion and the Economy of Violence in Mid-Ming China.* Honolulu: University of Hawai'i Press, 2001.

Robinson, Ronnie. "Tai Chi Interview-Gerda Geddes." http://www.Taiji-europa .eu. August 10, 2014.

Rosenbaum, Art. "S.F. Fans Can Boo with Best of 'Em." *San Francisco Chronicle,* May 17, 1959.

Shahar, Meir. *The Shaolin Monastery: History, Religion, and the Chinese Martial Arts.* Honolulu: University of Hawai'i Press, 2008.

Sharman, Lyon. *Sun Yat-sen, His Life and Its Meaning: A Critical Biography.* Stanford CA: Stanford University Press, 1934.

Skoss, Meik. "Jujutsu and Taijutsu." *Aikido Journal*, no. 103 (1995). http://www.koryu.com/library/mskoss8.html. Accessed July 28, 2014.

Smith, Robert W. *Martial Musings: A Portrayal of Martial Arts in the Twentieth Century*. Erie PA: Via Media, 1999.

Snowden, Jonathan. "The Phantom Punch Hits 50: Ali, Liston, and Boxing's Most Controversial Fight Ever." http://www.BleacherReport.com. May 25, 2015. Accessed June 3, 2015.

"Styles Make Fights: A Brief History Lesson." http://www.BoxingNews24.com. December 31, 2014. Accessed June 5, 2015.

Tadman, David, and Steve Kerridge, eds. *Bruce Lee: The Little Dragon at 70*. Los Angeles: Bruce Lee Enterprises, 2010.

Takaki, Robert. *Strangers from a Different Shore: A History of Asian Americans*. Boston: Little Brown, 1989.

Tchen, John Kuo Wei. *Chinese American: Exclusion/Inclusion*. New York: New-York Historical Society, 2014.

Thomas, Bruce. *Bruce Lee: Fighting Spirit*. Berkeley CA: Blue Snake Books, 1994.

"Timing." http://www.LeoTFong.com. October 2008. Accessed January 2015.

Tosches, Nick. *The Devil and Sonny Liston*. Boston: Little, Brown, 2000.

Tracy, Al. "Professor William K. S. Chow." http://www.TracysKarate.com. July 17, 2009. Accessed August 2, 2014.

Tracy, Will. "Kenpo Karate Setting History Right 1956–1959." http://www.KenpoKarate.com. August 8, 1999. Web. Retrieved August 2, 2014.

Trevino, Chris. "Bruce Lee Put U.S. Martial Arts on the Grand Stage in Long Beach 50 years Ago." *Long Beach Press-Telegram*, August 1, 2014.

Tsui, Bonnie. *American Chinatown: A People's History of Five Neighborhoods*. New York: Free Press, 2009.

Tzu, Sun. *The Art of War*. Minneapolis: Filiquarian, 2007.

"An Unnoticed Struggle: A Concise History of Asian American Civil Rights Issues." The Japanese American Citizens League, 2007–8. http://www.Jaclseattle.wordpress.com. Accessed May 4, 2015.

U.S. Senate Joint Special Committee. *Report of the Joint Special Committee to Investigate Chinese Immigration, February 27, 1877*. Washington DC: Government Printing Office, 1877. Reprint, Manchester NH: Ayer, 1979.

Vaughn, Alexa. "Jesse Glover, Bruce Lee's First Student, Dies at 77." *Seattle Times*, June 29, 2012.

"Violent Repose." *Time*, March 3, 1961, 51.

Wada, Jack. "Master Choy," Takemusu Scribblings, July 7, 2008. http://www.jack wada.blogspot.com. Accessed January 15, 2015.

Weisskopf, Michael. "The Last Shaolin Kung Fu Master." *Washington Post*, in the archives of Warren Chan.

"William Dozier; TV Producer, 83." *New York Times*, April 26, 1991.

Wing, Rick L. *Showdown in Oakland: The Story behind the Wong Jack Man–Bruce Lee Fight*. Self-published e-book, 2013.

Wing Woo, James. *Sifu*. Self-published, 2012.

Woods, Frank. *Dancer in the Light: The Life of Gerda Pytt Geddes*. Dyce, Aberdeen, Scotland: Psi Books, 2008.

Wong, Doc-Fai. "Great Grandmaster Lau Bun." http://www.PlumBlossom.net. 2012.

———. "Fut Gar: Southern China's Traditional—and Practical—Approach to Com bat Proficiency." *Inside Kung-Fu*, July 1985. http://www.PlumBlossom.net.

———. "Remembering Lau Bun." *Inside Kung-Fu*. July 2002. http://www.Plum Blossom.net.

Wong, T. Y. *Chinese Kung-Fu: Original "Sil Lum" System*. San Francisco, 1962.

Wong, T. Y., and K. H. Lee. *Chinese Karate Kung-Fu: Original "Sil Lim" System For Health and Self Defense*. San Francisco: Oriental Publishing, 1961.

Yarick, Ed. "The Steve Reeves I Know and Remember." *Muscle Mag International*, May 1976, 33–36.

"Yip Man: Wing Chun Legend and Bruce Lee's Formal Teacher." http://www .BlackBeltMag.com. August 12, 2013. Accessed November 15, 2014.

Zimmer, Ben. "Take Note, Grasshopper, of Kung Fu." *Wall Street Journal*, January 10, 2014.

———. "How 'Kung Fu' Entered the Popular Lexicon." *Visual Thesaurus*. January 14, 2014. http://www.visualthesaurus.com/cm/wordroutes/how-kung-fu -entered-the-popular-lexicon/. Accessed January 26, 2014.

INDEX

Illustrations in the gallery are indicated by *fig. 1*, *fig. 2*, and so on.

Jeet Kune Do system, 144–45

Joe, Allen: fitness culture's influence on, *fig. 12*, 77–78; image of, *fig. 25*; late-night martial arts sessions, 188; relationship with Bruce Lee, 76, 78–79, 82, 104, 144, 186

Johnson-Reed Act, 87

Jones, LeRoi, 110

Judkins, Ben, 42, 44, 46, 151, 175, 182

judo, 59, 89–90, 115. *See also* Jay, Wally

jujitsu, 89

Jun Fan Institute (Oakland), 113, 114, 123, 137–38

Jun Fan Institute (Seattle), 8, 103

Kamaga, Clifford, 112, 146

Kano, Jigoro, 89

karate, 59, 68, 74, 89–90

Kawachi, Ken, 91

Kennedy, Brian, 45

Kennedy, John F., 86, 109

kenpo, 94–95, 191

Keung, Chan "Bald Head," 137–38, 141, 149, 207

Kimura, Mits, 91

Kimura, Taky, 66, 118, 144

Kin Mon (martial arts school), 152; in the 1964 New Year parade, 108; challengers to, 68–69, 184; *Home* show appearance, 39, 173; role in Chinatown, 37, 59; tong racial exclusion code in, *fig. 5*, 39, 146–47; training focus in, 68

Kono, Tommy, 78

Kubota, Tak, 117–18

kung fu: anglicization of term, 74; assessment of fights in, 69; compared to karate, 68; definition of

term, 43; emphasis on softness in, 16, 114; introduction of term, *fig. 8*; iron body training in, 64; origins of, 41, 43; popularization of, in U.S., 151; styles in the Bay Area, 84–85

Kuo Lien Ying, 153

Kurosawa, Akira, 143

The Lady from Shanghai (film), 127

Lai, Brandon, 153

LaLanne, Jack, 77

Largusa, Ben, 118

Lau Bun: in the 1964 New Year parade, 108; and Bruce Lee, 57–58, 129, 179; death of, 151; descriptions of, 13, 164; images of, *fig. 2, fig. 3, fig. 4*; immigration agents story, 22–23, 168; martial arts abilities of, 22–23, 165; martial arts background of, 21–23, 84; and the racial exclusion code, 112, 147; role in Chinatown, 13–14, 23, 59, 136. *See also* Hung Sing (martial arts school)

Lee, Agnes (Bruce's sister), 49, 55, 178

Lee, Bruce: birth of, 33–34; birth of son, 150; books written by, 101, 129–30, 193; breaking the racial code, 67, 183, 209; childhood years, 29, 49–52; citizenship papers of, *fig. 1*; as a dance instructor, 28, 47–48, 81; evolution of approach, 55, 82–83, 92, 124–25, 143–46, 188; fight against Yoiche Nakachi, 65, 67–68, 69–70; images of, *fig. 1, fig. 13, fig. 14, fig. 18, fig. 20, fig. 22, fig. 24*; introduction to Chinatown, 29–36; late-night martial arts sessions, 84–87, 93–94, 112–14, 125, 188; and the Long Beach tournament, 115–21,

Wong, YC, 153

Wong Jack Man: challenge to Bruce Lee, 134–36, 204; debates surrounding Bruce Lee fight, 142–43, 145–46; fight against Bruce Lee, 137–41, 205; impact of Bruce Lee fight on, 149–50, 152, 210; martial arts style, 112

Wong Sheun Leoung, 54–55

World War II, 35, 38, 49, 86, 91

Wu, Ronald "Ya Ya," 134, 137–38, 141, 207

Yang Cheng Fu, 102

Yarick, Ed, 77–78

Yee, Coby, 108, 111

Yeun Hai, 22

Yip Man. *See* Ip Man

youth culture, 109–10, 147–48

Zen Buddhism, 39, 40